*To Caucasus,
the End of all the Earth*

To Caucasus,
the End of all the Earth

An illustrated companion to the Caucasus
and Transcaucasia

FITZROY MACLEAN

And they knew they were come to Caucasus,
at the end of all the earth
KINGSLEY

JONATHAN CAPE
THIRTY BEDFORD SQUARE LONDON

FIRST PUBLISHED 1976
© 1976 BY SIR FITZROY MACLEAN
JONATHAN CAPE LTD, 30 BEDFORD SQUARE, LONDON WC1

ACKNOWLEDGMENTS

My thanks are due to Mrs Clissold, Mrs Cookson, Miss Thorburn and
Mrs Macpherson for their patient help in preparing the text.

BRITISH LIBRARY CATALOGUING IN PUBLICATION DATA

MACLEAN, FITZROY, BARON MACLEAN
TO CAUCASUS, THE END OF ALL THE EARTH.
ISBN 0-224-01170-7
1. TITLE
914.7'9'0485   DK 511.C1
CAUCASUS – DESCRIPTION AND TRAVEL

PRINTED IN GREAT BRITAIN BY
JOLLY & BARBER LTD, RUGBY
AND BOUND BY WM. BRENDON & SON LTD
TIPTREE NR. COLCHESTER, ESSEX

Contents

FOR VERONICA

my favourite
fellow-traveller

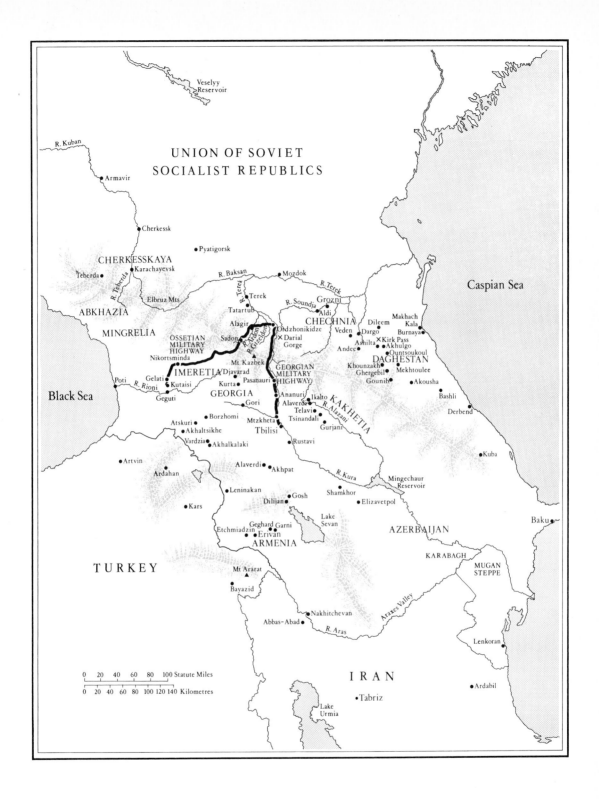

UNION OF SOVIET
SOCIALIST REPUBLICS

Veselyy
Reservoir

Caspian Sea

R. Kuban

Armavir

Cherkessk

Pyatigorsk

CHERKESSKAYA
Karachayevsk
Teberda   R. Baksan   Mozdok
                                                                                        R. Terek
                                           R. Terek   Terek
                        Elbruz Mts   Tatartub   R. Soundja   Grozni
ABKHAZIA   Alagir   Aldi
                                              Sadon   CHECHNIA   Dileem   Makhach
MINGRELIA   Ordzhonikidze   Veden   Dargo   Kala
                        OSSETIAN   × Darial   Ashilta × Kirk Pass   Burnaya
                        MILITARY   R. Gizeldon   Gorge   Andee   Akhulgo
                        HIGHWAY   Ountsoukoul
        Nikortsminda   Mt Kazbek ▲   Khounzakh   DAGHESTAN
                                                        GEORGIAN   Ghergebil   Mekhtoulee
                Gelati   Djavarad   GEORGIAN MILITARY   Gounib   Akousha
Poti   IMERETIA   Kurta   Pasanauri   HIGHWAY)
        R. Rioni   Kutaisi   Bashli
        Geguti   GEORGIA   Gori   Ananuri Ikalto
Black Sea   Alaverdi Telavi   KAKHETIA   Derbend
                        Atskuri   Borzhomi   Mtzkheta Tsinandali R. Alazani
                        Akhaltsikhe   Tbilisi   Gurjani
                Vardzia Akhalkalaki   Rustavi   Kuba
        Artvin
                Ardahan   Alaverdi Akhpat   R. Kura   Mingechaur
                                                                        Reservoir
                Kars   Leninakan   Shamkhor Elizavetpol
                                Dilijan Gosh
                        Etchmiadzin Geghard Garni   Lake   AZERBAIJAN   Baku
TURKEY   Erivan   Sevan
                                ARMENIA   KARABAGH   MUGAN
                                                                        STEPPE
                        Mt Ararat ▲
                        Bayazid   Lenkoran

        0 20 40 60 80 100 Statute Miles   Araxes Valley
        0 20 40 60 80 100 120 140 Kilometres   Nakhitchevan
                                Abbas-Abad   R. Aras   Ardabil
                                                    I R A N
                                                        Tabriz
                                        Lake
                                        Urmia

I · *The Mountain of Languages*

In the days before the last war, when Soviet Central Asia was a for-
bidden zone, the spirit of contradiction, which, my wife says,
largely dictates my actions, used to take me whenever possible to those
legendary cities of Turkestan, Samarkand and Bokhara. But now that
you can go more or less anywhere you like in the Soviet Union, it is
first and foremost to the Caucasus and to Transcaucasia that I feel
myself drawn.

Most people are fascinated by frontiers, and, if ever there was a
frontier, it is the Caucasus – the great mountain barrier stretching from
the Black Sea to the Caspian, dividing Europe from Asia, West from
East, Christendom from Islam.

From the earliest times the Caucasus has been a region of high
romance. To the ancients it was the End of the World. Beyond it, all was
fable and mystery. Here Jason and the Argonauts came in search of the
Golden Fleece. 'And at day dawn', we read in Kingsley's *Heroes*, 'they
looked eastward, and midway between the sea and the sky, they saw
white snowpeaks hanging, glittering sharp and bright above the clouds.
And they knew that they were come to Caucasus, at the end of all the
earth: Caucasus the highest of all mountains, the father of the rivers of
the east.'

Here, in the magic land of Colchis, Medea cast her spells. Here
Prometheus was chained by the gods to Mount Kazbek and an eagle sent
to tear out his heart. Here, gold-guarding griffins and one-eyed
Arimaspians carried on their perpetual war. And here dwelt the man-
hating Amazons. 'I will transport thy city beyond Mount Kaf,' cried the
magician in the *Arabian Nights*, 'and turn all its people into stones.' And
Sir John Mandeville tells us how somewhere amongst the mountains of
Georgia there is a country 'all covered with darkness, so that it hath no

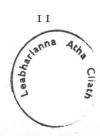

light that no man may see through and no man dare come into that country for darkness; and nevertheless, they of the country thereby say that they may sometimes hear therein the voice of man and horse crying, and cocks crowing, and they know full well that men dwell there, but they know not what manner of men.' Here, too, the frontiers of three countries meet – Persia, Turkey and the U.S.S.R. And here or hereabouts, in the Caucasus and the Anti-Caucasus and in the highlands of Armenia, in this vast tangle of mountains and valleys running this way or that, you will find a kaleidoscopic jumble of races and nations, languages, religions and civilizations such as exists nowhere else in the world.

All through the ages, the deep valleys and pathless mountains of the Caucasus have served to split up the population into innumerable tribes and to preserve in isolation the scattered remnants of the various races who in the course of history have passed this way or been washed up and stranded here on the flood-tide of some migration or invasion. If you cross the watershed between two deep valleys, you can find two tribes living a few miles from each other who speak a different language, profess a different religion, and belong to an entirely different race from their neighbours. And this pattern is repeated again and again throughout the whole region. The Mountain of Languages, the Arabs called it. 'We Romans', wrote Pliny, 'conducted our affairs there with the aid of one hundred and thirty interpreters.'

One tribe – the fair-haired Khevsurs – trace their origins to the Crusaders and within living memory still wore chain armour with a cross emblazoned on it back and front. The Abkhazians, according to some the handsomest race of all, claim descent from Prometheus himself. There are even, if you know where to look for them, Celts who play the pipes and dance reels and have other Highland habits, and the tombstones in the old graveyards bear the same intricate ribbon patterns as in our own Western Isles.

Transcaucasia, the land beyond the Caucasus, is divided today into three Soviet Socialist Republics: Georgia, Armenia and Azerbaijan. Azerbaijan, before becoming part of Persia and now, more recently, of Russia, was a Tartar khanate, or rather several Tartar khanates, not so very different from their neighbours across the Caspian. The history of the two Christian countries stretches back beyond their conquest by

Russia into the mists of antiquity. We are all, I suppose, descended from Noah. The Armenians and Georgians are more specific. While the former trace their descent from Noah's great-great-grandson, Haik, and call their country Hayastan, or Land of Haik, the latter claim that they go back to Haik's brother Karthlos and call themselves Kartvelhi or Karthlians and their country Sakartvelo or Karthli. The name Georgian, which Western Europeans later quite incorrectly sought to derive from St George, the country's patron saint, comes originally from the Arab or Persian *Kurj* or *Gurj*.

Quite certainly the Armenians have existed as a nation for a very long time. Few people or countries have a longer history. As their country has been constantly overrun by foreign invaders, it is scarcely surprising that their racial origins should be obscure, though there is a strongly held theory linking them with the Phrygians. Their language (and this is quite a separate problem) is, unlike that of their neighbours the Georgians, Indo-European of a rather special kind. Mention of their forerunners, and probably forefathers, the Urartians, is made in an Assyrian inscription of the thirteenth century B.C. And by the ninth century Urartu, as Armenia was then known, was one of the most powerful states in the Middle East and had become a serious rival to the Assyrians. Writing in 594 B.C., the prophet Jeremiah mentions the Kingdom of Urartu as an enemy of Babylon and we hear of clashes between the two. But four or five years later Urartu had been finally overthrown by the Medes.

The transition from Urartu to Armenia, in so far as there was one, seems to have taken place during the sixth century B.C. By 521 Armenia, as it was already called, had become a satrapy of the Persian Empire of Darius the Great, being listed as such in the famous inscription at Behistun near Kermanshah. It is also mentioned as part of Persia by Herodotus, who, writing in the middle of the fifth century B.C., comments favourably on the proficiency of the Armenians as innkeepers.

The Persians held sway over Armenia for almost two hundred years, from 521 to 334 B.C. Xenophon, who with his Ten Thousand traversed the area during the winter of 401 to 400 B.C., has left a famous account of it in which he complains of the appalling cold. Having travelled over the same route with my wife in an open Land Rover at much the same

13

time of year as he did, I can sympathize with him on this score. However, our journey had plentiful compensations, and so, one gathers, did his.

On their way through the country, Xenophon tells us, the Greeks captured the state tent of Governor Tiribazus of Armenia, complete with a set of silver-footed couches and some drinking cups. These they immediately put to very good use, having been provided by some hospitable local villagers with 'old wines with a fine bouquet'. Also 'an extremely strong beverage' made from barley, which they were obliged to dilute before they could drink it, but which they found 'extremely good when one got used to it'. When Xenophon went to see how his troops were getting on in their camp, he found them, he tells us, 'faring sumptuously ... there was no place from which the men would let them go until they had served them a luncheon and no place where they did not serve on the same table lamb, kid, pork, veal and poultry together with many loaves of bread.' In another place he found them feasting in their quarters 'crowned with wreaths of hay and served by Armenian boys in their strange foreign dress'. Clearly a good time was had by all. Through the centuries Armenian hospitality has in no way diminished and to the modern traveller Xenophon's account of his experiences has a most familiar ring.

For a time, the Armenians took advantage of the dynastic quarrels of their Persian overlords to win a greater measure of autonomy. But, with the victory of Alexander the Great over the Persians at Arbela in 331 B.C., they found themselves brought abruptly under Macedonian suzerainty. Henceforward Armenia, under a succession of rulers, enjoyed varying degrees of independence as part of the sphere of Graeco-Oriental influence which Alexander of Macedon left behind him.

For the space of forty years or so, from 95 to 50 B.C., King Dikran or Tigranes the Great ruled over an independent Armenian empire extending from the Caspian to the Mediterranean and from Mesopotamia to the Pontic Alps, and Armenia emerged once more as a major power in the Middle East, only to fall in the end under the dominion of Rome. Subsequent rulers sought, with varying degrees of success, to play the Persians off against the Romans and *vice versa*. Following the defeat and capture of the Roman Emperor Valerian by the Great King Shapur I in A.D. 260, Armenia again became part of

Persia. But in 286, under Diocletian, Rome recovered her former losses and it was under Roman auspices that King Trdat or Tiridates III was restored to the throne of his ancestors.

With the conversion of Tiridates in the year 303 by his cousin, St Gregory the Illuminator (whom he had previously kept confined for fourteen years in a well full of reptiles), Armenia came to be the bulwark of Christianity in Asia. This was a full generation before Christianity reached Rome. Henceforward the Armenian Church was to play a vital part in the affairs of the Armenian nation. A hundred years later, at the beginning of the fifth century, the invention of a special Armenian alphabet by a holy man named Saint Mesrop gave fresh impetus to its work and influence, making it at long last possible for the gospels and much else besides to be distributed and read in the vernacular.

But the Persians still kept up their pressure; the Armenian nobles were divided amongst themselves; and towards the middle of the fifth century Armenia was again conquered by Persia. For a considerable time the Armenian Christians had to endure savage persecution at the hands of Persian fire-worshippers. Then, in the seventh century, came conquest by the Arabs and the rapid spread of Islam throughout the Middle East with the result that the Armenians exchanged one form of oppression for another. During the centuries that followed, what had once been the territories of Armenia were bandied about between the Persians, the Byzantine Emperors and the Mohammedan Khalifs of Bagdad.

In the ninth century Armenia briefly regained a measure of independence and some of her former glory and for a century and a half a small Armenian kingdom, with its capital at Ani, flourished under the Bagratids, a princely Armenian family who also held sway in the neighbouring kingdom of Georgia. This was the high point of medieval Armenian civilization and prosperity. At Ani and elsewhere Armenian architecture and the other national arts blossomed and flourished, achieving a harmonious blend of eastern and western influences which has found a happy echo in the architecture of present-day Soviet Armenia. But in 1064 both Armenia and Georgia were again overrun, this time by the Seljuk Sultan Alp Arslan, and, as the Turkish invasion swept on to the Caucasus and the Black Sea, Ani, with its magnificent churches and palaces, was sacked and burnt and has remained a ghost-town ever since. Only in far away Cilicia did a dynasty of Armenian kings continue for a time to rule over a kind of Armenian enclave.

The existence of Armenia as an independent or even semi-independent state was now at an end. During the centuries that followed, its remnants were fought over by Mongols, Turks and Persians, and a great part of the inhabitants scattered far and wide over the world. But the Armenian people survived. Thanks to the stubborn tenacity which is an outstanding characteristic of their race, they somehow managed, despite persecution and massacre, to retain their identity as a nation. In this the Armenian Church, independent since the fifth century of both Rome and Byzantium, continued to play a vital part. The Armenians, wherever they were, clung to their religion with a zeal made all the more desperate by the knowledge that it was now all that remained of their nationhood, and through the centuries the Katholikos of Holy Etchmiadzin, to this day the Head of the Armenian Church throughout the world, acted as a national as well as a religious leader.

The recorded history of Georgia, like that of Armenia, goes back a long way. Archaeological discoveries point to a high degree of civilization in the Bronze Age and before. Colchis was known to the Greeks and already open to Greek influence in Homer's day. Indeed, it is more than probable that both Medea and her father Aeëtes, King of Colchis, were in fact historical characters and that Jason and his Argonauts actually came to Western Georgia on some kind of quest, probably commercial in character. 'Aeëtes', writes Strabo in his *Geography*, 'is believed to have ruled over Colchis and the name Aeëtes is still in use among the people of that region. Again Medea the Sorceress is a historical figure and the wealth of the regions round Colchis, derived from mines of gold, silver, iron and copper, suggest an adequate reason for the expedition.'

In classical times, Xenophon traversed Georgia on his way to the sea in the year 400 B.C. and seventy or eighty years later we hear of it as a dominion of Alexander the Great. Mtzkheta, the ancient capital, has been an inhabited town for two or three thousand years. After Alexander there followed various dynasties of semi-independent native kings, living in uneasy proximity to their Persian and Armenian neighbours. For a time around 100 B.C., Colchis became part of the dominions of

16

Mithridates Eupator, King of Pontus. But in 66–65 B.C., following Pompey's invasion of Georgia or, as the Romans called it, Iberia, both Colchis and Eastern Georgia fell under Roman hegemony though not under Roman occupation. The kings of Iberia were made 'friends and allies of the Roman People' and Roman influence became paramount.

For all this, the Georgians maintained a certain measure of independence and in A.D. 114 a second invasion of Georgia, this time by the Emperor Trajan, became necessary. Nor did they sever all links with their Persian neighbours. For a time, as the years went by, Roman and Persian influence existed side by side. Then, in about the third century A.D., with the gradual waning of Roman power in the east and the rise of the Sassanid dynasty in Persia, Persian influence started to predominate.

It was under a Persian-born king, Mirian, founder of the Chosroid dynasty, that in about the year 330 Georgia was converted to Christianity by Nino or Nouni, a holy slave-woman from Cappadocia or thereabouts. St Nino first won the confidence of Mirian's queen, Nana, by miraculously curing her from a mysterious complaint. Next, King Mirian, while out hunting, found himself suddenly enveloped in total darkness which as suddenly dissolved when he invoked Nana's new God. Work on a Christian church in Mirian's capital Mtzkheta was at first held up owing to the difficulty of hoisting the central pillar into position. But one morning the pillar was found hovering miraculously in mid-air, after which it neatly lowered itself on to its base and the church was completed on time. Confronted with so many indisputable proofs of the potency of the new religion, most Georgians, following the example of their Royal Family, hastened to embrace it. Some, however, the mountain clans in particular, persisted in their pagan practices – much to St Nino's disgust. Indeed near Kola, in southwestern Georgia, some stubbornly heathen peasants threw their children into a pit and stoned them to death, rather than allow them to become Christians. The children, poor little things, are rightly numbered among the martyrs of the early Georgian church.

The first church at Mtzkheta was made of wood and was only later replaced by a stone building. It bore, in recognition of its miraculous construction, the name of *Svetitskhoveli*, the Church of the Life-Giving Pillar. According to some accounts, it was built on the spot where

Christ's Coat without a Seam was found, after being brought there direct from Golgotha by a wandering Jew named Elioz, no doubt a founding father of the flourishing Jewish community which has existed in Georgia since very early times.

The conversion of Georgia to Christianity, which conveniently coincided with that of the Emperor Constantine, was an event of more than purely religious importance. Like Armenia a generation earlier, Georgia became an outpost of Christian civilization in the Middle East. Henceforward, the Georgian Church played a big part in the life of the nation and their Christian faith helped them, like the Armenians, to preserve their national identity and unity through all the vicissitudes of the centuries that followed. 'The kernel of the religion of the Cross', an Arab writer was to call them.

The Chosroid dynasty, founded by King Mirian (who, like Nino, was in due course canonized), ruled in Georgia for two centuries, establishing a feudal system based on nine *Eristavs* or Provincial Governors, who held civil and military power under the King, and helped him to control the numerous and turbulent territorial nobility. Perhaps the most famous of the later Chosroid monarchs was King Vakhtang, surnamed Gorgaslan, the Wolf-Lion, a kind of Georgian King Arthur, who reigned from about 446 to 510 and amongst other things moved the capital of Georgia from Mtzkheta to Tbilisi and secured independent status for the Georgian national church which, like the Armenian, henceforward became autocephalous, electing its own Katholikos-Patriarch.

After the death of King Vakhtang, who had made himself master of Abkhazia, Ossetia and a large part of Armenia, the Georgian monarchy was so weakened by internal dissension and by the intermittent struggle between Byzantium and Persia for control of the Caucasus that in the middle of the sixth century the reigning King of Persia was able to abolish it altogether and assume direct control of Georgian affairs. During the next two or three hundred years local princes and tribal chieftains ruled over as much territory as they could effectively control under Persian or Byzantine or, after the Arab invasion of the seventh century, Arab overlords.

Meanwhile in the marchlands of Georgia and Armenia a new dynastic force had arisen; the Bagratid princes of Speri or Ispir. The Bagratids had already held high office in Armenia for five or six centuries, moving into Georgia towards the end of the eighth century. It was not long before they had assumed complete control there. Settling in south-western Georgia, Ashot Bagration the Great (780–826) was granted by the Emperor of Byzantium the title of *Kuropalates* or Guardian of the Palace, after which, taking advantage of the remoteness of his imperial suzerain and, for that matter, of the Arab Khalif of Bagdad, he very soon established himself as *de facto* ruler of Iberia, and a century later, in 866, his descendant Adarnase IV Bagration formally assumed the title of King of the Georgians. It was a title that was to remain in his family for the best part of a thousand years.

The Bagrations claimed descent from the union of David and Bath-sheba and displayed on their heavily laden coat of arms the Lion of Judah, David's sling, the Psalmist's harp, Solomon's scales and Christ's Coat without a Seam. 'I', ran their title, 'Bagration, King by God's Grace, Heir of our Saviour Jesus Christ, Son of King Solomon and King David, Lord of Lords, Heir of Moses.' And it is related that in St Petersburg, before the Revolution of 1917, at least one elderly Princess Bagration always wore mourning on the feast of the Assumption of the Virgin Mary on the grounds that it had been a family bereavement.

Under the new dynasty the unification of Georgia continued and in 1008 King Bagrat III became King of both Eastern and Western Georgia, his reign coinciding with a period of high achievement in church architecture, notably in the great cathedral churches at Kutaisi in Imeretia, at Alaverdi in Kakhetia and finally at Mtzkheta, where another magnificent cathedral was built on the site of St Nino's little wooden church.

Tbilisi, meanwhile, remained in Moslem hands. These were bad years for the cause of Christianity in the Middle East. During the second half of the eleventh century the Seljuk Turks from Central Asia under their great leader Alp Arslan swept westward into Asia Minor, capturing, as we have seen, the Armenian capital of Ani, devastating large parts of Georgia and finally inflicting a decisive defeat on the Byzantines at Manazkert to the north of Lake Van in 1071, the same year in which they took Jerusalem. Georgia, under Bagrat IV and George II, was overrun and humiliated. It was not until towards the end of the century, when the feeble George II abdicated in favour of his sixteen-year-old son David IV, that there were signs of an improve-ment, an improvement which was reinforced by the timely arrival of the

Crusaders in the Middle East in 1097 and their capture of Jerusalem in 1099.

David IV, who has gone down in history as Agmashenebeli, the Builder or Restorer, was not only a great patron of the arts, but also an outstanding statesman and military leader, who between 1110 and 1121 won a series of brilliant victories over the Seljuk Turks, drove the Moslems from Tbilisi and after almost four hundred years of occupation successfully annexed large parts of the former kingdom of Armenia. King of the Forests, the Turks called him mockingly at the onset of his campaigns, but they soon learned to fear and respect him as a master of both guerrilla and conventional warfare. Soon Georgian influence, military, political and economic, extended from the Black Sea to the Caspian and Georgia became the centre of a new prosperity and culture which was to endure for several generations. It was during David's reign and under his personal supervision that the splendid monastery was built at Gelati where he himself lies buried and where, at the Academy he endowed, the great philosopher Joane Petritsi founded his famous school of neo-Platonist metaphysical philosophy. Though a staunch Christian, David was no bigot. Indeed, after capturing Tbilisi, he quickly granted an amnesty to the Moslem inhabitants. 'He soothed their hearts', says a contemporary Moslem writer, 'and left them alone in all goodness.' In fact he even spared their feelings by forbidding the pork-loving Georgians to bring their pigs into the Moslem part of the town.

David the Builder died in 1125. What he had begun was, after fifty years of stagnation, no less ably continued by his great-granddaughter Tamara who reigned, at first as co-regnant with her father, George III, from 1178 to 1213, and then on her own. Under her Georgia's power and prestige may be said to have reached their zenith. Like her great-grandfather, Queen Tamara was a considerable military leader. After Constantinople had been sacked by the so-called Fourth Crusade in 1204, she set up at Trebizond on the Black Sea a new Byzantine Empire which was to endure for two and a half centuries, installing as Emperor her own kinsman, Alexius Comnenus, a member of the Imperial Family who happened to have been brought up in Georgia. She also launched a number of successful expeditions against Persia, raiding Ardebil, Tabriz and Kazvin and occupying part of Azerbaijan. Tamara was married first to the Russian Prince George Bogoliubskoi from Suzdal near

Moscow, a vicious, drunken adventurer, whom she found it necessary to divorce and indeed expel from Georgia for sexual and other misconduct, and secondly to David Soslan, a prince from Ossetia, to whom she bore a son and a daughter, her own immediate successor, King George IV and Queen Rusudan, who later succeeded her brother. A subsequent attempt by George Bogoliubskoi to usurp the Georgian throne with Turkish support was successfully repelled.

It was during Queen Tamara's reign, according to tradition, that the great Georgian epic poet, Shota Rustaveli, author of *The Knight in the Panther Skin*, lived and flourished, becoming her Chancellor of the Exchequer, falling desperately in love with her and ending his days, broken-hearted, at a monastery in Jerusalem. Some later scholars, however, have maintained that Rustaveli did not in fact write *The Knight in the Panther Skin*, that he did not live in Tamara's time, that he therefore could not have fallen in love with her or held high office under her and, finally, that in all probability he never existed at all. A version which, if we accept it, leaves us with a fine but anonymous allegorical epic poem of great breadth of vision, harmoniously fusing the currents of neo-Platonist philosophy and eastern romance; and a town called Rustavi, which, it is thought, would have been Rustaveli's birthplace had he ever been born, and is today the site of a gigantic metallurgical combine, which is the pride of all Georgia. In one of his ballads the poet Lermontov shows Tamara in a somewhat unkind light, as a heartless harridan who caused her discarded lovers to be thrown to their destruction from a castle in the Caucasus, where the traveller is still shown at least one site ideally suited for this purpose. Those who have made a deeper study of Georgian history, however, deny the whole story, though admitting that it did not take her long to get rid of George Bogoliubskoi.

Queen Tamara, whatever her merits or demerits, and the former almost certainly outweighed the latter, died in 1213. Two years later, in 1215, Jenghiz Khan, who was now well and truly launched on his career of conquest, took Peking and then, leaving China for the time being, turned westwards, his arrival being heralded in Georgia by travellers' tales of 'a strange people, speaking a strange tongue' and sweeping all before them. By 1221 the Mongols had overrun all Persia and reached the frontiers of Transcaucasia, utterly defeating the Armenian and Georgian armies that were sent against them. George IV and the flower of Georgian chivalry were routed. Soon Azerbaijan, Armenia and Georgia had all been annexed. Tbilisi was taken and Tamara's twenty-nine-year-old daughter Queen Rusudan, who had succeeded her brother George on his death in 1223 and who, according to one well-informed source, was 'fearless only in her lusts', was forced to take refuge in the mountains of Imeretia.

The Mongol invasions put an end to Georgia's Golden Age and, for the time being, to her independence: henceforward her kings became vassals of the Mongol Il-Khans. Early in the fourteenth century, it is true, there were some signs of a national revival, but during the last two decades the whole of Transcaucasia became a battleground for Tamerlane, who repeatedly overran and devastated the country with his armies in the course of his far-flung campaigns against the Persians, the Turks and the Golden Horde whose Khan, Toktamish, he finally defeated at Tatartub on the River Terek in April 1395. Soon, in Georgia, the towns and palaces and monasteries of an earlier age lay in ruins, while their erstwhile inhabitants took refuge in the mountains. Trade was at a standstill and the grass grew on what had once been busy highways.

The last king of a united Georgia was Alexander I, who reigned from 1412 to 1443. Under his sons the country was divided up into three smaller kingdoms, each ruled over by a different branch of the Bagration family and each at variance with the other. A strong, resolute monarch might have united Georgia, but, as W. E. D. Allen puts it, 'here were no cold, wary Tudors, whetting their axe for their distant cousins, but a pack of Christian gentlemen, wasting the land in chivalrous fracas.' Henceforward the senior branch of the Bagratids reigned over the Kingdom of Karthli, namely Tbilisi and the rest of central Georgia. From Kutaisi a second branch governed Western Georgia or Imeretia and a third, based on Telavi, governed Eastern Georgia or Kakhetia, while several lesser princely families set up as minor monarchs on their own in various outlying areas: the Dadianis in Mingrelia, the Gurielis in Guria, the Gelovanis in Svanetia, and so on.

By 1453, following the fall of Constantinople to the Ottoman Turks, the Black Sea had become a Turkish lake and Georgia was now completely cut off from Western Christendom. With the loss of their national unity, the Georgians became an easy prey for their southern neighbours. In 1510 the Turks, who had inherited the Mongol tradition of military efficiency, invaded Imeretia and sacked Kutaisi and soon after this the Shah of Persia attacked Karthli. Towards the end of the sixteenth century the Turks took advantage of the disturbed state of Persia to seize the whole of Transcaucasia including Persian Azerbaijan. But, following the accession to the Persian throne in 1587 of the great Shah Abbas, the situation was quickly reversed. The Turks were driven out of Eastern Georgia and every possible step taken to turn it into a Persian province, starting with liquidation or deportation of any potentially troublesome Georgians.

It was not until the middle of the seventeenth century that the lot of the inhabitants of Central and Eastern Georgia became more tolerable, following the arrival in Tbilisi of what would today be termed an operator: one Khusran-Mirza, an elderly and illegitimate member of the Bagration family, who had become a Moslem and gone over to the Persians, with whom he possessed considerable influence and whom he showed great skill in conciliating. Marrying (according to both Christian and Moslem rites) Kateran Abashidze, the daughter of a great Georgian noble, he now assumed, with Persian support, the style of King Rostom I of Georgia, and from his delightful palace overlooking the Kura ruled in Tbilisi for twenty-six years with good sense and moderation. The Georgian patriots, needless to say, detested this elderly cynic as much as the Persian ways he introduced, 'luxury and high living, dissipation and unchastity, dishonesty, love of pleasure, baths and unseemly attire, lute and flute players'. But a probably more objective French traveller, the Chevalier J. Chardin, gives another view. 'Everywhere', he writes, 'he re-established peace and order, and governed with much clemency and justice.'

Over Imeretia, meanwhile, and the lesser principalities of Western Georgia, the Turks retained a loose suzerainty, leaving the population very much to their own devices, but sending an occasional punitive expedition to discipline some wayward prince and exacting in the meantime a regular tribute of handsome young male and female Georgian or Circassian slaves, whose good looks were at a premium in the slave-market of Constantinople.

Thus, in the centuries that followed, Georgia remained, in practice, partitioned between Persia and Turkey. There were periods when the Bagratid kings in Tbilisi enjoyed a somewhat greater measure of independence, but for most of the time they were little more than satraps of the Shah, hovering judiciously between Christian and Moslem religions and dividing their time no less judiciously between Tiflis and Isfahan. In the eighteenth century, it is true, during the long reign of King Hercules II, there came a partial revival of their power. But by now the Georgians were beginning to come under pressure from the north as well as from the south.

2 Northern Neighbour

For a good many hundred years there had been contacts of a kind between the peoples of the Caucasus and their northern neighbours. Already in the tenth century Russian raiders, dragging their boats overland, had appeared on the waters of the Caspian, while others waged war on and off against the tribes of the north-western Caucasus and gained a foothold on the Peninsula of Taman. In the thirteenth century Queen Tamara of Georgia had, as we have seen, been briefly married to George, son of Prince Andrew Bogoliubskoi, and in 1319 Michael of Tver was assassinated near Derbend. In 1492 King Alexander of Kakhetia sent an embassy of friendship to Ivan III of Moscow, and in the mid-sixteenth century, after capturing Kazan and Astrakhan, Ivan the Terrible took Kakhetia under Russian protection and sent the King a Russian bodyguard. He also took a Circassian princess as one of his many wives. But sustained relations between the Russians and the tribes of the Caucasus began only with the Cossack invasion of the Terek delta in the second half of the sixteenth century.

The Cossacks were marauding border-bands of Russian nomad horsemen, many of them originally outlaws or exiles or fugitives from justice, who first made their appearance during the troubled times which followed the Tartar and Mongol invasions. Gradually they came to occupy most of the disputed frontier areas to the south and east of Russia and Poland, whence they harassed and attacked their Moslem neighbours, driving back the Tartar hordes and so adding ever more territory to the Empire of the Tsars, whose suzerainty they had eventually come to accept. Some of their expeditions were successful and others, including an attempt in 1594 to capture the strategic fortress of Tarku in Daghestan, were less so, but by the end of the sixteenth century the Cossacks had firmly established themselves along the River Terek, holding it against all comers in the name of the Tsar, intermarrying and living on more or less amicable terms with the local tribes and their princes. Nor did they confine their military operations to their own immediate neighbourhood. In 1716 the Cossacks from the Terek sent a force of some eight hundred men, commanded by Prince Bekovich-Cherkasski, to join Peter the Great's ill-fated expedition against the remote Central Asian Khanate of Khiva, far away beyond the Caspian. Of these only two returned to tell the tale, Prince Bekovich-Cherkasski himself having been flayed alive and his skin, stuffed with straw, hung up above the principal gate of Khiva.

Six years later, in 1722, Peter sent a more successful expedition into the Caucasus, capturing Derbend on the Caspian and further strengthening the Cossack positions on the Terek. This process of reinforcement and consolidation was to continue on and off for the next hundred years, forts being built and Cossack garrisons and settlements installed, until, finally, what was known as the Great Cossack Line stretched right across the northern Caucasus, from the Black Sea to the Caspian for almost five hundred miles without a break, and came to form an integral part of the defences of the Empire. 'The Cossacks', wrote the great General Suvorov, 'are the eye of the Army.' The Advance-Guard of the Advance-Guard was another name that was given to them.

Originally the Cossack Line had been defensive in character, but, as time went on, the plight of Christian Georgia was to provide the Russians with a pretext for pressing on across the main range of the Caucasus and confronting the encroaching Turks and Persians. Through the centuries the early Mongol and Tartar invasions had been followed by continual acts of aggression and penetration on the part of successive Sultans of Turkey and Shahs of Persia. But, until the eighteenth century, the Russians had been too remote to be able to respond effectively to the appeals for help which from time to time reached them from the Christians of Transcaucasia.

In 1723, in the course of a war with the Persians, the Russian General Matiushkin had, it is true, followed Peter the Great's capture of Derbend by taking Baku (much to the delight of Peter, who called the captured city 'the key to all our business') and also by occupying the adjoining Persian provinces of Ghilan and Mazenderan. But in the following reign, under the Empress Anne, these conquests had been surrendered and the Russians had of their own accord once again fallen back to the Terek Line.

For the Georgians, the consequences of Russian intervention in the

Caucasus, followed as often as not by subsequent changes of plan, were not always happy. Thus King Vakhtang VI of Karthli, a most enlightened and progressive monarch, fell heavily between several stools when, having agreed in 1722 to help Peter the Great and having refused, at his request, to give his suzerain the Shah the support he needed against the rebellious Afghans, saw Persia suddenly collapse into chaos and Turkey take advantage of this to march into Georgia and occupy his capital of Tbilisi, with the result that he himself ended his days in exile in Astrakhan, where the Russians, after a good deal of equivocation, eventually agreed to grant him asylum.

After this unhappy episode there was an understandable decline in Russian influence in Georgia and it was not until well into the long reign of King Hercules II (1744–98) that a fresh *rapprochement* took place between the two countries.

Hercules is described as having 'a greenish brown complexion', a melodiously sweet voice and 'such a quickness of apprehension that at the opening of any subject he understood the whole extent of it' – no doubt a useful asset for anyone in his situation. In his formidable queen Darejan he was to find a consort worthy of him. As a young man, he had given loyal service to Nadir Shah of Persia, and in 1744 the latter had rewarded him by making him King of Kakhetia, while his father Timuraz II reigned over Karthli. It was thus that on his father's death in 1762, Hercules became king of a combined East Georgian Kingdom.

The curse of Georgia at this time was incessant raiding by the Moslem mountain tribes of the Caucasus, constantly egged on by their Turkish co-religionists. To this extent King Hercules shared a common interest with Russia. For the past thirty years and more the Russians had been content to stand on the Terek Line. But with the accession to the throne of Catherine the Great in 1762, attention was once again focused on the Caucasus. In 1763 a fort was built at Mozdok on the Terek and later converted into a stronghold which was to serve as a cornerstone for the Russian conquest of the Caucasus. But the fortification of Mozdok was not only distasteful to the local Moslem Kabardan and Ossetian tribesmen. It also offended their protector, the Sultan of Turkey, who, after protesting without effect in St Petersburg, in 1768 declared war on Russia.

The ensuing war was to last for five years and to be fought by the Russians with varying fortunes and on several different fronts: on the

Danube, on the Dniester, in the Crimea and in the Caucasus itself, where the Georgians gave the Russians such help as they could. One of the most spectacular successes of the Caucasian campaign was achieved by General von Todtleben, a German soldier of fortune in the Russian service, who, after winning lasting fame in 1760 by his brilliant capture of Berlin for the Empress Elizabeth, had in the following year, by one of those sudden reversals of fortune which are such a feature of Russian life, been arrested by his own officers and, after a lengthy inquiry, condemned to be hung, drawn and quartered for high treason. Now, in 1769, having been reprieved by Catherine and re-promoted to the rank of Major-General, he assembled some 400 men and four guns, and, crossing the main range of the Caucasus by way of the Darial Gorge, took Tbilisi. The following year, after asking for and receiving reinforcements, he marched into Imeretia, took by storm the fortress of Bagdat, restored Kutaisi, the capital, which had been in Turkish hands for 120 years, to the local ruler, King Solomon I of Imeretia, and, routing without difficulty a Turkish army of 12,000 men who attempted to bar his way, laid siege to Poti on the Black Sea Coast.

At this juncture, having become involved in a series of complicated three-cornered quarrels and intrigues between Russians, Georgians and Imeretians, General von Todtleben, who in his relations with the Georgians at any rate had not always shown himself the most tactful of men, was suddenly recalled by Catherine. Three years later, leaving the Georgians and Imeretians to fend for themselves, the Empress decided, as suddenly, to withdraw all Russian forces to the Cossack Line. The war continued inconclusively for another two years in the northern Caucasus and the neighbouring Nogai steppes, with the Cossacks fighting against a much stronger combined force of Turks and Moslem tribesmen. Indeed, according to tradition, the Russians were on one occasion only saved from disaster by the timely appearance of Saints Barnabas and Bartholomew, who reduced the infidels to panic by riding along their front, mounted on white horses and clad in shining raiment. In gratitude for which a special chapel was later built on the scene of the battle to commemorate the helpful intervention of the two Apostles. In July 1774 the Russians and Turks signed the peace treaty of Kutchuk Kainardji. This formally forbade the Turks to give official help or encouragement to the Moslem tribes of the Caucasus, but did not in practice prevent them from continuing to do so.

The Russians, for their part, now concentrated once again on strengthening the Cossack Line (which they carried westwards from Mozdok as far as the Sea of Azov) and on generally consolidating their power on both flanks. Meanwhile the Moslem tribesmen fought among themselves and waged a desultory and inconclusive guerrilla war against the Russians who reacted against this harassment with varying degrees of violence. Thus in 1775, on instructions from Catherine, the Russian General Medem attacked the Outsmi of Karakaitagh on the Caspian, who had kidnapped one of the Empress's favourite scientists, Academician Gmelin. Having ravaged the Outsmi's dominions, General Medem next pushed south and temporarily reoccupied Derbend, whose ruler, a vassal of Persia, then retaliated by massacring the crew of the next Russian merchantman to be wrecked on the shores of the Caspian. Again, in 1782, Catherine's lover, Prince Gregory Potyomkin, annexed the adjoining peninsula of the Crimea, until then under Turkish suzerainty, and enforced Russian rule there with such ferocity that a large part of the Tartar inhabitants fled to Turkey.*

Soon after this, on orders from Prince Potyomkin, who personally presided over Catherine's eastern policy, the famous General Suvorov summoned the neighbouring Nogai Tartars, an offshoot of the Golden Horde who roamed over the Kuban Steppe to the north of the Cossack Line, to a great *durbar* and feast on the shores of the Sea of Azov. When they reacted unfavourably to his announcement that they were to be deported *en masse* to the Urals, he massacred all he could and hunted down and routed the remainder. For his presence of mind and resourcefulness on this occasion Suvorov was awarded the Order of St Vladimir (First Class), and the fertile steppes, now empty, were quickly repopulated with Cossacks and other Russian settlers. In this manner, the Russians, while consolidating the Cossack Line, secured their flanks and rear and, consciously or subconsciously, prepared the way for an eventual advance across the main range of the Caucasus.

The Treaty of Kutchuk Kainardji had put an end to any formal Turkish claims on Imeretia and Georgia, and in the north-west had fixed the River Kuban as the frontier between Russia and Turkey. The main threat to Georgia now came from Persia and, when in 1783 the new

---

* History sometimes repeats itself. It is interesting to note that in 1945, after the Second World War, the Soviet Government found it necessary to deport the remaining Tartar population of the Crimea to Central Asia and liquidate their Autonomous Republic on account of the apparent lack of enthusiasm of the inhabitants for the Soviet cause.

Shah, Ali Murad, sought to reimpose on the Georgians the suzerainty which his predecessors had once claimed, King Hercules II of Georgia at once appealed to Russia for help. The Commander-in-Chief of the Russian forces in the Caucasus, Lieutenant-General Count Paul Potyomkin, a cousin of Catherine's lover Gregory, was quick to seize the opportunity thus offered.

His first care was to build and garrison a fort, strategically sited to the north of the main range at the key point where the River Terek issues from the mountains, and connected by a line of fortified posts with Mozdok. To this he gave the name Vladikavkaz, or Ruler of the Caucasus. He next charged eight hundred of the soldiers under his command with the task of converting the rough bridle path, which at this time was still the only line of communication from Vladikavkaz across the mountain passes to Tiflis, into something more closely approaching a road. Work on the new road, eventually to become famous as the Georgian Military Highway, went ahead so fast that the following autumn Count Potyomkin himself was able to drive all the way from Vladikavkaz to Tbilisi in a carriage drawn by eight horses. He was followed on 3 November, 1783 by two Russian Jaeger battalions with four guns. The day they entered Tiflis was, as it happened, a bleak one and there were those in Tbilisi who said that the Russians had brought their climate with them. Early in 1784 Catherine formally took King Hercules II of Georgia under her protection and on 24 January he signed a document acknowledging himself her vassal.

In February 1784 General Suvorov returned to Russia and Count Paul Potyomkin took over command of both the Caucasian and the Kuban Army Corps, becoming in May 1785 the first Viceroy of the Caucasus, with his seat of government at Ekaterinograd on the Terek, where he built himself a handsome Viceregal Palace.

Meanwhile a new and highly significant character had appeared on the scene, the forerunner of others who were to prove a perpetual thorn in the flesh of the Russians.

The origins of the famous Moslem tribal leader Sheikh Mansur are mysterious. The first official Russian military reports to make mention of him stated that he had been born in Chechnia. According to other sources, he was a Tartar from Orenburg who had received his religious education in Bokhara. But many years later a series of documents were found in the State Archives at Turin in Northern Italy which threw an entirely new light on the subject. These were a number of letters written by the supposed Sheikh to his father which, if genuine, showed that he was in fact a certain Giovanni Battista Boetti, born in Italy at Monferrat, where his father was a notary. After running away from home at the age of fifteen, Giovanni Battista had, after various adventures, become a Dominican monk and been sent as a missionary to the Middle East, where, from a Christian preacher he had, in the course of further adventures, managed to convert himself into a Moslem prophet. The real truth of the matter will probably never now be discovered. But, whatever the mystery surrounding Sheikh Mansur's origins, there can be no doubt that as a guerrilla leader he was extremely successful.

On learning the extent of the new prophet's activities in Chechnia, Count Potyomkin at once sent a strong force into the forests and mountains of Chechnia to take him prisoner. Events now followed a pattern which, with the years, was to become increasingly familiar. The Russians stormed Aldi and burned it to the ground. But Sheikh Mansur escaped and on the return march the Russian expeditionary force was ambushed in the dense forest and almost annihilated.

Following this first victory the Sheikh's fame spread throughout the Caucasus, and fresh insurgents flocked to join him. Encouraged by this, he launched a series of daring attacks against a number of strongly fortified Russian positions and in each case was driven off after a fierce fight. These set-backs, the most important of which took place in 1785 at Tatartub, the ford across the River Terek where Tamerlane had defeated Toktamish in 1395, somewhat dampened the spirit of his followers. But Sheikh Mansur, undaunted, now took refuge with the Turks on the Black Sea coast and within a year had won as much influence and authority over the Circassians of the west as he had ever possessed over the Chechen tribesmen of the east. Under his leadership the Circassians once more began to raid the Kuban Steppe, attacking and burning Cossack villages, carrying off cattle and even threatening the town of Rostov itself.

With the renewed outbreak of war between Russia and Turkey in 1787, Sheikh Mansur became a greater menace than ever and Count Potyomkin, determined to eliminate him for good, sent out a number of strong columns across the Kuban Steppe to put him down. But, though several times defeated in battle, each time he managed to escape and finally again took refuge with the Turks, this time at Anapa on the Black Sea coast, a strongly fortified position still in Turkish hands near the mouth of the Kuban River.

For the Turks, Anapa, which, with the help of French engineers, had by now been turned into a first-class fortress, was a position of vital importance, serving as it did both as a base and as a jumping-off place for their religious, political and para-military operations in the Caucasus. For the Russians, it represented a corresponding threat and its possession soon became the central issue of the campaign. A first Russian expedition in 1788 withdrew when they realized the strength of the fortress they were to attack. In January 1789 a second force of eight thousand men managed to reach their objective after a painful approach march during which they were continuously harassed by the Circassian tribesmen along their route, but failed in the ultimate assault on Anapa and suffered appalling casualties during their retreat to the Kuban. A victory over a numerically much stronger Turkish force that autumn somewhat restored Russian morale and prepared the way for a third attempt to capture Anapa. This was made in June 1791, when General Count Gudovich with an army of 15 battalions of infantry, 3,000 sharpshooters, 54 squadrons of cavalry and 2 regiments of Cossacks with 50 guns, finally stormed the fortress and, 'exasperated by their long resistance', put the Turkish garrison of 15,000 men to the sword. One of the few prisoners taken was Sheikh Mansur, who was first carried off to St Petersburg for inspection by the Empress and then imprisoned on the notoriously insalubrious Island of Solovyetsk in the White Sea, until quite recently still in use as a repository for problem prisoners. There, some years later, he died, having first, according to the Turin archives, dispatched a final letter to his aged father in Italy asking for his forgiveness and signing himself, for the last time, Giovanni Battista Boetti, Preacher.

The war with Turkey was brought to an end by the Treaty of Jassy in January 1791. Trouble, meanwhile, was brewing in another quarter. Although Catherine had in January 1784 formally established her suzerainty over Georgia, the two Russian battalions sent there the year before had quickly been withdrawn. Thus, in the long run, Russia's brief intervention served only to exasperate Persia without producing any seriously deterrent effect and in 1795 the eunuch Aga Mohammed Shah invaded Georgia, sacked Tbilisi and massacred the inhabitants by hundreds. 'On this glorious occasion', wrote a Persian chronicler, 'the valiant warriors of Persia gave the Georgian unbelievers a foretaste of what they might expect on the Day of Judgement.' King Hercules II, now seventy-five, and his troops fought gallantly in defence of the city, but were borne down by overwhelming odds. Once inside the walls, Aga Mohammed's soldiers raped any women they fancied, at the same time neatly ham-stringing the virgins among them by cutting their right leg-muscles, so that for the next half-century or so Tbilisi was full of limping ladies.

Catherine's immediate answer to this outrage was to declare war on Persia, and Count Valerian Zubov, the twenty-four-year-old brother of her latest lover, Count Platon Zubov, was appointed Viceroy of the Caucasus with supreme command over the Russian armies in the field. Against all probability the choice proved an excellent one. Count Valerian's appointment was quickly justified by his daring and successful conduct of operations. Though Aga Mohammed threw eighty elephants into the battle, he was soundly defeated at Dandja and Derbend, being later murdered by his own servants while he slept, and Baku and Kuba fell to the Russians in rapid succession. Soon the Mugan Steppe and all the territory along the Caspian as far as the mouth of the Kura River were in the hands of the Russians and the Persian province of Azerbaijan was at their mercy. But at this moment, in November 1796, Catherine the Great died. Her son Paul I at once gave orders to put an end to the campaign and withdraw to the line of the Terek; Count Valerian Zubov was relieved of his command; the conquered Khanates on the Caspian recovered their limited independence and Persia her sovereignty over them.

It was not long, however, before events forced Paul to revise his ideas and once more turn his attention to Transcaucasia. After reigning wisely and more or less successfully for fifty years, King Hercules II of Georgia had finally died in January 1798 at Telavi in Kakhetia and had been succeeded by his weak, slothful, middle-aged and gluttonous son, George XII. Having failed in the first place to secure the succession for any of her own children, George's stepmother, the formidable Queen Darejan, was soon striving, by all the means at her disposal, to dethrone him and replace him by her own son, Prince Yulon. Tbilisi was seething with intrigue and unrest. To the Persians the temptation was irresistible. Encouraged by the confusion prevailing in Georgia and made bolder by the Russian withdrawal, Fath Ali, the new Shah of Persia, addressed to the unfortunate George XII letters, couched in the most uncompromising terms, demanding the immediate surrender of his eldest son as a hostage and threatening a fresh invasion of Georgia if he failed to comply with this request. Simultaneously the Persian army moved menacingly to the Georgian frontier.

The new Tsar's reaction to these threatening moves was to order General Knorring, his commander in the northern Caucasus, to be ready, should the need arise, to cross the mountains in strength and at the same time to assure the King of Georgia of Russia's determination to protect him against any attack. The Shah now vacillated. Egged on by another of King George's brothers, Prince Alexander, who had gone over to the Persians, he first crossed the River Aras. But then, dismayed at the actual prospect of war with Russia, wisely decided to withdraw.

For the time being the threat to Georgia had receded. But to King George XII, now in his turn dying of dropsy in Tbilisi, it seemed evident that his country's best hope of survival lay in union with Russia. From his deathbed he sent to St Petersburg a special embassy, begging the Tsar to 'take Georgia under his full authority'. On 18 December, 1800 Paul published a manifesto formally accepting this offer and George died ten days later. The Tsar's proclamation has a contemporary ring. He assumed this additional burden, he declared, not from any wish to extend his already vast Empire, but from motives of humanity and in response to the heartrending appeals of the suffering people of Georgia.

The Emperor Paul, as it happened, did not survive his neighbour for long. Barely three months later, in March 1801, he was assassinated and succeeded by his eldest son, Alexander, who quickly confirmed the annexation.

3 God, Hurrah and the Bayonet

With Paul's death many of those who had held appointments under Catherine returned to favour. Amongst them was Prince Paul Dmitrivich Tsitsitsvili or Tsitsianov, a Georgian of Russian upbringing who had served with distinction under Suvorov in Poland and under Zubov in the Caucasus and who in September 1802 was appointed Inspector-General of the Cossack Line and Commander-in-Chief in Georgia, in succession to General Knorring.

Tsitsianov, who during the next four years was to play an important part in Transcaucasia, was endowed with exceptional courage, energy, ability and determination. In addition to being a first-class fighting soldier, he was also an outstanding administrator. Born and bred in Russia, he was completely loyal to his adopted country, seeing Georgia's best hope for the future in union with Russia. At the same time his innate knowledge of his own people and of their character gave him advantages which no Russian could have possessed.

Prince Tsitsianov's first task on assuming his new responsibilities was a delicate one. In order to put an end to the innumerable intrigues with which the old Royal Palace in Tbilisi was seething, the decision had been taken to remove to Russia the remaining members of the former Georgian Royal Family, who were clearly likely to constitute a focal point for hostile and discontented elements. Old Queen Darejan – 'that Hydra', as Tsitsianov called her – was still in residence, manfully persisting in her attempts to put her son Prince Yulon on the throne. Several of the other princes, including, as we have seen, the late King's brother Alexander, had already taken refuge in Persia, whence they hoped to return in due course. But for Tsitsianov the most immediate threat was from King George's widow, Queen Mariam, who, hoping to see one of her sons succeed him, had from the first bitterly opposed her husband's decision to abdicate. She was, as it happened, Tsitsianov's own cousin, having, like him, been born a Tsitsitsvili, and was now openly intriguing against the Russians.

On his arrival at the Palace, General Lazarev, whom Prince Tsitsianov had sent to secure her person, was dismayed to find the Queen in her bed, from which she utterly refused to move. Worse still, her son and daughter now drew their daggers and attacked one of his officers. Thereupon General Lazarev himself approached the royal bedside. This was what the Queen had been waiting for. Drawing out her own dagger from underneath the bedclothes, she drove it into him with all her strength, killing him instantly.

As can readily be imagined, this whole episode caused a sensation in Tbilisi. But it also greatly simplified Tsitsianov's task. Despite a spirited attempt by the Khevsurs, or, according to other accounts, the Ossetians, to rescue her on her way across the mountains, Queen Mariam was now deported under guard to Russia as a common criminal, leaving Tsitsianov free to settle down, undisturbed, to the serious business of government. Old Queen Darejan, for her part, somehow managed to stay on in Tbilisi for another whole year before being finally deported to Russia by the long-suffering Tsitsianov in October 1803. After seven years in close confinement in an Orthodox convent at Voronezh, Queen Mariam was ultimately released and spent the next forty years or so in relative freedom in Moscow. On her death in 1850 her body was brought back to Georgia and buried there with full royal honours. Today her portrait, sallow and disagreeable-looking with an unpleasingly pursed-up mouth, hangs in the Picture Gallery at Tbilisi. It is easy to see that she could have been good with a knife.

As for Prince Tsitsianov, it soon became apparent that he had ideas of his own about the best way in which to govern the dominions entrusted to his care. 'I', he wrote to the Tsar, 'adopt the opposite system to that used hitherto. Instead of paying subsidies and giving gifts to these people in the hope of mitigating their highland manners, *I* demand tribute of *them*.' The diplomatic communications he addressed to the native Khans were framed in language which carried a readily comprehensible message. 'Is it', he wrote, 'reasonable for the fly to enter into negotiation with the eagle? Your bullet won't kill five men. My cannon, loaded with ball or with shrapnel, will mow down thirty at a time.' When the nominally independent Djaro-Byelokani tribesmen refused to hand over the princes of the Georgian Royal House who had sought asylum with them, their territory was promptly invaded. 'My blood boils like water in a kettle; my limbs tremble with rage,' Tsitsianov wrote when he heard that these same tribesmen had defeated the troops he had sent against them and killed their commander. And to the Sultan of Elisou, who had dared ally himself with them, his language was even more direct. 'Shameless Sultan, with the soul of a Persian', he wrote. 'So you still dare to write to me. Yours is the soul of a dog and the understanding of an ass ... Know that, until you become a loyal vassal of my Emperor, my only desire will be to wash my boots in your blood.' In the end both Elisou and the Djaro-Byelokani submitted, took the oath of allegiance to the Tsar and paid the tribute demanded of them.

Each month brought news of fresh conquests. In January 1804 the Khanate of Gandja was invaded and its Khan killed on the grounds that centuries earlier, in the days of good Queen Tamara, it had been part of Georgia. 'Five hundred Tartars', wrote Tsitsianov to the Tsar, 'shut themselves up in a mosque, meaning, perhaps to surrender, but an Armenian told our soldiers there were some Daghestanis among them and this was a death-signal for them all, so great is the exasperation of Your Majesty's troops against these people for their raids into Georgia and the guerrilla war they wage.' Mingrelia followed next and in April 1804 Imeretia, its ruler King Solomon II (whose portrait, heavily moustached and florid-looking, also hangs today in Tbilisi) submitting reluctantly and with the worst possible grace. 'Our Prince', wrote one of Tsitsianov's officers gleefully, 'makes music with bombshells and bullets and forces every Khan to dance to his playing.' But, whatever Tsitsianov's methods, it is impossible to deny their effectiveness. By the end of 1804 the territories of the ancient Georgian monarchy, divided up four hundred years before, had, thanks to him, been reunited under the Tsar and Russia's dominions in Transcaucasia now stretched from the Black Sea to the Caspian.

Sooner or later Tsitsianov's forward policy was bound to lead to trouble with Turkey and Persia, both of which had at one time or another claimed suzerainty over the greater part of the khanates he had annexed. In June 1804, with ten thousand men and twenty guns, he marched on Erivan in Armenia, still nominally an independent khanate and at that moment invested, as it happened, by a Persian army of 30,000 men. For once Tsitsianov failed in his objective and Erivan was occupied by the Persians. In the ensuing campaign, however, he several times defeated Persian forces vastly superior to his own in strength and managed to annex a number of other khanates to Russia. Finally the Shah himself, who, with an army of 40,000 men had marched out to meet him, once again had second thoughts and withdrew across the River Aras without striking a blow.

Tsitsianov's aim was to consolidate Russia's hold both on the Black Sea and on the Caspian, thus safeguarding her position against Turkey on the one hand and Persia on the other. With this in mind, having first built the fort of Redout Kalé on the Black Sea in Mingrelia, he now turned his attention to the Caspian and Baku. After a seaborne expedition, commanded by one of his subordinates, had been driven off somewhat ingloriously by a neighbouring Khan, the Viceroy decided to see what he could do himself. Following a difficult approach march through the mountains of Shirvan (which he annexed on the way), he arrived on 30 January, 1806, with 1,600 men and ten guns, at the frontier of the Khanate of Baku and, in a typically forthright manner, invited its ruler, Husayn-Kouli-Khan, to surrender his capital. Husayn-Kouli signed his assent, and on the appointed day rode out with a mounted escort, apparently to hand over the keys in person to Tsitsianov, who advanced to meet him accompanied only by his aide-de-camp, Prince Eristov, a fellow Georgian. No sooner, however, were Tsitsianov and his A.D.C. within range than the Khan and his party drew their pistols and opened fire on them, killing both the Viceroy and Eristov. Simultaneously the guns of Baku opened up on the Russians, who, demoralized by the loss of their leader, withdrew northwards in confusion. Tsitsianov's head and hands were now cut off and sent in triumph to the Shah, with whom Husayn-Kouli was anxious to ingratiate himself. His body was buried beneath the walls of Baku, where it was to remain for the next five years, before being finally dug up in 1811 and reburied in Tbilisi in the Sion Cathedral which Tsitsianov had endowed with a fine campanile only a few years earlier.

Tsitsianov's death was to be the signal for renewed trouble throughout the Caucasus. His successors lacked his outstanding qualities. By the end of 1806, it is true, both Derbend and Baku and the intervening Khanate of Kuba had been forced to surrender and duly annexed to Russia; but, further north, in the mountains, the Ossetians had risen and the Kabardans and the tribes beyond the Kuban were again raiding Russian settlements. In western Georgia, meanwhile, King Solomon II of Imeretia was openly defying his new masters; the Khan of Baku, who had taken refuge with the Persians together with the Georgian ex-Crown Prince Alexander, had invaded Georgia from Erivan; a Persian army was marching on Shusha; the ever-turbulent Djaro-Byelokanis had again rebelled; and a number of other khans had seized the opportunity to throw off their allegiance and attacked Russian outposts. As soon as one uprising was put down, another broke out.

With Napoleon now threatening the Vistula, no reinforcements could be expected from European Russia. A temporary armistice was patched up with Persia, but in 1807, thanks to Napoleon's skilful diplomacy in the Middle East, war broke out again with Turkey. For the next five years it was as much as the Russians in the Caucasus, under commanders of varying merit, could do to hold their own against the periodic attacks of the Turks and Persians and constant harassing by the insurgent tribesmen. Finally, in 1812, the year of Napoleon's invasion of Russia, the latent unrest in Georgia came to a head and soon all Kakhetia was in turmoil. Everywhere the Russian garrisons were besieged by the insurgents. In Tbilisi itself, where the suppression of the independent Georgian Church had caused great indignation, trouble was brewing. Raiding parties of Lesghians penetrated the outskirts of the city and to the north in the mountains the rebellion had reached Ananuri and spread into Ossetia. There was trouble from the Black Sea to the Caspian. It was not long before, in the main range of the Caucasus, between Vladikavkaz and Tbilisi, all the mountain tribes had risen, Christians and Moslems alike.

In May 1812 a treaty, bringing peace with Turkey, was signed at Bucharest. Though it restored to the Turks everything they had lost for years past, it at least brought a measure of relief to the hard-pressed Russians, who could now concentrate their limited resources against their remaining enemies. The Ossetian tribesmen, threatening Tbilisi from the north, were now quickly beaten and dispersed and the road cleared to Vladikavkaz. In October the former Crown Prince Alexander of Georgia and his armed bands of Daghestanis were finally defeated in Kakhetia and a few days later the main Persian army was utterly routed on the banks of the River Aras with the loss of 10,000 men. 'God, hurrah, and the bayonet', wrote the Russian commander jubilantly, 'have brought victory to His Most Gracious Majesty.'

Fighting for the Persians on this occasion at the head of the Persian troops they had trained, were two British officers, Major Christie, the son of the auctioneer, and Captain Lindsay, both, not unnaturally, under strict orders not to take part in any hostilities against a country with which Great Britain was now allied against Napoleon. Determined, in these circumstances, not to be taken alive, Christie, though shot in the neck, managed to kill six Russians before he himself was finally dispatched by a Cossack. Amongst the arms captured by the Russians were eleven cannon of British manufacture, inscribed, or so the angry Russians said, 'From the King of Kings to the Shah of Shahs'.

Crossing the snowy Mugan Steppe in December 1812 the Russians next stormed the Persian fortress of Lenkoran on the Caspian, recently rebuilt with the help of British engineers, and massacred the Persian garrison who were holding it. 'The extreme exasperation of the soldiers at the obstinacy of the defence', wrote the Russian commander to the Tsar, 'caused them to bayonet every one of the 4,000 Persians composing the Garrison. Not a single officer or man escaped death.'

Next year, in October 1813, peace between Russia and Persia was signed. Under a treaty concluded at Gulistan, Persia abandoned her claims to Georgia, Imeretia, Mingrelia, Abkhasia and Daghestan and Russia was confirmed in her possession of Baku, Derbend and the other khanates and territories she had recently acquired, including the hard-won frontier fortress of Lenkoran. A successful Russian campaign against the rebellious Khevsurs rounded off the year 1813 and, now that there was no longer any hope of active help from Turkey or Persia, there was less trouble from the other mountain tribes. One of those who held out longest against the Russians was King, or, as he preferred to call himself, Tsar, Solomon II of Imeretia, the last of the Bagratids to hold power. In 1810, though surrounded by Russian troops, he had stubbornly refused to submit and, rejecting a Russian ultimatum, took to the mountains. Then, after he had eventually been hunted down and taken in custody to Tbilisi, he had managed to escape from his captors and sought refuge with the Turkish Pasha commanding the frontier fortress of Akhaltsikhe. At this the people of Imeretia once again rose enthusiastically against the Russians and had to be crushed by armed force, after which a Russian administrator was installed in Kutaisi and martial law declared. From his place of refuge Tsar Solomon now appealed personally to Napoleon himself, calling on him as supreme head of Christendom to 'take cognisance of the act of pitiless brigandage' which the Russians had committed against him. But his letter only reached Napoleon as the Emperor was setting out for the Russian campaign of 1812 and by the time he returned there was little he could do for poor Solomon, who died in exile in 1815, and was buried in the Cathedral of St Gregory of Nydsa at Trebizond. Simultaneously with the end of the war in Europe, peace, of a kind, had come to the Caucasus.

4 *Yermolov and Paskevich*

Such was the situation when in 1816 one of the great Russian national heroes of the Napoleonic wars, General Aleksei Petrovich Yermolov, who had been Chief of Staff to Barclay de Tolly during the Russian Campaign and Commander of the combined Russian and Prussian Guard at the taking of Paris, was appointed Commander-in-Chief in Georgia and the Caucasus and, for convenience, Ambassador Extraordinary to the Court of Persia.

Yermolov's reputation had preceded him. Pushkin wrote,

> Bow down thy snowy head, O Caucasus,
> Submit! Yermolov comes.

The new Commander-in-Chief was not yet forty. His formidable appearance, gigantic stature, massive shaggy head set on powerful shoulders, arrogant manner and utter disregard for any kind of danger were well calculated to strike terror into his adversaries. He also inspired complete confidence in those he led. For all the arrogance he displayed in his dealings with his equals and superiors, he never failed to ensure that the soldiers under his command had everything they needed, was always ready to share with them the hazards and hardships of war and enjoyed nothing better than sitting round the camp fire, laughing and joking with them. In this way he won their devotion and had soon greatly improved the morale of the Army of the Caucasus.

Yermolov's policy towards the natives of the territories over which he now held sway and which were already known to him from his service as a lieutenant-colonel of nineteen in Count Zubov's Persian War of 1796, is best summed up in his own words: 'I desire that the terror of my name should guard our frontiers more effectively than fortresses and that for the natives my word should be a law more inevitable than death. In the eyes of Asiatics condescension is a sign of weakness and from pure humanity I am inexorably severe. One execution saves hundreds of Russians from destruction and thousands of Moslems from treason.' Such, in a couple of sentences, was Yermolov's system. *Yarmoul*, the natives called him, and the story of the punitive forays carried out on his orders was to be passed down from one generation of tribesmen to another in story and song – the songs being mainly laments. 'He was', wrote a Russian historian some years later in a pregnant phrase, 'at least as cruel as the natives themselves.'

The theory behind Yermolov's policy was as direct as his method of applying it. It was simply that the whole of the Caucasus must at all costs become an integral part of the Russian Empire and that the continued existence of independent or semi-independent states anywhere in the area could not be tolerated. To this purpose he now addressed all his very considerable energies and talents.

Such was the frame of mind in which Yermolov, having paused briefly in Tbilisi to assume formal command, now continued his journey to Teheran, in order to fulfil without delay the other, diplomatic, portion of his mission. The Shah, Aga Mohammed's nephew, Fath Ali, to whom Yermolov was accredited as Ambassador Extra-ordinary, still cherished hopes of somehow regaining control of the khanates and other territories which he had ceded to Russia under the Treaty of Gulistan three years earlier. Yermolov's instructions were to disillusion him on this score, but at the same time to establish genuinely friendly relations with Persia while as far as possible eliminating British influence in Teheran.

In order to widen his knowledge of the problem, he travelled by way of the disputed khanates and, having done so, reached his destination more deeply convinced than ever of the vital strategic and political importance of incorporating them once and for all in the Russian Empire.

In the end Yermolov did not meet the Shah until July 1817. When he did, his tactics, based on a sound understanding of human nature rather than on any extensive diplomatic experience, were to inundate Fath Ali himself with the grossest flattery, while making it quite clear to his ministers that, if the Russians could not achieve their aims by peaceful means, they would not hesitate to resort to war. The fact that he was Commander-in-Chief as well as Ambassador served to underline this message, as did his physical appearance and consciously arrogant manner. 'I relied', he wrote afterwards, 'on my wild beast's muzzle, my gigantic and terrifying frame and my capacious throat. They were

clearly convinced that anyone who could shout so loud must be right . . .
they seemed to hear, not my voice alone, but the roar of 100,000 men.'
He also let drop in the course of his audience the impressive but no
doubt completely unfounded claim that he himself was descended from
Jenghiz Khan, subsequently recording that 'the Shah looked with no
little respect on the descendant of so redoubtable a conqueror.'

Whether because of the flattery, or the threats, or because of his
fictitious relationship with Jenghiz Khan, Yermolov got his way. The
Shah, it appears, was much impressed by his visitor and readily agreed
to give up his rather tenuous claim to the khanates, which Yermolov
had in his own mind long since decided to turn into Russian provinces.
Having thus successfully concluded his diplomatic mission to Persia,
the new Commander-in-Chief now returned to Tbilisi, determined to
lose no time in putting his other theories into practice.

Already on his first arrival in Tbilisi in 1816 Yermolov had found,
both north and south of the mountains, much that disturbed him from a
military point of view. On his return from Persia he at once applied
himself to the task of putting things right.

He first turned his attention to the Terek Line. Here there was
continual unrest among the tribes. Raids were frequent. Guerrilla
warfare was intermittent. No one's life was safe outside the forts.
Yermolov's plan was to build a fresh chain of fortresses across the tribal
areas designed to control the country around.

The first to be built was *Grozni*, or Fort Formidable, sited on the left
bank of the River Soundja in the heart of Chechnia. Right in the middle
of it Yermolov caused a *zemlianka* to be built, a kind of dug-out in
which he himself took up his quarters.

No sooner had the foundations of the new fort's six bastions been
laid, on 10 June, 1818, to the accompaniment of prayers and the
ceremonial firing of cannon, than the Chechens, resenting this invasion
of their privacy, started to snipe at the Russian camp. Yermolov
decided to set a trap for them. He arranged for a single gun to be
abandoned, temptingly, at a pre-arranged point on which all the other
available artillery was then trained. When, as he had expected, the
Chechens arrived to take possession of the gun, the Russian gunners
opened fire with devastating effect. Unused to the effects of accurately
aimed artillery fire, the survivors sought to gather up their dead and
wounded. But again the fatal barrage came down and at the final count

'two hundred dead Chechens and as many wounded ... served as a good lesson and took away their taste for night attacks.'

By the autumn of 1818, trouble was brewing in the mountains of Daghestan. The building of Grozni had disturbed not only the Chechens but their neighbours to the south and south-east. The ruler of Avaria, who held the rank of a Major-General in the Russian Imperial Army, now conferred with the Khans of Mekhtoulee, Karakaitagh, Tabassaran and Kazi-Koumoukh and with them decided to take concerted action in defence of their mutual interests. On getting wind of this, Yermolov at once sent a couple of battalions to Karakaitagh. But there disaster overtook the Russians. Having imprudently advanced as far as Bashli, the principal town of the area, they soon found themselves surrounded by vast numbers of tribesmen and in the end were lucky to escape to Derbend with a total loss of twelve officers and five hundred men. Their defeat was a signal for rejoicing throughout Daghestan, while in Persia the news of the tribesmen's victory was greeted with feasting and cannon-fire.

But by now Yermolov himself, with a much larger force and fourteen guns, was moving on Mekhtoulee. Paraul, the capital, was sacked and the ruler put to flight, together with his ally, the Khan of Avaria; the people of Mekhtoulee made their submission to the Russians; and the Khanate was abolished. At the same time Bashli, the scene of the Russians' earlier setback, was retaken and utterly destroyed. The Russian success was complete. It was the Russian artillery, against which the natives had no defence and which was quite new to them, that had won the day. 'Such convincing proof of our rights', wrote Yermolov, with disarming frankness, 'could not fail to give me the advantage ... It is very interesting', he continued, 'to observe the first impact of this innocent instrument on the heart of man and I thus learned how convenient it was to have the one, when not immediately able to gain control of the other.'

Yermolov, meanwhile, continued to build forts in the tribal areas. Grozni was followed in 1819 by *Vnezapnaya*, Fort Surprise, sited in eastern Chechnia at the foot of the Salatau Range as a barrier against the warlike tribes of Central Daghestan, the two being later connected by a chain of smaller forts. In 1821 *Burnaya*, Fort Stormy, built on the rocks overhanging Tarku, near the present town of Makhach Kala, was to complete the line of forts which now linked Vladikavkaz to the Caspian.

In 1819 the Emperor, at Yermolov's request, sanctioned a substantial increase in the strength of the Georgian Army Corps. This enabled him to have under arms a permanent effective force of at least 50,000 men. The regiments composing the Corps, usually including the soldiers' families, were stationed at strategic points throughout the Caucasus in solid, well-sited buildings, protected by strong fortifications. These constituted what amounted to self-contained military colonies which, amid a perennially turbulent and hostile population, served as useful rallying-points in times of trouble. What is more, men remained with the colours for a full twenty-five years and this, as well as the almost continuous fighting, produced in these regiments of the Caucasus a unique family feeling and *esprit de corps*. Indeed, it was not unusual for father and son to be fighting side by side in the same unit.

In the summer of 1819 the tribes, having recovered their spirits during the winter, again attacked the Russians, both north and south of the line. This time Yermolov was ready for them. Ably supported by his Chief-of-Staff, General Velyaminov, and by General Prince Madatov, a dashing cavalry leader from Karabagh, who, as a tribesman himself, possessed an insight into the native character unshared by any Russian, he embarked on a series of successful punitive expeditions which led to one khanate after another submitting and being annexed by Russia. In a matter of months Tabassaran, Karakaitagh, Akousha, Shirvan, Shekeen and Karabagh were all taken and Russian troops at last penetrated into the innermost valleys of Daghestan. 'The subjugation of Daghestan', Yermolov reported to the Emperor in the summer of 1820, 'is now complete; and this country, proud, warlike and hitherto unconquered, has fallen at the sacred feet of your Imperial Majesty.' It was, it is true, a slight exaggeration – there were still areas in western Daghestan where the Russian writ quite certainly did not run – but an exaggeration that, in the circumstances, might seem excusable.

Yermolov's methods were as usual savage. Again and again the Russians took villages by assault and gave no quarter. As for the treaties he concluded with the native princes, he interpreted them, by his own admission, 'as Moslems interpret the Koran, namely, according to circumstances.' In St Petersburg, as victory followed victory, his stock stood higher than ever. But in the Caucasus he was helping to build up an enduring legacy of hatred for Russia and the Russians. On occasion even the Tsar felt bound to remonstrate with him. 'The news of a house being blown up in which sixteen innocent people perished for one who was guilty is extremely disagreeable to me,' wrote Alexander to his Commander-in-Chief. 'There was', replied Yermolov, with his habitual directness, 'no other way to destroy the villain.'

But although, as Yermolov claimed, an uneasy peace had for the time being been imposed on Daghestan, the same could not be said of Chechnia. Here, in 1824, after six years of peace a popular rising broke out which was partly inspired by religious fanaticism and partly by sheer hatred of the Russians and all they stood for. Yermolov's subordinate commanders did their best, cutting down the forests, burning the native villages and massacring the inhabitants, as their Commander-in-Chief had directed. But for all this, the revolt continued to spread. The two senior Russian generals in the area were killed and the Russians suffered other setbacks. Yermolov now intervened personally and, after one short, sharp campaign, peace of a kind was restored.

Meanwhile there had been a sudden change for the worse in Yermolov's personal fortunes. In December 1825 his patron Alexander I had died unexpectedly at Taganrog and had been succeeded, not by his next brother, Constantine, who had abdicated his rights to the succession, but by the latter's younger brother, the Grand Duke Nicholas, a gloomy, rigid, suspicious tyrant who now ascended the throne as Nicholas I. 'I know nothing so terrible', wrote Alexander Herzen of the new Tsar, 'as those cold, colourless, pewter eyes.' And, in case it be objected that Herzen was prejudiced, we even have the testimony of our own Queen Victoria. 'The expression of his eyes', she wrote in 1844, 'is terrible ... I have never seen anything like them.'

This sudden shift in the succession, amongst other contributory causes, touched off the December Rising in St Petersburg, where some regiments had shouted for *Konstitutsia*, a constitution, many of them in the belief that they were loyally cheering the wife of the Grand Duke Constantine. Subsequently a number of liberal-minded young officers were executed or sent to Siberia for their real or supposed participation in the rebellion.

Alexander had been Yermolov's friend and protector. Nicholas did not trust him. On Alexander's death Yermolov had made the natural, but manifestly unfortunate, mistake of proclaiming Constantine as

Tsar. And although the Commander-in-Chief quickly corrected his initial error, the doubt thus sown in Nicholas's suspicious mind continued to rankle. 'Yermolov', he wrote in 1826 to one of his closest advisers, 'I trust least of all.'

In the summer of 1826 Nicholas had sent a special mission to the Persians to announce his accession, bringing lavish presents and headed by Count Menshikov. And now, while Count Menshikov was still in their country, without warning they suddenly crossed the River Aras and invaded Karabagh.

Yermolov, although he had for some time past repeatedly warned St Petersburg of the possibility of an attack and asked for reinforcements to ward it off, was, in the atmosphere now prevailing, naturally blamed for what had happened. Worse still, things did not go well for his troops. The border provinces were quickly overrun. Everywhere Russian garrisons were taken by surprise and in many cases were wiped out or forced to surrender. Elizavetpol (formerly Gandja; now Kirovabad) opened its gates to the invaders; Baku was besieged; the garrison of Lenkoran were driven to take refuge on an island in the Caspian; the German colony established by Catherine the Great at Ekaterinenfeld was utterly destroyed and the surviving inhabitants carried off to be sold as slaves in Istanbul.

And all this while Yermolov remained inactive in Tbilisi, sending instructions to his subordinates to stand and fight and complaining of the High Command's failure to send him reinforcements. For once his own fighting spirit and his will to win seem to have failed him. He felt, he said, that he was no longer trusted. Before long the panic had spread to Tbilisi itself, where the aged and articulate Princess Bebutov, who had endured the horrors of Aga Mohammed's invasion in 1796 and had no wish to repeat the experience, was giving free vent to her feelings. At length, stung to action, Yermolov roused himself sufficiently from his torpor to despatch his best commander, Prince Madatov, against the enemy with a striking force of 2,000 men. With these, on 2 September, Madatov won a brilliant victory over five times the number of Persians at Shamkhor. Elizavetpol was recaptured and confidence to some extent restored.

But by now Nicholas, distrusting Yermolov, doubtful of his military capacity, and impatient at his continued inactivity, had decided to place the conduct of operations in the Caucasus in other hands. On 1 Sep-

Old Tbilisi

Old Tbilisi

tember, his favourite, Prince Paskevich, had arrived in Tbilisi with instructions to take over command of the troops in the field with direct responsibility to the Emperor. On 10 September, a week after Madatov's victory at Shamkhor, Paskevich arrived at the front and assumed command, bringing with him the long awaited reinforcements from Russia. Four days later, the Russians engaged and routed the main Persian Army of 60,000 men and twenty-six guns. The tide had turned. The issue of the war was no longer in doubt.[*]

Though officially Yermolov remained in supreme command, his position was now clearly impossible. From the outset his relations with Paskevich had been unendurably strained. It could only be a question of time before they reached breaking point. Meanwhile Paskevich, in his private reports to the Tsar, blamed Yermolov for everything that had gone wrong and accused him of obstructing him and intriguing against him. It was not long before he declared that either he or Yermolov must go.

There could be no doubt which it would be. In March 1827, six months after Paskevich's arrival, Yermolov tendered his resignation to the Tsar. But already a letter was on its way to him depriving him of his command and severely reprimanding him in the name of His Imperial Majesty. On 29 March Paskevich was appointed Commander-in-Chief.

The day before, Yermolov, 'the once all-powerful pro-consul', to borrow his own phrase, had left Tbilisi for ever, having first had to plead with junior officials for an escort to accompany him on his way across the mountains. At Taganrog he turned aside to visit the scene of the death of his benefactor Alexander, 'with whom', he wrote, 'was buried all my good fortune.' He was just fifty.

Yermolov did not receive another appointment, but spent the rest of his long life in modest retirement. As the years went by the old man's former failings were forgotten and he became to an ever greater extent the hero of the Russian army and people, who saw in him the embodiment of their country's glorious past, one of the great Russian commanders in the war against Napoleon and the man who prepared the way for Russia's ultimate conquest of the Caucasus.

---

[*] The Russians claimed that on this occasion the Persian artillery was under the command of British officers. In fact the only British soldier present was Sergeant Dawson of the Royal Artillery, who, more or less single-handed, saved fourteen of the guns from capture by the Russians.

With Yermolov out of the way, Paskevich was free to pursue as he thought best the advantages gained the previous year. The war against the Persians was taking longer than had been expected and the Russians, as usual outnumbered, had to win a number of hard-fought battles before they could claim the ultimate victory.

The main objective of the Russian plan of campaign, so far as one existed, was the capture of Erivan, the capital of the Persian-protected Khanate of that name and a fortified city of some strength. Only a dozen miles from Erivan was the monastery of Etchmiadzin, the seat of the Armenian Katholikos.

In June 1827, Paskevich, bringing with him fresh reinforcements, joined the advance guard of his army, which, after successfully occupying Etchmiadzin, was now investing Erivan. He next moved south against the neighbouring frontier Khanate of Nakhitchevan and the fortress of Abbas-Abad, occupying both. Meanwhile further north in Armenia things were going a good deal less well. That year the summer heat had been exceptional, Russian morale was at a low ebb, and, after two months without any rain at all, the Russian force besieging Erivan had been obliged to raise the siege and withdraw. Encouraged, the Persian garrison, led by the Khan of Erivan, sallied out and, with additional support from the main Persian force, attacked the small Russian garrison in Etchmiadzin with the object of then crossing the mountains and devastating Tbilisi. Throughout the ensuing battle, the venerable Patriarch Narses V of Armenia, praying hard to the God of Victories, bravely held aloft the monastery's most precious relic, the Roman soldier's spear which at the Crucifixion had pierced the side of Christ and was stained with His blood. For a time it was touch and go, but in the end Etchmiadzin was saved, though at heavy cost, and the Persians withdrew into Azerbaijan.

By this time a sharp deterioration in Russia's relations with Turkey had made it more necessary than ever for her to take Erivan before she found herself fighting two wars at once. Towards the end of September the siege was actively resumed under Paskevich's command and on 2 October Erivan finally fell into the hands of the Russians. For this feat of arms Paskevich was awarded the Order of St George and given the right to use the surname Erivanski. In fact, much of the credit for the capture of Erivan was due to the brilliant technical directions of a former officer of the Imperial Engineers named Pushchin, who had been reduced to the ranks for his part in the plot of December 1825 and who, after the victory, was somewhat reluctantly advanced to N.C.O., for Nicholas I was not a man who easily forgot or forgave past misdemeanours.

When Paskevich marched north to Erivan in September, he had put two of his subordinates, Prince Eristov and Count Muraviov, in charge of the small Russian force which he had left in the area of Nakhitchevan on the River Aras, with instructions to stay on the defensive on the line of the Aras and not make more than minor diversionary moves beyond it. But neither Eristov nor Muraviov were suited by nature for a purely defensive role. Having easily driven off a Persian force which advanced to attack him and then received intelligence that the Persians were in fact completely demoralized, Muraviov decided on his own initiative to push on into Persia and make a bid for Tabriz, the capital of the Persian province of Azerbaijan, which was barely a hundred miles away. On learning of this plan, Eristov, who was in command, agreed. On 13 October the Russian advance guard reached the outskirts of Tabriz. The Persian garrison fled in disorder in the direction of Teheran. The gates were opened and later the same day Eristov and Muraviov entered the ancient city unopposed.

It was at this point that Eristov received the news that Erivan had fallen. To the message of congratulations which he now sent to the Commander-in-Chief, he added the information that he himself had, without really trying, captured Tabriz. Paskevich, though not usually a man to tolerate indiscipline in his subordinates, seems to have taken this surprising announcement in fairly good part, and a week later himself entered Tabriz at the head of his army, accompanied, strangely enough, by the British Minister to Persia, Sir John Macdonald.

Peace negotiations were now opened in which the Shah's medical adviser, Dr McNeill from Colonsay, who enjoyed his complete confidence, played a leading part as did his fellow West Highlander, Sir John Macdonald. These dragged on for some months owing to the Shah's reluctance to pay over the large sum of money demanded of him by the Russians and also to his hope that war might soon break out between Russia and Turkey. But Persia was now at Russia's mercy; Teheran lay open to the invading army; and in the end a treaty of peace was signed in February 1828 at the village of Turkmenchai.

Under this treaty Russia retained possession of the Khanates of Erivan and Nakhitchevan, while Persia paid Russia an indemnity of twenty million roubles and undertook to allow any Armenians who so desired to emigrate freely from Persia to Russian territory – a concession of which large numbers took advantage. Paskevich had urged on the Emperor that the whole of Azerbaijan, including Tabriz, should now also be annexed, on the grounds that, once this had been done, the British, whose influence in Persia he resented, might as well 'pack up and go back to India'. But to this, Nicholas, anxious not to alarm the other European powers unduly, refused to agree.

Barely a month after the conclusion of peace with Persia in March 1828, Paskevich received a despatch from St Petersburg, informing him that Russia was at war with Turkey. At least Russia was not now fighting two wars at once; but even so the task which confronted Paskevich was a formidable one. His garrisons were weak and widely scattered and he had no field force available for immediate use. The Turks were on the whole better soldiers than the Persians and their army more numerous. The whole frontier from Ararat to the Black Sea lay open to attack by Turkey. And in the northern Caucasus the Turks not only held a considerable stretch of the Black Sea coast on the west, but in the east exercised considerable influence over the Moslem tribes of Chechnia and Daghestan.

The instructions which Paskevich now received from the Emperor were, first, to do everything he could to divert pressure from the Russian front on the Danube and, second, to seize from the Turks any places that would round off and secure the Russian frontier in Asia Minor and the Caucasus, notably the Pashaliks of Kars and Ardahan and the fortresses of Anapa and Poti on the Black Sea. To achieve these objectives, Paskevich could not hope, if allowance were made for troops on garrison duty, to muster a fighting force of more than twelve or fifteen thousand men.

Paskevich began his operation by a brilliant and audacious attack on the extremely strong Turkish fortress of Kars. Again Pushchin (now restored to the rank of lieutenant) played a decisive part in organizing and preparing the Russian assault and after a siege of three days the fortress fell before any reinforcements could reach it. This time Paskevich recommended Pushchin for the Order of St George. But once more Nicholas refused to relent and it was not until thirty years later that Pushchin, still soldiering on, finally received the decoration in question from Nicholas's son, Alexander II, by when, presumably, whatever he had or had not done in December 1825 had long since been forgotten. Meanwhile, ten days before Kars, the key Turkish fortress of Anapa on the Black Sea had fallen to a combined Russian land and naval force and Poti had followed three days later.

Paskevich's next major objective was Akhaltsikhé, another fortified town of great strategic importance, occupying a reputedly impregnable position on the River Kura and held by a garrison of 10,000 Turks. 'You may sooner snatch the moon from the heavens', ran a Turkish saying, 'than the crescent from the mosque of Akhaltsikhé.' The Russians arrived before the town at the beginning of August and at once laid siege to it, bringing up heavy guns with which to batter its fortifications. On 14 August, having received news that a strong Turkish force was on its way to relieve Akhaltsikhé, Paskevich decided to storm the town next day. A fierce battle ensued; by dawn on 16 August the rest of the town was in Russian hands and on the 17th the fortress itself finally surrendered. By the end of August the Russians had also taken Ardahan and the whole of the Pashalik of Bayazid. 'Your Majesty's flag', Paskevich reported to the Tsar, 'is now flying over the head-waters of the Euphrates.'

The Russians were by this time only sixty miles from Erzerum, the chief city of Anatolia. But winter was approaching and any further advance was postponed until the spring. In the Caucasus Paskevich had achieved all his principal objectives. But the Turkish armies were still in the field. Indeed in mid-winter they made a determined attempt to recapture Akhaltsikhé. Meanwhile, it was still important to divert pressure from the Balkan front.

The spring of 1829 found Akhaltsikhé again menaced by the Turks, who were also advancing on Bayazid and a number of other Russian-held positions. By May the Russian centre and both flanks were under pressure. But now the Russians in their turn took the offensive; a number of successful engagements followed; and in mid-June Paskevich set out from Kars to march on Erzerum at the head of a force of some 1,200 infantry, 500 cavalry and 70 guns, which, though outnumbered more than three to one by the two Turkish armies which faced them, enjoyed the incalculable advantage of superior leadership.

Always a daring and decisive commander who planned his campaigns in advance with unfailing care, Paskevich was at his best during the days that followed. After a brilliant approach march across the mountains, he next by a skilful manoeuvre engaged and defeated the enemy force confronting him before its commander could join up with the main Turkish army and then immediately pushed on to Erzerum. There, on 27 June, the Turkish Governor and Commander-in-Chief and his demoralized garrison capitulated without a fight and, for the first time in five centuries, an army of infidels entered the capital of Anatolia. In four months Paskevich's little army, with the strength of barely one modern division, operating hundreds of miles from its base, had fought its way across three hundred and fifty miles of hostile mountainous country; defeated and dispersed a Turkish force of 80,000 men and 200 guns; killed 10,000 of the enemy and captured 5,000, including two Commanders-in-Chief complete with batons and banners.

The campaign continued for some months in a desultory fashion – longer in fact than it need have done – for, though the news did not reach Paskevich until almost a month later, peace between Russia and Turkey had in fact already been signed on 2 September at Adrianople.

The peace thus concluded was to endure for a quarter of a century. Of her latest conquests Russia retained only Anapa, Poti and Akhaltsikhé. For the time being the political arguments outweighed the military, and Kars and Ardahan were restored to Turkey. But once again the Russians were careful to ensure that the local Christians and in particular the Armenians were allowed, if they so wished, to emigrate to Russia, and, when the Russian army finally crossed the frontier, they took with them some 90,000 Christian refugees.

The Russians had soundly defeated both Persia and Turkey. Their southern frontiers with these two powers had been extended and adjusted to their liking. In the Caucasus it now only remained for them finally to impose their will on the turbulent mountain tribes over which they claimed sovereignty. But this, in some ways, was to prove the most arduous task of all and the resulting struggle was to last without interruption for the next thirty years.

5 *The Imam Shamyl*

With its foothills, the main range of the Caucasus stretches from east to west for about six hundred and fifty miles. Of this total the highest mountains, at the centre of the range, account for some four hundred miles, the foothills on either side falling away gradually for another hundred miles or so on the west to the Black Sea and to the Caspian on the east. With the tribes occupying the central massif, the Ossetians and Kabardans to the west of the Georgian Military Highway and the Ingushes, Khevsurs and Pshavs to the east, the Russians were to have relatively little trouble. They continued, it is true, to rob and raid spasmodically. But in general they accepted the rather remote rule of the Tsar without question. Trouble during the years that followed was to come, rather, from the Cherkess or Circassians, whose forests stretched from the slopes of Elbruz to the Black Sea Littoral and who continued to fight the Russians on and off, with or without Turkish help, from the end of the eighteenth century down to the year 1864; and from the warlike tribes of the eastern foothills, the Chechens in their dense beech-forests and the various tribes who ranged over the barren mountain plateau and tablelands of neighbouring Daghestan.

It might have been thought that, with no real hope of outside support, these tribes would now, with more or less good grace, have accepted Russian rule. But this was not so. Successive Viceroys and Commanders-in-Chief of the Caucasus – Tsitsianov and Yermolov in particular – had done nothing to endear the Russians to their subject races. There was also another powerful force at work. In addition to the strong national feeling which set it off, the war which now broke out was in essence a religious war, a war inspired by fanatical hatred of the *giaour*, the infidel, as well as of the foreign oppressor. For a war of this kind – a war of resistance – to succeed, two things are necessary. A strong, all-pervading idea. And also a leader. While the Russians were congratulating themselves on the relative ease with which they had subjugated the Caucasus, such a leader was waiting in the wings.

55

The Imam Shamyl, as he is known to history, was born in the mountain village of Ghimri in north-eastern Daghestan in the last decade of the eighteenth century. From early youth he was known for his devoutness and dedication to the Moslem faith and for his extreme physical toughness, exceptional even among the hardy highlanders of Daghestan. Shamyl's first teacher and friend was another, older boy from Ghimri, called Kazi Mulla. Though both boys later studied under some of the most learned religious teachers in Daghestan, Shamyl always said in after life that he had learnt more from Kazi Mulla than from anyone else. In Daghestan the Russian conquest had coincided with a religious revival known as Muridism after the Murids or Mohammedan holy men who inspired it. It was thus natural that the war of resistance against the foreign invader should have become merged in a *jihad* or *ghazavat*, a holy war against the infidel. National liberation, clearly, was a condition of religious revival and reform, and resistance to an oppressor the ideal justification for a holy war.

Though both were from the start active in the new movement, it was not Shamyl but Kazi Mulla who first took over its leadership and first assumed the title of Imam. Kazi Mulla began to preach at Ghimri in 1827. At first he did not openly preach resistance to the Russians, but towards the end of 1829 he judged that the moment had arrived to throw off all pretence and call on his followers to gird themselves for war.

From the date of his first call to open resistance until his death in action three years later Kazi Mulla's career was a stormy one. His first attacks, characteristically, were directed against such neighbouring tribes or rulers as did not show immediate readiness to join in his war against Russia. His own plans were, to say the least of it, ambitious. 'When we have driven the Infidel from the Caucasus and taken Moscow', he would say, 'we will go on to Stambul, and, if we find the Sultan a religious man, strictly obeying the precepts of the Shariat, we will not molest him. If not, woe unto him! We will bind him with chains and his Empire shall pass to the Faithful.'

Such sentiments, confidently and forcibly expressed and backed where necessary by violence, could not fail to impress. Soon most of Daghestan was up in arms and Kazi Mulla acclaimed on all sides as Imam. The greater part of the following year was taken up with further punitive expeditions against neighbours reluctant to join in the forthcoming struggle. But in May 1831, after some preliminary skirmishing

with the Russians, Kazi Mulla boldly attacked Vnezapnaya, Fort Surprise, and then ambushed and heavily defeated the Russian force which
was sent to its relief. At the same time, beyond the mountains, another
of the Murid leaders, Hamzad Beg, having successfully roused the
warlike Djaro-Bielokanis, inflicted in his turn a disastrous defeat on a
Russian force sent against him, in the course of which two Russian
battalions completely lost their nerve and fled – much to the distress of
Prince Paskevich, who, after four successful years, was about to leave
the Caucasus to assume command in Poland.

The insurgents were quick to follow up their initial success. In
August Kazi Mulla appeared on the Caspian littoral, laying siege to
Derbend and raiding Kizhai on the lower Terek. Other Russian setbacks followed. Paskevich had been succeeded by Baron Rosen, a
run-of-the-mill general officer with a reputation as a *bon viveur*. He did
not much like what he found. 'I arrived here', he wrote in December
1831, 'at a time of very great disturbance. Never were the mountain
tribes so insolent or so persistent.'

The Russians now made a determined attempt to bring the situation
under control. In order to quell the Circassians on the Black Sea, the
Abkhazian coast was occupied as far as Bombor; the Djaro-Bielokanis
were, for the time being, pacified; and Russian authority was firmly
established in Ossetia, both north and south of the mountains. But
much still remained to be done. Early in 1832 Kazi Mulla again
appeared in Chechnia and actually threatened Vladikavkaz and, with it,
Russia's communications with Georgia. It was now that the new
Commander-in-Chief took the decision to resort to a policy of massive
punitive raids and in August 1832 himself set out at the head of a force
of 9,000 men and twenty-eight guns to harry Lower Chechnia, 'laying
waste settlements, destroying the harvest, driving off flocks and herds
and attacking the enemy wherever they had the audacity to assemble in
any numbers.' He was accompanied by his Chief-of-Staff, General
Velyaminov, who had held the same appointment under Yermolov,
and whose policy it was that was now being implemented.

First-hand accounts bear witness to the character of the campaign.
'The road', writes one of those who took part in the expedition, 'lay
through dense forests of lofty trees ... Fighting went on from beginning to end of each day's march: there was the chatter of musketry,
the whistle of bullets; men fell; but no enemy was seen. Puffs of

smoke in the jungle alone showed where they were lurking and our soldiers, for want of anything better, took aim by that.'

But the Russians did not let themselves be put off. 'Small columns were sent out to ravage the enemy's fields and dwellings. The *auls* blaze; the crops are mown down; there is a rattle of musketry and the thunder of guns. Our Tartar allies come in with severed heads tied to their saddle-bows; there are no prisoners – the men give no quarter.'

On 18 August Kazi Mulla achieved one more success, ambushing a Russian force in the forest, killing the commander and inflicting heavy casualties on his column. But already the tide was turning. A week later Baron Rosen's task force, making lavish use of artillery against which the Chechens were defenceless, stormed and burned Ghermenchug, the largest settlement in Chechnia, most of its defenders dying in the blazing houses, rather than give in. 'We want no quarter', said one of them, on being summoned to surrender. 'The only grace we ask of the Russians is to let our families know that we died as we lived, refusing to submit to foreign dominion.'

Next Greater Chechnia and then one area after another were subjected to the same treatment, until in all eighty villages had submitted and sixty-one had been totally destroyed. By now Kazi Mulla and Shamyl had fallen back on Daghestan, determined to make a final stand in their native village of Ghimri. The Russian attack on Ghimri, carefully planned and put into execution by General Velyaminov himself, was launched on 17 October. 'Five hundred Murids were surrounded by ten thousand Russians,' said an old man who had been there at the time, telling the tale sixty years later. The defenders made their stand at a point three or four miles above the village where they had thrown a triple line of stone fortifications across the ravine. In the end, after much bitter fighting, they were reduced to some sixty Murids, still holding out in two small *saklias* or stone huts. Of the sixty in the end only two were to escape alive. One was Shamyl, who, leaping clean over the heads of a line of Russian soldiers about to open fire on him, cut down three of them before a fourth ran him through with his bayonet. Plucking the bayonet from his own chest, he then used it to dispatch its owner and thus made his escape into the woods. There, during the weeks that followed, his wife Fatima and her father, Abdul Aziz, a famous physician, somehow nursed him back to health from the bayonet wound and the other injuries he had received.

Shamyl had escaped. But when the Russians came to examine the Murid dead who lay piled in front of the two stone huts, they found amongst them one who in the moment of death had assumed the Moslem attitude of prayer, with one hand grasping his beard while the other pointed to heaven, and whom, to their delight, they were able to identify as the Imam Kazi Mulla. After publicly exposing Kazi Mulla's body for several days so as to bring home their loss to the tribesmen, the Russians set out on the return march, convinced that Murid resistance had been crushed once and for all and that their hold on Daghestan was now assured.

With Kazi Mulla dead and Shamyl out of action, Hamzad Beg was now elected Imam, a mediocre leader and a man of equivocal character. Hamzad was only to survive as Imam for two years, during which resistance to the Russians remained at a low ebb. In September 1834 he was assassinated in the mosque at Khounzakh in pursuance of a blood-feud, which he had started by murdering the sons of the Khan of Avaria. He was succeeded as Imam by Shamyl who, on learning of his death, had at once made his way to Ashilta in Avaria and there assumed command.

It was a couple of years before Shamyl could again build up resistance to its former pitch, but by the beginning of 1837 insurgence was again widespread. The Russians had by now come to realize the nature and extent of the Murid threat and the need for effective action to contain it. In May 1837 a picked expeditionary force of some 5,000 men and eighteen guns was despatched against Shamyl's headquarters at Ashilta. The ensuing campaign, which cost the Russians many lives and considerable effort, lasted for most of the summer. But, while achieving certain local and tactical successes, it failed in its main purpose, which was to stamp out resistance in Daghestan and Chechnia and bring Shamyl to book. Once again, the Russians, after long and painful approach marches through difficult country, used the advantage which their artillery gave them to batter and storm fiercely-defended native *auls* and then massacre any survivors who fell into their hands. But, as usual, their more mobile adversaries, ably led by Shamyl, would fade back into the mountains and forests and then attack them again where they least expected it.

The autumn of 1837 had, as it happened, been chosen for a State visit by Nicholas I to Transcaucasia and, on the strength of various over-optimistic reports from the commanders on the spot, it was decided that this would be an appropriate occasion on which to celebrate the final pacification of the Caucasus and also the formal submission to the Tsar of the Imam Shamyl. For this purpose it was clearly necessary to establish contact with Shamyl, and in September a preliminary meeting was arranged in the mountains between the Imam and the Russian field-commander, General Kluke von Klugenau.

The ensuing scene in that wild mountain valley, beneath the towering peaks of the Caucasus, must have been a curious one. On one side Shamyl, tall, turbaned and austere, with his pale face and massive hennaed beard, and an escort of two hundred fierce-looking native horsemen. On the other, with Yevdokimov his A.D.C., and an escort of a dozen Cossacks, Klugenau, a square, Teutonic figure on his charger; 'very tall', writes a contemporary, 'stoutly built, brusque in manner, hot-tempered to the point of insanity.' As was to be expected, the talks which now opened between the two leaders, as they sat together on a cloak spread out on the ground, produced no positive result. The conclusion of the meeting was even less productive. As the two leaders rose to take leave of one another, Klugenau put out his hand to take Shamyl's. But at this moment Surkhai Khan, one of the Imam's most fanatical followers, gripped his leader's arm to stop him from defiling himself by physical contact with an infidel. This infuriated Klugenau, who, already not in the best of tempers, responded with the most insulting gesture he could think of, hitting out at Shamyl's turban with a crutch he was using. Seeing what was happening, both escorts reached for their weapons and for an instant the lives of the principal protagonists hung in the balance. Fortunately, however, Shamyl showed his usual physical dexterity and presence of mind. Catching the General's crutch in mid-air with one hand, he seized Surkhai Khan's half-drawn dagger with the other and shouted at his escort to stand back, while at the same time urging Klugenau to withdraw without delay. But the General, for his part, simply stood there, pouring out a torrent of abuse at Shamyl and his followers, until finally dragged away by the coat-tails by his horrified and much embarrassed *aide-de-camp*, Yevdokimov, who eventually persuaded him to get back on to his horse and ride home. To a subsequent letter from Klugenau, Shamyl replied as follows: 'From the poor writer of this letter, Shamyl, who leaves all things in the hand of God. This is to inform you that I have finally decided not to go to Tiflis, even though I were cut to pieces for refusing, for I have often had experience of your treachery, and this all men know.'

A day or two later, on 29 September, 1837, the Emperor Nicholas started on his tour of the Caucasus. Landing on the Black Sea coast, he travelled in state by way of Kutaisi, Etchmiadzin and Erivan to Tiflis, arriving there in a downpour of rain on 21 October after an uncomfortable journey, during which he had been badly bitten by fleas. On his arrival in Tiflis he was shown Shamyl's letter. This did nothing to soothe his already savage temper. Nor, for that matter, did the reports which now reached him of corruption in high places, notably on the part of the Governor-General's own son-in-law, Prince Dadiani, Colonel of the Georgian Grenadiers, honorary A.D.C. to the Emperor and a scion of one of the greatest families in Georgia. At the ensuing ceremonial parade the Tsar vented his outraged feelings by ripping off Prince Dadiani's epaulettes, thus reducing him at a stroke to the ranks and shortly afterwards to suicide. This episode, we are told, 'alarmed the officers commanding the various regiments, speculation being so general that there are few, if any, whose conduct would bear close investigation.' It also cast a blight on the State Ball held next night. From Tiflis the Tsar made his way across the mountains to Vladikavkaz and thence to Moscow. On his return home, to round off his tour, he gave orders for Baron Rosen to be dismissed from his post as Commander-in-Chief.

Shamyl, for his part, spent the year 1838 strengthening his military position and building up his authority over the tribes. Returning to the mountains of Daghestan, he established his headquarters on the rock of Akhulgo, a natural bastion rising six hundred feet above the River Koisu, which, according to local tradition, Shaitan, the Devil, had with Allah's permission built as his own lair. Here, on the summit of the rock, with the river flowing round it like a moat, Shamyl had a two-storeyed house built for himself by some of his numerous Russian prisoners and here he established himself with his favourite wife Fatima and her two sons, Djemmal-Eddin and Kazi Mohammed. With him, too, was another of his wives, Djavarad and her baby, and Shamyl's mother, Bahou Messadou.

Early in 1839 the Russian Government again decided that effective measures must be taken to check Shamyl's growing might. In addition to a proposed punitive expedition against the tribes of the Black Sea

coast, who were still giving trouble in the west, a plan was drawn up by
the new Commander-in-Chief, General Golovin, and modified by Tsar
Nicholas himself. This aimed at the final conquest of Chechnia and
northern Daghestan and in particular the capture of Shamyl's new
capital of Akhulgo and the utter destruction of his power. With these
objects in view, no less than 9,000 men were concentrated at Vnezapnaya in Chechnia and 3,000 more at Temir-Khan-Shura in Northern
Daghestan.

The campaign began, as the others had done, with a series of savage
battles for individual native strong points of secondary strategic value.
But towards the middle of June Shamyl made the mistake of allowing
himself to be besieged by a strong Russian force on the rock of
Akhulgo. With him were some 4,000 men, women and children, of
whom not more than a thousand were combatants, and only limited
supplies of food and water. By thus allowing himself to be pinned
down, he had sacrificed a guerrilla's most precious asset, his mobility,
and now presented a ready-made target to a much stronger enemy force.

Even so, his position on the rock was immensely strong. Individual
outposts, fiercely defended, fell to the enemy. But, despite much preliminary artillery bombardment, successive attempts by the Russians
to take the rock itself by storm were all successfully repulsed, with
heavy losses on both sides.

From the middle of July until the middle of August there was a
deadlock. The pure mountain air was polluted by the stench of count-
less unburied corpses lying out under the blazing sun. More and more
men fell sick. The Russians were beginning to feel the strain. But so was
Shamyl. His provisions were running out and water could only be
brought up from the river below under fire from the Russian snipers.
Negotiations for a truce were opened between the two sides, but came
to nothing. The Russians demanded Shamyl's submission and the surrender as a hostage of his eight-year old son Djemmal-Eddin, while the
tone of Shamyl's replies 'was such as no Russian general could properly
listen to.'

On 17 August the Russians again attempted to storm the rock. Again,
after a fierce battle, they failed. But by now Shamyl's position was
desperate. Under the merciless rays of the August sun, the rock was
littered with dead and dying. Surkhai Khan, his right hand man, who
had figured so fiercely in his encounter with General Klugenau, was

dead. The women and children were starving. Under a white flag, the Imam sent his son Djemmal-Eddin over to the enemy as a hostage.

Negotiations for the surrender of Akhulgo were now re-opened, but again failed and on 21 August orders were once more given for a general assault. A desperate battle ensued, lasting on and off for a week. 'Every stone hut', wrote an eye-witness, 'every cave, had to be taken by force of arms. Though doomed, the highlanders utterly refused to surrender and defended themselves to the last. Women and children, with stones or daggers in their hands, flung themselves on to our soldiers' bayonets or threw themselves in despair over the cliffs to certain death. It is hard to picture all the scenes of this terrible, fanatical struggle. Mothers killed their children with their own hands – anything rather than let them fall into the hands of the Russians. Whole families perished under the ruins of their stone huts. Some of the Murids, though exhausted by their wounds, still sought to sell their lives dearly. Pretending at first to surrender their weapons, they then treacherously killed those about to take them ...'

But in the end Akhulgo was taken. The siege had lasted for eighty days and had cost the Russians dear in killed, wounded and sick. But at least they had achieved their object – or so they hoped. Anxiously they searched through the piles of enemy dead, in every cave and amid the ruins of every house, seeking the one body they really wanted to find. Painstakingly they interrogated every prisoner. Shamyl's son was now in their hands. His sister had jumped to her death. It appeared that at least one of his wives had died in the siege. But of the man himself there was no sign.

It was not until some days later that the Russians learned what in fact had happened. On the night of 21 August, realizing that all was now lost, Shamyl, his wives Fatima and Djavarad and their children and a few faithful followers, had hidden in a cave in the mountainside above the river. The next night, after first drawing the enemy's fire by sending a raft laden with dummies drifting down the river, the little party had crept along the river bank under cover of darkness and then turned inland up a ravine. Here they ran into a Russian patrol. In the ensuing encounter Shamyl and little Kazi Mohammed were wounded and Djavarad and her baby killed. But Shamyl himself managed to dispatch the Russian commander whose patrol then fled. At least they were now through the Russian lines and, after further adventures, which included a skirmish with a treacherous group of villagers from Shamyl's own birthplace, Ghimri, they finally crossed the river and made good their escape into the mountains.

'Very good', wrote the Tsar on the somewhat optimistic report of the Akhulgo operations which he received from the commander on the spot. 'But it's a pity that Shamyl has escaped ... We must see what happens now.' In fact nothing much happened for the next six or seven months. During the winter the Russians marched in strength through Lower Chechnia without meeting any resistance; the natives seemed cowed; and further reassuring reports were sent to St Petersburg. 'In Chechnia', wrote General Golovin's Chief of Staff, 'no serious unrest, no general rising need be anticipated.'

Tbilisi

Old Tbilisi

Ikalto

Alaverdi, Georgia

Kutaisi, the Bazaar

Kutaisi, the Flower Bazaar

Kutaisi, in the Bazaar

6 Guerrilla War

The decision was now taken to build three more forts as part of a fresh line of defence in Chechnia. At the same time the rumour spread that the Russians were proposing to disarm the Chechens, settle them on the land as ordinary peasants and call them up for military service in the Russian Army. This was all that was needed to set the country ablaze once more. In March 1840, before the Russians had finished building the first of their forts, the whole of Chechnia was up in arms, with Shamyl at the head of the insurgents, his authority stronger than ever. By the end of the year the rising had spread to Daghestan. Soon the war in the mountains was raging more fiercely than ever. Meanwhile encouraging news was now reaching Shamyl from the Black Sea coast, where the Circassians and other western tribes, stirred up and armed by an enterprising young Scottish politician and publicist named David Urquhart – Sheikh Daud they called him – and his two friends Long-worth and Bell, had successfully stormed several Russian forts and massacred the garrisons.

In Chechnia Shamyl now showed himself as much a master of forest fighting as of the mountain warfare he had waged hitherto. The Russians, it is true, won individual engagements, such as the battle on the River Valerik in July 1840, for his gallant part in which the poet Lermontov was mentioned in despatches. But Shamyl had learned by the experience of the past ten years. Avoiding pitched battles as far as he could, he kept constantly on the move, making sudden raids on enemy settlements and sometimes within twenty-four hours threatening points as much as eighty or ninety miles apart. Meanwhile his subordinate commanders were doing the same from the borders of Daghestan in the east to the country round Vladikavkaz in the west. One of the more successful of these Murid leaders on the western flank was Akhverdi Mahoma, who from one of his raids brought back as a present for Shamyl a beautiful sixteen-year-old Armenian Christian captive called Shouanete who with the years was to become his favourite wife of all. Another was Hadji Murad, an equivocal figure, but a man of great influence in his own country, Avaria, and a considerable partisan leader, who, after a period of submission to the Russians, had also thrown in his lot with Shamyl.

It had been Hadji Murad who, to revenge the young sons of the Khan of Avaria, brutally slaughtered by the Murids, had with his brother Osman murdered Hamzad Beg, the Second Imam, in the Mosque at Khounzakh in 1834. Osman had himself been killed in the ensuing brawl. But Hadji Murad had escaped in the confusion and, resentful of Shamyl's pre-eminence among the tribes, had decided to join the Russians, who for their part were always ready to play off one tribal chieftain against another.

For five or six years Hadji Murad had prospered. Then, in 1840, another local leader, Akhmet Khan of Mekhtoulee, had denounced him to the Russians for double-dealing. He had been arrested, kept chained to a cannon by the detestable Khan of Mekhtoulee and then despatched to Russian Headquarters under an escort of an officer and forty-five men.

It was winter and the passes over the mountains were deep in snow. Hadji Murad's hands were tied as he plodded along through the snow and for good measure he was roped to a Russian. But he had not given up hope. Picking his moment carefully, he waited until he and his escort were passing along a narrow ledge above a yawning chasm. Then with a violent jerk he threw himself over the edge, dragging his guard with him in a sudden flurry of snow and loose stones.

It was inconceivable that either guard or prisoner should have reached the bottom alive. Peering over the edge, the men of the escort could see nothing. On reaching General Headquarters the officer in charge of them had reported the loss of his prisoner and of one of his own men and been reprimanded for his carelessness. It never entered anyone's head that Hadji Murad could still be alive.

In fact, though the Russian soldier had been killed outright, Hadji Murad had somehow survived his fall. His skull was cracked and a leg and some ribs broken, but he was still alive. First cutting the Russian's throat for good measure, he painfully dragged himself to the nearest *aul*. There he lay up until he was strong enough to move on. Early in 1841 he addressed himself to Shamyl, offering him his help against the Russians. 'Accept', he wrote, 'my arm and my vengeance. You learned its worth when I fought against you ... Will you try it once more, now that I offer to fight alongside you?' Shamyl replied at once. 'Our hands', he wrote, 'are outstretched to welcome you.' Then he appointed Hadji Murad his first Naib and publicly proclaimed the news of his accession to the ranks of the Murids. Soon the mountains were once more in a ferment.

In Daghestan as in Chechnia, thousands now flocked to Shamyl's standards. Here, though heavily outnumbered, the Russians, under Shamyl's old acquaintance General Kluke von Klugenau, managed to win a number of battles and even recaptured and held Ghimri. But the fact remained that here too, within a year of his defeat at Akhulgo, Shamyl was once again the leader of a people in arms.

Whenever it was necessary, Shamyl imposed his authority with relentless severity. Wherever he went, he was accompanied by his Executioner, carrying a huge long-handled axe, with which to lop off here a hand and there a head at his master's bidding. In June 1840, after a dispute over the custody of two Chechen prisoners, Shamyl ordered the right eye of a village elder to be gouged out.

That night his victim escaped and, snatching a dagger from one of his guards, broke into Shamyl's room and managed to stab him several times before being cut down by the Imam's bodyguard who also accounted for his two brothers who had joined in the affray. To conclude the argument, Shamyl now gave orders for the eight surviving members of the man's family to be shut up in their house and burnt alive. His order was at once carried out.

General Golovin, who was no doubt informed of such incidents, had by now come to have a truer appreciation of his adversary's character and capabilities. 'We have never', he wrote, 'had in the Caucasus an enemy so savage and so dangerous as Shamyl. Owing to a combination of circumstances, his power has acquired a religious-military character, of the same nature as that by which, at the birth of Islam, Mohammed caused three-quarters of the globe to tremble. Shamyl has surrounded himself with blind executants of his will. Inevitable death awaits all who incur the slightest suspicion of disloyalty. Hostages are killed mercilessly if the families from which they are taken prove false. The rulers he has set up over the various communities are his slaves, blindly loyal, possessing in their turn absolute power of life and death. Our first aim must be to suppress this terrible despotism.'

With this aim in view, General Golovin and his staff, by now rather less optimistic, were working out their plan of campaign for the ensuing year, which in due course was submitted to and approved by the Emperor. Everywhere existing defences were strengthened and new forts built. The troops already in the northern Caucasus were reinforced by the Fourteenth Infantry Division, comprising sixteen Battalions, the Emperor letting it be known that he hoped that with these additional resources General Golovin 'would produce corresponding results'. An army of 12,000 men was to take the field in Daghestan, while in Chechnia an only slightly less numerous force was to march to and fro, 'devastating the land with fire and sword'.

In the course of 1841, Chechnia was duly devastated; a new fortress built; and an enemy strong-point retaken. But when, after another season's desultory campaigning, the Russian troops regained their winter quarters, Shamyl's position was stronger than ever before. The ensuing year's campaign followed the same pattern. The Russians, at considerable cost to themselves, won a number of minor victories and suffered a number of minor setbacks, while all the time, throughout Chechnia and Daghestan Shamyl's power waxed greater and spread.

That winter found General Golovin's Chief of Staff intriguing with the Emperor behind his Commander-in-Chief's back, while General Golovin, for his part, reported unfavourably to St Petersburg on his Chief of Staff's conduct of operations. Meanwhile, at a lower level lesser generals bickered unceasingly among themselves. In December, 1842, both General Golovin and his Chief of Staff were recalled. Not a moment too soon, one feels, for Russia's imperial interests: by the end of 1842 the Russians had in four years lost, in killed, wounded and missing, over 400 officers and nearly 8,000 men and had achieved little or nothing to justify it.

The following year was to prove even more disastrous for the Russians than the four previous years had been. General Neidhardt, the new Commander-in-Chief, was no great improvement on his predecessor. On his appointment he offered to give its weight in gold to anyone who would bring him Shamyl's head. Not long after, a Tartar horseman galloped up to the gates of General Neidhardt's headquarters and, after handing in a letter, galloped off again into the mountains. The letter was from Shamyl. He thanked the Commander-in-Chief politely for the compliment he had paid him, but regretted that he could not return it. He would not, he said, give a straw to anyone who delivered General Neidhardt's head to him.

Shamyl used the first part of 1843 to reorganize his forces. In particular he raised from every part of the areas he controlled a picked body of armed horsemen, known as *mourtazeks*, who were chosen one from every ten households and who must at any time be ready to spring into action at a word from the Imam. The *mourtazeks*, who wore the characteristic black Caucasian *cherkess*, with its two rows of cartridge cases across the chest, and either turbans or high sheepskin hats, were divided into tens, hundreds and five hundreds under commanders of corresponding rank. Those who had sworn to die for Shamyl received additional rations and wore a green cloth patch on the front of their sheepskin hats. In recognition for their onerous responsibilities, the *mourtazeks* were relieved of all ordinary work, the other villagers being obliged to feed their horses for them, till their land and reap their crops. For a guerrilla war of the kind Shamyl was waging, such a system had everything to recommend it. It was ideally suited to the highland temperament. It required no elaborate commissariat – his troops found their own food and horses. And it enabled him to gather and disperse his forces at will and at the shortest possible notice. From his own headquarters he could threaten the enemy wherever he chose and keep them continually guessing. At any moment a strong striking force of *mourtazeks* could swoop on the Russians where they least expected it and then, before they had time to react, fade back into the forests and mountains.

No one was better aware than Shamyl of the weakness of the Russian position in Daghestan or more determined to exploit it. The Russian forces of occupation were scattered in small units, occupying weak positions, over a vast area of difficult and essentially hostile country, either with long straggling lines of communication or, more usually, no communications at all. While strategically on the offensive, they were tactically everywhere on the defensive – a disastrous position for an occupying force. Their morale, too, was none too good. They presented, in short, an ideal target for guerrillas, and commanding them in the field was Shamyl's old adversary, General Kluke von Klugenau, a courageous and competent, but not always very imaginative commander. In August 1843 Shamyl decided that the moment had come to strike a decisive blow.

From his spies Klugenau had received news of a massing of Murid forces. But on 16 August he reported that they had dispersed and that all was again quiet. Ten days later Shamyl set out with a strong force from his headquarters at Dileem in Eastern Chechnia and in twenty-four hours appeared before Ountsoukoul in north-western Daghestan. Here he was joined simultaneously by two of his principal lieutenants, Kibit Mahomá from Tilitl and Hadji Murad from Avaria. Their combined force was now 10,000 strong.

The year before, the people of Ountsoukoul had openly declared against Shamyl, had surrendered seventy-eight of his Murids to the Russian forces of occupation, and had admitted a Russian garrison. Shamyl had two objects: to punish the inhabitants of Ountsoukoul and to destroy the Russian garrison. No sooner had he arrived before Ountsoukoul, than a Russian force of some five hundred more men was hastily sent to relieve it. Before they could reach their destination, they were outflanked and utterly defeated, losing nine officers and 477 men killed. Ountsoukoul was now at Shamyl's mercy. He first took the native *aul* and dealt with the inhabitants. Two days later the Russian fort surrendered. The commander, Lieutenant Anosov was, with unwonted chivalry, allowed to keep his sword as a mark of respect for his gallant conduct in not surrendering sooner.

It was now that General Kluke von Klugenau appeared on the scene with another 1,100 men, gallant, but as usual hopelessly outnumbered and even more hopelessly outmanœuvred. After much floundering about and one disastrous skirmish, he finally fell back on Khounzakh, the capital of Avaria, where on 14 September he was joined, with 5,000 more men, by Major-General Prince Argulenski-Dolgoruki, who had fought his way up from southern Daghestan to relieve his superior officer.

And there Shamyl left them. In barely three weeks the Russians had lost in killed, wounded and prisoners over 2,000 officers and men, while he had captured fourteen cannon and taken all the Russian strongholds in Avaria except Khounzakh. For Khounzakh, Shamyl had other plans. A siege and pitched battle against strongly entrenched regular troops did not appeal to him. He accordingly moved rapidly to Eastern Chechnia and attacked Vnezapnaya, Fort Surprise, and the neighbouring Russian fort of Andreyevo. With a fresh threat developing in Chechnia, the Russians could not keep the bulk of their forces tied up in Avaria. And so Klugenau returned to his Headquarters and in due course orders were given for Khounzakh to be evacuated.

Towards the end of October Shamyl again assumed the offensive and by mid-November every Russian garrison in northern Daghestan was once more threatened. By the end of the year, when Shamyl decided that the time had come for him to withdraw to Avaria, most of them, after many troop movements and much fighting, had been relieved or evacuated. But the Russian losses since the beginning of the campaign in August now amounted to 92 officers and 2,528 men as well as 27 guns and 12 fortified places.

In guerrilla warfare, with its ever-shifting zone of hostilities, those who usually suffer worst are the non-combatant population, forever caught between conflicting forces and at the mercy first of one side and then of the other. In the Caucasus the tribesmen who submitted to the Russians were branded as traitors by the Murids, while those favouring the insurgents were held to be guilty of rebellion against the Tsar. This was true both in Daghestan and Chechnia, particularly in those fringe areas where neither side exercised absolute control and which were therefore constantly changing hands. Thus in Avaria Shamyl's savage rule was detested by many, but the Russians were no more popular. 'One could not help noticing', writes one Russian commentator, 'that the position of the natives in those parts of Daghestan which had submitted to us was extremely burdensome. Oppressed by our demands, they murmured against us and went over to the enemy at the first opportunity.'

In lowland Chechnia the inhabitants now found themselves left to fend for themselves as best they could, while Shamyl carried the war into the mountains of Daghestan. Finally, in despair, they decided to send four delegates to ask him either for adequate protection or for permission to make such terms as they could with the Russians. To put such a proposition to a leader of Shamyl's character required considerable courage. The Imam's personal Executioner, with his long-handled axe, was never far away. In the end, the Chechen delegates decided to approach Shamyl through his mother, Bahou Messadou, a pious old lady, to whom her son was known to be devoted. With the help of a bribe of 2,000 roubles to an amenable *mulla*, an interview with the *Khanum* was arranged and that same evening the old lady set out to call upon Shamyl. Exactly what passed between mother and son can only be surmised. What is certain is that the old lady emerged from the long interview with her eyes red and swollen from much weeping, and that the Imam, for his part, shut himself up in the mosque to fast and pray, while outside the building his faithful Murids congregated to join their prayers to his.

At length, after three days and three nights of suspense, the doors of the mosque opened and Shamyl emerged, pale and drawn, and, ascending with the two attendant Murids to the roof, showed himself to the excited crowd. The Chechens, he announced, forgetful of the oath that bound them, wished to submit to the Infidel. They had sought his own mother's intervention and, because of this, he had thought it right to inquire the will of Mohammed, the Prophet of God. The answer he had received from Mohammed had hit him like a thunderbolt: it was the will of Allah that whoever had dared transmit to him the shameful message of the Chechens should receive a hundred strokes of the whip.

No sooner were these words out of the Imam's mouth than the two attendants seized his mother, tore the shawl from her shoulders and started to lay into the old lady for all they were worth. After five strokes, she fainted, while Shamyl, displaying extreme emotion, threw himself at her feet. A few moments later, however, he rose and announced that he had himself been granted the right to bear the blows allotted to his unhappy mother. Then, baring his shoulders, he handed two great whips to his attendants and stood unflinching while they delivered the remaining ninety-five strokes. After this, resuming his robes, he strode down into the crowd, calling loudly for the wicked Chechens who had brought down such a terrible punishment on his poor mother.

At once the four were dragged forward and thrown down at his feet, while the crowd looked on with wild surmise, wondering what terrible fate was about to be inflicted on them. But again there was a surprise in store for them. 'Go back to your people,' said Shamyl sternly to the four delegates, 'and, in reply to their foolish demand, tell them all that you have seen and heard.' After which there was no further talk of defection from the Chechens.

And now the insurrection against Russian rule was spreading beyond the Imam's own area of operations, to the Caspian littoral in the east and to the Moslem tribes both north and south of the main mountain range. For Shamyl, 1843 had been another year of success, but to the Emperor

Nicholas it had brought nothing but frustration. Again he decided that determined action must be taken to pacify the Caucasus. General Neidhardt, he decreed, was to 'go into the mountains, scatter and disperse Shamyl's hordes, utterly destroy his organization, take possession of all the most strategic points in the mountains and fortify and hold as many as seemed necessary.' For this purpose the Army of the Caucasus was to be reinforced by another 26 battalions and 40 guns, as well as substantial fresh drafts to fill the depleted ranks of the units already there. 'From such gigantic resources', he added, in a phrase that was becoming familiar, 'I expect corresponding results' – and expected them, he made clear, before the end of 1844. And he went on to talk of 'political means' and subversion and negotiations with the tribal leaders. But Shamyl, for his part, simply let it be known that the penalty for any dealings with the enemy was death, and left it at that. And so, in the event, the year 1844 came and went; immense efforts were made by the Russians; minor victories were won and setbacks sustained by both sides; Shamyl reacted with his usual ruthlessness at any sign of disloyalty on the part of the population and at the end of the year emerged with his standing and prestige still further strengthened.

7 *Count Vorontsov*

The spring of 1845 found Tsar Nicholas busy with the preparation of yet another plan of campaign and calling once more for early and decisive results. Meanwhile General Neidhardt had been replaced by the famous Count Michael Vorontsov, who had distinguished himself thirty years earlier in the war against Napoleon and now, at sixty-three, was appointed Viceroy of the Caucasus as well as Commander-in-Chief.

Born in 1782, Michael Vorontsov had been brought up in England, where his father, Count Simon, had been Catherine the Great's ambassador to George III and where his sister had married Lord Pembroke. It is now known that it was old Simon who at an advanced age hid under the timbers of the raft in the middle of the River Niemen at Tilsit in 1807 and, with his legs dangling in the icy river, listened to the whole of Alexander's secret conversation with Napoleon, which he at once passed on to the British Government. Like his father, Michael was an Anglophile and spent as much time as he could in England, racing at Epsom and leading the life of a Regency buck. Sir Thomas Lawrence's portrait of him was a sensation. He married Countess Elizabeth Branitski, said by some to be Prince Potyomkin's daughter by his favourite niece, Alexandra. (All four of Potyomkin's nieces became, at one time or another, their uncle's mistresses.) In any case it was to Elizabeth that Prince Potyomkin left all his vast wealth and when she married Michael Vorontsov she brought with her a dowry of thirty million roubles, two hundred thousand serfs, the famous Potyomkin diamonds, innumerable salt mines and endless estates. She also possessed considerable beauty and even greater charm. This she exercised all too successfully on the poet Pushkin, who in 1823 was briefly attached to her husband's staff at Odessa and whose mistress she became and remained until her husband suddenly had him posted elsewhere.

It was while Count Michael Vorontsov was living at Odessa as Governor General of Southern Russia in the 1820s that he built his great castle of Alupka near Yalta in the Crimea, employing the English architect Edward Blore to construct for him on the shores of the Black Sea a dream-palace of green stone from the Urals in a mixture of styles, variously recalling Windsor Castle, the Brighton Pavilion and the Taj Mahal. He also created with the help of a German expert, a magnificent botanical garden a short distance outside Yalta, which to this day is one of the glories of the Crimea, and a second no less splendid botanical garden in Tiflis.

With Count Vorontsov, attracted by his name and reputation, came a brilliant galaxy of fashionable officers. With their smart uniforms, magnificent chargers, grooms, chefs, soldier-servants, luxurious tents and frequent French catch-phrases, the newcomers were in marked contrast to the rough, hard-bitten veterans alongside whom they were now serving. '*Ecoutez, mon cher!*' they kept saying to each other, and sneering at their uncouth comrades at arms. Each general had a large staff and a camp-area marked by his own personal pennon, red, red and black, red and white, silver and white and so on. 'There never', wrote an English naval officer, who found two of them at their toilet, 'was seen more luxury displayed in that department than by these Petersburg guardees.' And he goes on to tell of their silk dressing-gowns and their 'dressing cases of English manufacture ... filled with jug and basin of solid silver.'

The Emperor's latest plan provided for a large-scale punitive expedition, designed to penetrate deep into the mountains, pin down Shamyl and capture his new stronghold of Andee in north-western Daghestan – 'that nest' – utterly defeat him and establish a Russian base there. But Count Vorontsov himself, after talking to his generals, who had had some experience of these things and of the Emperor's plans, was less optimistic. 'If God', he wrote to the Minister for War on 25 May, 'is not pleased to bless us with success, we shall nevertheless have done our duty, we shall not be to blame.' And again on 30 May: 'I dare not hope for much success from our enterprise, but I will of course do all I can to carry out the Emperor's wishes and justify his confidence.' Next day the expedition set out, its two component columns from Chechnia and Daghestan coming together on 3 June and continuing their march into the mountains together.

Count Vorontsov's force consisted of 21 battalions of infantry, 16 *sotnias* of cavalry, 4 companies of sappers and 46 guns, as well as some sharpshooters and native cavalry, amounting in all to some 18,000 men. His plan was to approach Andee through the mountains from the east by way of the Kirk Pass. By 5 June he had reached the pass, which he found to be undefended. His troops, who had hoped for an early victory, were disappointed not to meet the enemy. However they continued their march. The weather in the mountains now turned bitterly cold, as it can in the Caucasus even in June, and during the next week the Russians lost five hundred horses and suffered serious casualties from frost bite. So far, apart from a little skirmishing, they had hardly seen the enemy.

On 14 June the Russians reached Andee. They found it in ruins. Shamyl, who had a clear appreciation of the potentialities of the situation and knew that his right course was to avoid pitched battles with so strong an enemy and seek rather to lure him on into the mountains, had, on their approach, set fire to his headquarters and retired into the neighbouring hills, whence, after another skirmish, he withdrew northwards along the Aksai valley to his forest stronghold of Dargo, a dozen or so miles away in southern Chechnia. 'God', wrote the Emperor to Vorontsov on 9 July, when he heard the news, 'has crowned you and your brave troops with the success you deserved and shown once more that nothing can stop the Russians – the Orthodox Russians – when, with firm reliance on His help, they go where their Tsar tells them.'

The Russians had certainly gone where the Tsar had told them. The problem for them now, as Shamyl realized better than they did, was how to maintain themselves there. More than a third of the total force had been left behind to guard the lines of communication and special instructions given to hurry forward supplies. But it was already difficult to feed the forward troops and the men at Andee were on short rations. As for local supplies, Shamyl had destroyed everything for miles around. He had also made it clear to the inhabitants that he would not tolerate the slightest collaboration with the Russians and one Russian officer, coming back from an early morning ride, was disturbed to find in his path two severed shaven heads, with the inscription, 'Thus are punished the adherents of the Russian Government.' Already the feeling was beginning to gain ground that the Russians were lucky to have advanced as far as they had without disaster and would be even luckier to get back alive. And yet Dargo was barely ten miles away and Count Vorontsov still had ten thousand men with which to attack it.

For three weeks Vorontsov waited at Andee for provisions to arrive. But, when it became clear that they would not reach him in time, he took the decision to start for Dargo on 6 July, at the same time sending back part of his force to collect and bring on the provisions. The Russians started their march at four in the morning, just as it was getting light. But when the Commander-in-Chief emerged from his tent and called for his favourite charger, it was missing. One of his own native attendants had galloped off on it an hour earlier to warn Shamyl of the enemy's approach. By nine the whole Russian force had reached the fringes of the forest. Here, for a few hours, they halted and ate their rations. Chechnia lay at their feet, a mass of thickly wooded hills and valleys stretching away into the distance to where the plains began and the River Terek marked the position of the old Cossack line. From where they were, Dargo was barely five miles distant. To reach it, they had to follow a path leading along the ridge of a steep, thickly wooded mountain spur. Their way forward, they very soon found, was blocked at intervals of four or five hundred yards by the trunks of giant beech-trees neatly felled across it, while on either side the woods swarmed with hidden enemies.

After they had eaten and rested, the leading regiment, longing for action, asked leave to advance. Leave was given. They brandished their muskets above their heads and, when the bugle sounded, charged forward to the attack, led by their officers and even by some of the Staff. Rushing impetuously forward, they successfully surmounted the first six barriers. Another regiment followed and the way now seemed clear for the rest of the column to advance. But when the Commander-in-Chief set out to follow them, he and his Staff suddenly found themselves cut off by the enemy from their own advanced troops and caught in a devastating cross-fire at a point where the track narrowed between the second and third barriers. It was not until late that night that Count Vorontsov, after losing one of his generals and suffering a number of other casualties, finally extricated himself from this unpleasant situation and, joining up with his advance troops, fought his way through to Dargo, only to find the usual piles of blazing ruins, which Shamyl had left behind him, while he and his followers yet again faded back into the forest.

Once more the Russians were in an awkward situation. They had rations for five days. Ahead of them, almost thirty miles due north, at the far end of the Aksai valley lay the village of Gherzel-aul and relative safety. There was clearly a strong case for fighting their way through to it without delay. But in the event Count Vorontsov decided rather to wait for the arrival of the convoy bringing the rations.

Shamyl, meanwhile, had established himself on the high ground on the other side of the River Aksai, whence with four captured guns he proceeded to bombard the Russian camp below, while every evening at sunset, adding insult to injury, he caused a large band of Russian prisoners and deserters to march up and down in full view of their former comrades, playing the Russian Tattoo.

After enduring this for two days, Vorontsov finally retaliated by sending a strong force to attack Shamyl's position. By the time the Russians reached it, the enemy was nowhere to be seen and their comrades, watching from below, cheered at the ease with which they had attained their objective. It was only as the Russians were returning to base that the Chechens suddenly reappeared, descending on them like a pack of wolves, and killing and wounding nearly two hundred before they could regain their camp. Shamyl now quickly reoccupied his former position and that evening, while Count Vorontsov's men buried their dead comrades to the melancholy chanting of their Orthodox priests, the merry strains of the Russian Tattoo once more rang out across the river as the deserters' band marched and counter-marched in mockery at their misfortunes.

Russian morale was now at a low ebb. 'An inexplicable depression', writes an eye-witness, 'pervaded the army' – though in fact the expla-nation of their mood can scarcely have been far to seek. Next day, however, on 9 July, rockets were seen to go up from the point on the edge of the forest, whence the column had started their advance five days before. The convoy bringing the rations had, it seemed, at last arrived there.

The problem was how to bring it along the intervening ridge. In the end, a force of no less than 4,000 men, under General Kluke von Klugenau and two other generals, was detached from the main column and sent back to provide the necessary escort. It was to be famous in the annals of the Russian Army as the Biscuit Expedition.

The force set out back along the ridge on 10 July. All his military life Klugenau had been guided by Suvorov's famous maxim: 'The Head does not wait for the Tail.' On this occasion he followed it blindly. Soon his forward troops were separated from the centre and the centre from the rear. The barriers of tree-trunks had been re-erected. The enemy swarmed in among the Russians, cutting them off from each other and attacking them from every side, even sniping them from the branches of the great beech trees above their heads. The fighting, much of it hand to hand, lasted all day. The Russians suffered appalling casualties. It was not until nightfall that the survivors finally fought their way along the ridge and out of the forest into the open, where the provision train was waiting for them.

Klugenau's first impulse was to leave Vorontsov to fend for himself. But then he changed his mind and at first light on 11 July, after firing three cannon-shots to warn their comrades at Dargo that they were starting, the convoy set out once more to make their way back along the fatal ridge. Again the barriers were in position and this time the enemy were more numerous than ever. When the leading troops arrived at the point where the track narrowed, they found that Shamyl had a surprise in store for them: the barrier of tree-trunks was piled high with the Russian dead of the day before, stripped, hideously mutilated and stacked one on top of the other. The barrier itself was not held by the enemy, but as the advancing Russians halted to stare in horror at this appalling spectacle, they found themselves caught in a withering cross-fire from strategically placed strong-points on either side. The engagement that now followed was even more disastrous. In addition to the supplies they had come to fetch, Klugenau's force were now burdened by an ever greater number of wounded, whom they dared not abandon to their fate. As they straggled along the ridge in little groups, the enemy never gave them a moment's respite, keeping them under constant fire and harassing them continually as they sought to fight their way through, while Klugenau, for his part, his light-grey uniform riddled with bullet holes, led desperate counter-attacks like any company-commander and, when all his staff had been killed, sat his horse, an eye-witness tells us, under a hail of bullets, 'like the statue of the Commander in *Don Juan.*'

In the end, Count Vorontsov, realizing their plight, sent out a battalion from Dargo to help bring them in and that night the survivors of the Biscuit Expedition finally reached Dargo. In two days they had lost 2 generals, 50 officers and more than 1,200 men killed or wounded and 3 cannons captured. Of the provisions they had set out to fetch, hardly any were left.

Count Vorontsov's force had now been reduced to some 5,000 bayonets. He was burdened with more than a thousand wounded. He had practically no rations and was hemmed in on all sides by a formidable enemy. His only remaining hope was somehow, before they all starved, to fight his way through the thirty miles or so of forest which separated him from Gherzel-aul.

Some days before, Count Vorontsov had consulted General Freitag, an old hand at this kind of fighting, now commanding the Left Flank of the Cossack Line at Grozni, Freitag's answer was scarcely encouraging.

> Amongst the Chechens it is already no secret that your Excellency intends to come down to the plains from Dargo. 'We have not yet begun to fight the Russians,' they say. 'Let them go where they will, we know where to attack them.' And indeed they do know; in the forests all advantages are on their side, and they understand well how to make the most of them.
>
> Your Excellency has given me permission to express my opinions. I cannot justify such flattering confidence better than by being absolutely frank. On the downward march you will meet in the forest such difficulties and such opposition as, probably, you do not anticipate. I will not attempt to prove that the operation is well-nigh impossible; on the contrary, I feel sure that your Excellency will win through; but the losses will be enormous. You will find that the Chechens know how to fight when necessary.

And again:

> I promised to be frank, and frank I must be. Judging from your Excellency's letter, you seem to expect important results from the march through the forest to the plain. Allow me to say simply that you are being deceived. However successful your operations, they will have no influence on the subjugation of Chechnia.

Freitag's gloomy prognostications were abundantly justified. On 13 July Count Vorontsov's force set out from Dargo for Gherzel-aul. Their march was a repetition of previous disasters. Again the enemy harassed them and ambushed them at every stage. Again the forward troops lost touch with those in the rear. By 17 July they had covered barely fifteen miles – less than four miles a day. Gherzel-aul was still more than ten miles away. They had lost another thousand men. They

Kutaisi, the Spice Bazaar

Nikortsminda

The Georgian Military Highway, a side valley

The Black Aragvi

The Georgian Military Highway, the top of the pass

The Georgian Military Highway, a wayside shrine

were now carrying with them more than 2,000 wounded. Their rations had finally run out and they were starving. Their supplies of ammunition were also running low.

Seeing that he could advance no further, Vorontsov, who before leaving had despatched five different messengers to Freitag at Grozni in the hope that one at least might reach him, now decided to halt where he was and await the arrival of a relieving force. But there was still no answer from Freitag and no means of telling whether any of the five messengers had got through to him. And all the time the surrounding enemy kept up their attacks. The 17th of July went by and most of the 18th and still there was no sign of Freitag. 'If relief does not come soon', noted Prince Alexander of Hesse, who had been temporarily attached to Count Vorontsov's staff to gain experience, 'our whole force will be wiped out.' And then, just before sunset on the 18th the sound of cannon, echoing through the forest from the north, told them that at last help was on the way. Soon, looking through their telescopes, they could see the forward troops of the relieving force. 'The men', wrote Prince Alexander, 'have all begun to sing.'

Vorontsov's first message had reached Freitag in Grozni on 16 July and he had set out at once, covering almost a hundred miles in two days. By nightfall the two columns had made contact and two days later Vorontsov and what was left of his own force were safe in Gherzel-aul, while Shamyl, for his part, once again faded back into the forests and mountains. In this, their latest signally unsuccessful attempt to extirpate him, the Russians had altogether lost 3 generals, 195 other officers and no less than 3,433 men killed and wounded, while Shamyl's own losses had been negligible. In the circumstances, Count Vorontsov's claim that 'the mountain tribes have now learnt that we can reach them in places hitherto considered unaccessible,' did not really carry great conviction. But at any rate the Emperor, whose idea it had been, was pleased with the outcome of the expedition. 'Read with great interest', he wrote on his Commander-in-Chief's report, 'and with respect for the fine courage of my troops.' And on Count Michael Vorontsov he gratefully bestowed the title of Prince.

Shamyl, meanwhile, encouraged by his successes, was preparing to put into execution a plan which he hoped would imperil the whole Russian position in the Caucasus. While he himself had been fighting the Russians in Daghestan and Chechnia, the Circassians and other

Moslem tribes of the Black Sea littoral, heartened by the news of his victories, had been carrying on their struggle, though rather less effectively, in the Western Caucasus. From time to time emissaries were exchanged, but there was no real attempt to co-ordinate resistance. For Shamyl it was of the utmost importance that the western tribes should not abandon the struggle, and so leave the Russians free to concentrate all their available strength against him. His aim, on the contrary, was, if he could, to link the two wings of the resistance movement and so extend his influence from sea to sea.

The key to the situation lay in Kabarda, the wild upland area lying immediately to the north of the main range, between the valleys of the Terek and the Kuban. Since 1822 the Kabardans, a warlike race related to the Cherkess, had accepted Russian rule and abstained from open revolt. Situated as they were between the eastern tribes on the one hand and the western on the other, their submission to the Russians separated the two areas of operations and so greatly facilitated the Russian task. But now there were signs that, unsettled by news of the Murid victories, the Kabardans were beginning to stir. Already their princes were seeking contact with Shamyl. If he could induce them to rise, the forces at his disposal would be strengthened, the gap between east and west bridged and the Russians confronted by the most formidable coalition they had yet had to face. It was to this end that he now directed all his efforts and prepared as a first step to enter Kabarda in strength.

Early in April 1846 General Freitag, well informed as usual, got wind at his headquarters at Grozni of unusually important Murid forces massing in Chechnia. Greatly daring, he at once sent a message stopping the return to Russia of two battalions of Fifth Corps, which was at that moment being withdrawn from the Caucasus on express instructions from the Tsar, and diverting them to Nikolayevskaya, a Cossack settlement on the Terek, thirty miles north-west of Vladikavkaz. From Nikolayevskaya, they could cover the famous ford on the River Terek by the Minaret of Tatartub, where Tamerlane had defeated Toktamish in 1395 and Sheikh Mansur had been defeated by Count Potyomkin in 1785. For Freitag knew that, if Shamyl was intending to move west of Vladikavkaz, this was where he was bound to cross the Terek. Vladikavkaz itself was held by a garrison of 1,300 men, while Freitag's own little Army of the Left Flank, from its central position at Grozni could quickly be thrown in wherever it was most needed. Having made these dispositions, he then awaited further developments.

On 12 April General Freitag heard that Shamyl's force was at Shalee, only fifteen miles from Grozni, moving rapidly westwards. Gathering all the troops he could from his own and neighbouring commands, he set off in pursuit. Soon it was clear beyond a doubt that what Shamyl had in mind was the invasion of Kabarda. Realizing to the full the implications of such a move and more determined than ever to bring his adversary to action at the earliest opportunity, Freitag continued in hot pursuit, while at the same time notifying all concerned of the danger. By 16 April he was only a few hours behind him. On the 17th he learned that Shamyl with his main force was making for the minaret and on the 18th he caught up with him at the ford.

By this time Shamyl himself was already across but as his rearguard were crossing, they came under fire from Freitag's guns and an inconclusive engagement ensued. Freitag's position was not an easy one. He was in light marching order and short both of rations and ammunition. He was also heavily outnumbered by the enemy and very conscious that the Left Flank, for which he personally was responsible, was now dangerously exposed to an attack should Shamyl decide to double back across the Terek and take him in the rear. In spite of this he was determined to engage Shamyl regardless of odds.

Shamyl, too, had his problems. He had now reached the position from which he hoped to rouse the Kabardans to insurrection and so hold the Russians in check while he continued his march westwards. But it was an essential part of his plan that a force commanded by one of his *naïbs* should seize and hold the famous Darial Pass, thus blocking the Georgian Military Highway and preventing the arrival of Russian reinforcements from Tiflis. And this project, as it happened, had been nipped in the bud by the prompt action of General Gurko, until a few days before, Prince Vorontsov's Chief of Staff, who had happened to be travelling home that way and, seeing what was afoot, had at once assumed command and taken steps to secure the road. Moreover the success of Shamyl's plan depended on the active co-operation of the Kabardans, who, having witnessed the arrival of the formidable General Freitag hard on the Imam's heels, now hesitated to fulfil their part of the bargain.

And so, on 19 July, just as Freitag was preparing to attack him,

Shamyl, quickly changing his plans, abandoned his position on the River Terek and simply continued his way westwards into the mountains. Fearing for the Left Flank and thinking it wiser not to follow his adversary further west, Freitag now resolved to wait on events. Shamyl, meanwhile, finding the Kabardans still undecided and learning that the attack on the Darial Gorge had failed and that Russian reinforcements were reaching Vladikavkaz from Georgia, had decided to abandon his original plan and withdraw across the Terek. By 26 April he was back at the ford, and, successfully fighting off the Russian detachment he found there, was safely across it with the whole of his force before Freitag and the rest of his troops could come up with him. Twenty-four hours later he was sixty miles away and beyond pursuit.

If the Russians had missed an opportunity to pin down Shamyl and defeat him, Shamyl, thanks to the energy and presence of mind of General Freitag, had at least been forced to abandon an enterprise which, if successful, could drastically have changed the course of events in the Caucasus. And this, as their dispatches show, was recognized readily enough both by the Tsar and also by Prince Vorontsov, who for the second time in less than a year had every reason to be grateful to his subordinate.

As for Shamyl, though he had not succeeded in this particular enterprise, he had suffered little or no material loss and, despite everything, had retained the initiative, as he clearly demonstrated three months later by daring to bombard the great Russian fortress of Grozni. During the months that followed the Russians were given no peace either in Chechnia or Daghestan and ended the year, as usual, with a heavy list of casualties. And when the following summer Prince Vorontsov sought to storm Shamyl's stronghold of Ghergebil with a force of ten battalions of infantry strongly supported by cavalry and artillery, he was repulsed with heavy losses and forced to withdraw. Indeed it was not until a year later, in the summer of 1848, that the Russians, with a force of 10,000 men, finally captured the little mountain village, only to find that even now they were unable to hold it. Twenty years had passed since Kazi Mulla and Shamyl had first taken the field against the Russians. During those years the insurrection had prospered and spread and nowhere was there any sign of its being quelled. Indeed, Shamyl's influence and authority were stronger than ever before.

Since 1847 the Imam's headquarters had been situated beside the

River Khoulkhoulau at Veden in Chechnia, not far from Dargo, near the borders of Daghestan. Here he lived with his children and wives, each of whom had a suite of three rooms to herself. Of his eight wives, Fatima, his favourite, and the mother of his three sons, had died in 1845; the senior was now Zaidate, ill-favoured, but a descendant of the Prophet. With another of his wives, whom he had married only to please the Chechens, he had spent no more than a token three hours. Since Fatima's death the favourite of all was Shouanete, the beautiful Armenian who had been captured in Akhverdi Mahoma's raid on Mozdok in 1840 and who, though her rich relations sought to ransom her, always refused to leave the Imam. But for years Shamyl's constant companion and most regular guest was a plain black and white cat which had been given him by a Russian deserter and which always sat opposite him at table. To this little animal he was deeply devoted and would always see that it was happy and provided with special dishes of its favourite foods.

From Shouanete's cousin, Atarov, an Armenian merchant from Mozdok, who in 1850, greatly daring, somehow made his way there through the mountains to try to ransom his cousin, we have a first-hand account of Veden, or Dargo-Veden, as it came to be known. Shamyl's stronghold stood on a high plateau, surrounded by even higher mountains. Behind it was the thickly wooded hillside; in front, a precipice dropped sheer to a raging torrent far below, the River Chilo. Round the fortress was a stockade, its only entrance defended by blockhouses and by a single cannon of European make. Shamyl's own house was at the centre of the inner fortress, heavily guarded by a picked force of Murids. Adjoining it was a mosque. A tall watchtower dominated the scene.

Having finally reached his destination, Atarov offered the Imam great sums of gold as a ransom for his cousin. But it was of no avail. Shouanete declared that she was happy where she was, while Shamyl, for his part, only smiled and made the Armenian a present of a fine horse as a parting gift.

During the years that followed the capture of Ghergebil there was on the whole less action in the Caucasus, both the Murids and the Russians being more inclined to stand on the defensive. Shamyl was left in possession of Western Daghestan, including Avaria, and of most of

Chechnia, while the Russians built more forts and roads and consolidated their existing defences, and Prince Vorontsov occupied himself increasingly with the reform of the civil administration, a field in which he achieved considerable success.

The year 1851 had been marked by a sudden shift in the internal balance of the Murid forces. For ten years Hadji Murad had occupied a position second only to that of Shamyl as a partisan leader, winning lasting fame by his daring raids against the Russians. But now relations between him and the Imam had become strained. Hadji Murad had grown too powerful and too arrogant. When, towards the end of 1851, Shamyl proclaimed his second son, Kazi Mohammed, as his successor, Hadji Murad flew into a passion. 'The sword', he said, 'will decide who shall succeed – only the sword.' On hearing of this, Shamyl decided to eliminate him. But Hadji Murad, on learning what was in the wind, once again acted with characteristic speed and presence of mind. Taking four of his most trusted followers with him, he made his way by night to the nearest Russian fortress and there gave himself up to its commander, who happened to be Colonel Prince Simon Vorontsov, the Viceroy's son.

'If you want to boast of news from the Caucasus', wrote young Count Leo Tolstoi in a letter dated 23 December, 1851, to his brother Sergei, 'you may announce that the second personage after Shamyl, a certain Hadji Murad, has just surrendered to the Russian Government. He was the finest warrior and horseman in all Chechnia, yet he committed this baseness.' It was a theme which Count Tolstoi subsequently developed further in his book *Hadji Murad* which with time was to become more famous than its hero, but which, like this early comment, showed no very profound understanding for the tribesman's ethic or view of life.

Without loss of time, young Simon Vorontsov sent Hadji Murad to his father in Tiflis. There, dark, handsome, inscrutable and still slightly lame from his leap over the precipice, he caused a social sensation at the Opera and at the Viceregal receptions. Prince Vorontsov and his wife Eliza, still almost as attractive as when, twenty-five years earlier, she had been Pushkin's mistress, treated their guest with affability. But what Hadji Murad wanted was Russian support against Shamyl and arms with which to destroy his detested rival. With arms and guns, he kept repeating, he could raise the whole of Daghestan against Shamyl.

86

Meanwhile, the weeks were passing. His family were in Shamyl's power. Indeed rumour had it that the Imam had already put his son's eyes out. But the Russians, doubtful of his sincerity, only procrastinated, talking of an offensive in the spring once the snows had melted, in which he might possibly be allowed to join in a subordinate role.

In the end Hadji Murad decided to act independently. He would first escape from the Russians and then take Shamyl by surprise. On the pretext of an early morning ride, he and his four followers set out across country, followed as usual by an escort of five Cossacks. Choosing their moment, they turned on the Russians, cut them down, took their ammunition and then made off at full speed for the mountains. At mid-day, finding themselves still in open country, they decided to lie up in a wood and there await nightfall before proceeding further.

When the news of Hadji Murad's escape reached Tiflis, the garrison commander, gathering as large a force of Russians and native troops as he could muster, set out in pursuit. On the road, as luck would have it, he encountered an old man who had noticed five strange horsemen enter a wood. Within an hour the Russians had found and surrounded the wood.

Outnumbered five hundred to five, Hadji Murad and his men refused to surrender. Having cut their horses' throats, they made a rampart from the bodies and then met shot with shot as the Russians closed in on them. Finally, with several bullets in him, Hadji Murad, now in his death throes, rose to his feet and charged the enemy, *kinjal* in hand. But before he could reach them, another shot laid him low. Then his adversaries rushed him, the first to reach him being the son of his old enemy Akhmet Khan of Mekhtoulee, who hacked off his head in triumph while his companions, coming up with him, joined him in kicking and stabbing the bleeding corpse. The head was later embalmed and displayed by the Russians in the military hospital at Tiflis, 'in order', it was said, 'to reassure the public.' What happened to the body is not known. 'Thus, on 24 April 1852', wrote Prince Vorontsov, 'died Hadji Murad – died, as he had lived, with desperate courage. His ambition equalled his bravery and to that there was no bound.'

8 Prisoners of Shamyl

In October 1853 Turkey declared war on Russia, to be followed six months later by France and Great Britain. The Crimean War had begun. The Russians were now heavily engaged elsewhere and this should have improved Shamyl's chances. But Shamyl does not seem to have exploited the potentialities of the situation as fully as he might have done. Nor, for that matter, did the Allies do anything to help him despite his appeals for help. 'England', he wrote in a letter to Queen Victoria, 'must know of our ceaseless struggle against Russia ... We urge you, we beseech you, O Queen, to bring us help.' But there was no answer to his letters and the help he asked for never came. Nor was there much more response from his natural ally, the Sultan of Turkey, who, it is true, formally appointed him Viceroy of Georgia, but did nothing else to further his cause. And so the Russians continued to hold their own in the Caucasus, keeping the insurgents in check as well as the Turks, who suffered a series of devastating defeats, while their French and British comrades-at-arms waged war against Russia with only slightly greater success in the seclusion of the Crimea.

But, although during these years Shamyl undertook no major military initiatives, his Murids carried out one highly successful incursion into Georgian territory, which gave him the means of implementing a project on which he had long since set his heart.

In the second half of June, 1854, the young and beautiful Princess Anna Chavchavadze, a granddaughter of the last King of Georgia and wife of Colonel Prince David Chavchavadze, had set out from Tiflis with her family and retainers to spend the rest of the summer on her husband's estates at Tsinandali, pleasantly situated forty or fifty miles away to the north-east on a tributary of the Alazani River in a remote valley among the hills. With her went her five children, the youngest, Lydia, only seven months old, her sister Princess Varvara Orbeliani, whose husband's recent death in battle had left her a widow at twenty-five, a beautiful teenage niece, Princess Nina Baratova, and a far from foolish, pertly pretty thirty-two-year-old French governess, Madame Anna Drancy, the estranged wife of a Parisian *limonadier* and *restaurateur*. Princess Anna's husband, Prince David, who commanded the local militia, was on duty near by.

A few years before, both Princess Anna and Princess Varvara had spent several seasons at Court in St Petersburg; had been appointed Ladies-in-Waiting to the Empress; and had enjoyed the success assured by their noble birth and good looks. Now, with their children, they divided their time between Tiflis and their country estates.

Warnings from the military that they were acting imprudently in venturing so far in the direction of the mountains had gone unheeded. But by the beginning of July disturbing rumours and mysterious comings and goings in the immediate neighbourhood caused Princess Anna to wonder whether she had not made a mistake in ignoring the advice she had been given, and on the night of 3 July she finally decided to start back for Tiflis next morning.

But at daybreak, just as they were preparing to leave, came shouts and the sound of shooting from the garden; then the thunder of hooves and the sudden tumult of galloping horsemen, and then a great horde of wild Chechen tribesmen burst into the house and surged up the stairs and on through the rooms, seizing anything and anyone they could lay hands on.

One tribesman grabbed Madame Drancy and cleared the stairs with her at a leap. Another tried to take her away from the first, offering him three roubles for her. Others laid hold of the Princesses and the maids and the children. Downstairs in the hall the Chechens were fighting over the women. Madame Drancy, explaining shrilly that she was a French citizen and that they would come to regret what they were doing, finally fell to the lot of 'a turbaned monster', who dragged her out into the courtyard. Her clothes by now had been torn off her and she was dressed only in her stays and a pair of kid boots she had bought in the Rue de Rivoli. When she tried to get away from her captor, he gave her a vicious cut across her bare shoulders with his whip, repeating the process with irrefutable logic every time she attempted to reason with him. All this time Prince David's eighty-year-old Aunt Tinia was wandering about stark naked with arms outstretched and wispy hair hanging down her shoulders, praying loudly for death. Princess Anna, with her dress torn off and her black hair streaming down her back, was clutching her baby daughter, Lydia. Tearing the magnificent diamond ear-rings she was wearing from her ears, a tribesman tied her to his stirrup by one arm and then rode straight into the river, dragging her after him, while she tried desperately to keep her baby's head above water. Madame Drancy's tormentor pulled her up on to his horse behind him. The others were either thrown on to horses or dragged along behind them. The children were strapped on to saddles or stuffed head first into saddlebags and the raiding party, having looted and sacked the house and outbuildings and then set fire to them, set off at a gallop towards the mountains, a Georgian nurse who could not keep up with the horses on foot being dispatched with one well directed sabre-cut.

The raiders had just entered a narrow defile in the hills when some shots rang out and they found themselves under heavy fire from a Russian patrol. At this they wheeled round and made off as fast as they could in the opposite direction. By now Princess Anna's captor had hoisted her up behind him on his horse and was galloping as hard as he could go. Exhausted and distraught, she clutched her baby, head downwards, by one foot. But though she screamed to him to stop, he only galloped faster, urging on his horse and shouting gaily to his companions, while the baby's head banged against his stirrup and the horse's side. In the end Anna's weak grip loosened and the child fell to the ground under the trampling hooves of the oncoming horses, its dying wails drowned by its mother's shrieks and the excited cries of the Chechens, as, before the horror-struck eyes of Princess Varvara, galloping wildly behind her sister in her trailing widow's weeds, they rode right over the little body and on into the mountains to meet Shamyl.

Prince David, meanwhile, on duty at a neighbouring outpost, had no idea that morning of what was happening at his house. Then, some hours later, came the news that large numbers of tribesmen had come down from the mountains and were attacking in strength in the direction of the Alazani River. Taking four companies, he at once set out to head them off. But he was too late. He had not gone far when several columns of smoke on the horizon showed him that already half a dozen villages, Tsinandali among them, were on fire. By the time he reached the river the main body of raiders were safely back in the mountains. But some of his family silver, found in the saddlebags of one small party of Murids his men had managed to intercept, told him all too clearly

what had happened to his house. And next day, in the defile where the
main force of Murids had been ambushed and turned back, a party of
his men came on the bodies of several of his serfs and of his little
daughter Lydia.

Prince David did not reach Tsinandali and the smouldering ruins of
his house until two days later. At the edge of the wood, tied to a tree and
out of her mind, he found Maria Gaideli, his family's hundred-year-old
head nurse, who for longer than anyone could remember had brought
up successive generations of Chavchavadzes. She was wailing a funeral
dirge in a high, cracked voice. No one else was to be seen.

It took the prisoners a month of almost continuous travelling, across
ever higher mountains, over snowy passes, through rushing torrents
and beside ever deeper precipices, to reach Shamyl's rocky fastness of
Veden in Chechnia, known to his followers as the Great Aul. By the
time they arrived there, they were half naked and such clothes as they
still had were verminous and in tatters. They were also half starved,
having existed on a diet of *koumeli* or millet meal supplemented by
an occasional handful of rhododendron leaves and a strip or two of
leathery dried mutton, and dreadfully weakened by exposure and
exhaustion. And all the while Princess Anna, distraught and often
delirious, kept asking whether anyone had seen her baby daughter
Lydia.

Other terrible things had happened on the journey. Several of the
prisoners had died of hunger or exhaustion or disease. Others had been
slaughtered by their guards because they were too feeble to keep up.
Once one of the Murids had been so exasperated by a baby's wailing
that he had snatched it up and dashed its brains out on a rock, silencing
its mother's shrieks by driving his knife into her – much to the dismay
of the Princesses, whose children were also given to wailing. As was
usual in the mountains, most of the Chechens carried severed human
heads at their saddle-bows and Madame Drancy was particularly disturbed by a woman's hand with a gold wedding-ring on one finger,
which dangled from her own saddle and flapped against her bare thigh
as she rode. To make matters worse, she had no head for heights and
had to be driven past every precipice with a whip. On one slippery
bridge of rounded logs she lost her footing altogether and was only
saved from destruction by a Murid who caught her by her feet, still
encased in those elegant kid boots from the Rue de Rivoli, and held her

hanging head downwards over the abyss. Such wisps of underclothing as still remained to her were finally swept away while crossing a river, after which the Murids, finding her bruised and battered body still disturbing, ordered her to save them from any further temptation by covering it with a *burka*, a heavy goat-hair cape, which they provided for this purpose.

It was growing dark and raining heavily when they reached the Great Aul. Each of the women had been furnished with a great square of black silk and told to cover her face and head with it. Here no woman might appear unveiled in public, nor might she gaze directly on the Imam. The rain poured down, obscuring the mountain tops. Peering out from behind their veils, the Princesses and Anna Drancy contemplated with foreboding the high, forbidding stockade with its iron-bound gates, the guards with their long black cloaks and high black sheepskin hats, the watchtower and minaret and, towering above everything else, the soaring pinnacles of rock.

The gates were now opened and they passed into a large courtyard, crowded with men and horses and with wooden, galleried houses on three sides of it. Looking up, they caught sight for a moment of a gigantic, heavily bearded figure in a long white cloak, standing on a balcony above the courtyard and gazing down on them. '*La Allah, illa Allah*,' he intoned and then turned away. It was the Imam Shamyl.

From an inner courtyard the Princesses, their children and servants and Madame Drancy were led into a low, whitewashed room, some eighteen feet by twelve, lit by a single unglazed window 'no bigger than a pocket-handkerchief', and furnished with several frowzy mattresses and a teapot. Here all twenty-three of them settled down as best they could. It was to be their home for the foreseeable future.

Next day they were told that the Imam would see them that afternoon. When the time came, a plain wooden chair was placed in the gallery outside the door of their room and on this Shamyl, appearing in due course, seated himself, an impressive figure, accompanied as usual by his Bodyguard and his Executioner.

He did not take long in coming to the point. 'The Russian Sultan', he said, speaking through an interpreter, 'took my son away from me and, no matter how often I have offered distinguished prisoners in exchange, he has never given him back to me. They say that you are the granddaughters of the Sultan of Georgia. You are therefore fit persons to write to the Russian Sultan. If he will return Djemmal-Eddin to me, I will at once let you go. My people also want to hold you to ransom. I will discuss this with your families in due course. Meanwhile, if you conduct yourselves well, you will have nothing to fear. But if ever I find you seeking to deceive me or to escape, I will have you killed. To cut off heads is my right, indeed my duty, as Imam.'

Upon which, turning on his heel, he walked away, followed by his Bodyguard and Executioner, while Madame Drancy, frightened and indignant, broke into shrill lamentations.

Life for the captives during the months that followed was both monotonous and unnerving. It seemed to the Princesses unlikely that the Tsar would agree to release Djemmal-Eddin in return for them. They had also been told that in Shamyl's domains no woman was allowed to go spare for more than three months. The squalor of their crowded, stuffy room depressed them. They were in no circumstances allowed to go outside the seraglio or inner courtyard. This centred round Shamyl's own quarters, which consisted of three small rooms adjoining a little mosque. The women's quarters were situated all round the courtyard and gave on to the gallery. Their horizon was bounded by its wooden hutments and rough stone walls.

For company they had Shamyl's wives. Since Fatima's death the first among these was the shrewish Zaidate, the descendant of the Prophet, who hated all infidels and was as unpleasant to the captive Princesses as she could be. Next came Shouanete, the beautiful Armenian from Mozdok, once a captive herself, who was kind enough to them and with whom they could at least talk Russian. Then Aminete, the youngest and newest of the wives, a lovely eighteen-year-old Kist. She was still desperately in love with Shamyl's handsome second son Kazi Mohammed, whose playmate she had once been; but Shamyl, for reasons of his own, had preferred to marry Kazi Mohammed to Kherimat, the sophisticated, perfumed, extravagant daughter of Daniel Beg, the devious Sultan of Elisou, and had then married Aminete himself, later divorcing her on account of her sterility.

A favourite subject of conversation among the wives, and one which did nothing to reassure the captives, was what would happen to the Princesses if the ransom never came or if Shamyl were killed in battle. If Shamyl were by any chance to die, said Zaidate, so would they; she had definite orders to cut their throats. Again, if they were not ransomed, they would no doubt be distributed among the *naïbs*, and Zaidate, clearly jealous, seemed to fear that Shamyl might take the beautiful Anna for himself. As for pretty little Princess Nina, she, the story went, would stay behind, even if the others were ransomed, to be the bride of Djemmal-Eddin himself, when he returned to his people. At which Nina would run shrieking to her aunts.

In due course news of the Princesses' capture and imprisonment had reached Tiflis and after further delays letters and even an occasional parcel would arrive by long and difficult stages at the Great Aul. From her husband, Prince David, Anna had had a letter to say that he was doing everything he could to obtain their release. But the weeks and months went by; the winter and the snows came; their servants were taken away from them; and still there was no news.

Meanwhile, a thousand miles away in St Petersburg, a dispatch had at long last reached the Tsar from the Caucasus, emphasizing that only the return of Djemmal-Eddin could save the princesses from a singularly unpleasant fate. It was one dispatch amid the flood of bad news which, in that winter of 1854, was pouring in from the Crimea. But Nicholas, by now a dying man, remembered his wife's pretty Georgian Ladies-in-Waiting; realized that his commanders on the spot were powerless to save them; realized the nature of the fate that awaited them; and, setting aside for a moment more weighty matters, decided to take the action that was required of him. And so on a freezing day in December 1854, Lieutenant Prince Djemmal-Eddin Shamyl, then serving with his regiment in Warsaw, received orders to proceed at once to St Petersburg for an audience with the Tsar.

It was fifteen years now since the eight-year-old Djemmal-Eddin, dressed by his mother Fatima in his white *cherkesska* and white sheepskin hat, armed with a little *kinjal* and speaking no word of any language except his own, had been handed over to the Russians at Akhulgo, a real child of the mountains. From the Caucasus he had been taken directly to St Petersburg and there taught to speak Russian and brought up as a personal protégé of the Tsar until he was old enough to serve in the *Corps des Pages*, become an officer and then be posted to a suitable Russian regiment.

He was now a dark, good-looking, rather studious young man of twenty-three or four who usually wore the uniform of his regiment, the Vladimirski Lancers, only occasionally putting on his national dress. He had enjoyed life at Court and in the Army, had become a Russian in outlook and way of life and, though he recalled with pride that he was Shamyl's son, thought of himself, first and foremost, as a loyal soldier of the Tsar, to whom he was personally devoted. Of his parents and his childhood in the mountains he had retained only the haziest recollections.

But now, when the Tsar told him what was required of him, he did not hesitate for a moment and a few days later, at the beginning of January 1855, set out in a *troika* for the Caucasus, accompanied by a small escort of Cossacks.

It took his little party, travelling by *troika* and *tarantass*, the best part of a month to reach their destination and it was not until the beginning of February that he arrived at Vladikavkaz and once again beheld the rocky peaks of the Caucasus outlined against the winter sky. On his arrival he was made welcome by Prince David Chavchavadze, who had come to Vladikavkaz to meet him and who stayed with him during the weeks that followed. At Vladikavkaz, at Tiflis and at Hassif Yurt, the Russian General Headquarters, the leaders of garrison society vied with each other to entertain Shamyl's son, who, as they knew, was also aide-de-camp to the Tsar. He was the hero of the hour. Balls were given in his honour and the local beauties were delighted by his dancing, his elegance and his good looks. Any suggestion that he was sacrificing himself to save the princesses he brushed aside. Only once did he let fall a remark which made Prince Chavchavadze realize how much he regretted what he was leaving behind him. 'How strange life is ...' he said to Prince David, who had found him sitting, surrounded by books, in the Commanding Officer's library, 'just as I am beginning to appreciate the advantages of learning and am ready to apply myself to it with all my heart, fate takes me and plunges me back into ignorance, where I shall forget all that I have learned and start to move backwards like a crab.'

Meanwhile, the negotiations for the exchange were going far from smoothly. Now that he was certain of getting his son back, Shamyl, egged on by his *naïbs*, who minded more about the money, was concentrating on the ransom. The original sum mentioned had been 40,000 roubles; now he was asking for more and his demands were sharpened by threats.

'Today', wrote Princess Anna in a despairing letter to her husband, 'they were going to distribute us among the *naïbs*. We thought we were lost. But Kazi Mohammed and the Mulla asked Shamyl to send messengers to you for the last time ... What is to be done? It seems as though it were not God's will that we should see each other again in this world. I know that you have spared no effort to save us. But it is impossible to reason with these people. It is impossible to convince them that you cannot collect a larger sum. May God bless you and give you strength. I can add no more.'

By the same messenger came a letter for Prince David from Shamyl. 'I thank you', he wrote, 'for keeping your word in respect of my son. But this cannot end the negotiations. You must know that, besides my son, I require a million roubles and one hundred and fifty of my Murids whom you hold prisoner. Do not bargain with me. I will take no less. If you do not comply, I have resolved to distribute your family among the different *auls*. This would already have been done but for my son Kazi Mohammed who prevailed on me to give you one last chance to add to the paltry forty thousand roubles you originally offered me.'

To this outrageous communication Prince David responded with spirit. 'I shall not', he declared to the messengers, 'reply to your Imam any more. You can tell him from me that long ago, on the banks of the Alazani, I took an eternal farewell of my family. I can now only entrust them to God's mercy. These are my last words. If, by Saturday, you do not bring me the solemn acceptance of my offer, I swear by the Creator that on that day, I will leave Hassif Yurt and take Djemmal-Eddin with me. You may follow me for a thousand versts and beg me to return; but I will not. And you may do what you like with my family. They will not be mine. I shall have renounced them ... If they are made the slaves of your *naïbs*, I shall no longer recognize my wife as my wife nor my daughters as my daughters.'

Further exchanges followed, including a suggestion by the Murids of a side deal for Princess Anna only, at a greatly reduced price, while leaving her sister to her fate. At this Prince David threw himself at the messenger and had to be forcibly restrained. 'I will not', he shouted, 'allow even the youngest of my servants' children to be detained.'

Djemmal-Eddin, who had been present throughout the negotiations, was by now becoming more and more distressed by everything he had seen and heard. Noticing this, one of Shamyl's emissaries took him aside and sought to reassure him. 'Do not be upset,' he whispered. 'This

The Fiagdon Valley

Tsimitar

The Ossetian Military Highway

Beshtau

The Northern Caucasus

Teberda Valley

The foothills of Elbruz

Sanahin

is our way in the mountains ... All will be well in the end.' But for Djemmal-Eddin, already mortified by the conduct of his compatriots, this well-intended aside was the last straw. 'I am not upset,' he burst out, to the dismay of all present. 'I do not return to my native land with any joy ... I would go back to Russia tomorrow, if it were only possible.' After which the meeting ended in confusion; Shamyl's messengers were hurried from the room; and this phase of the negotiations came to an end.

Behind the scenes, meanwhile, a certain Isaac Gramov was playing an important part as a go-between. A multi-lingual Armenian serving as an officer in the Russian Army, he visited Shamyl more than once in the mountains and did his best to convince him that the sum for which he was now asking was not a realistic one. He also tried another approach. 'If I were you', he said to Shamyl, 'I should be content with the glory of the whole affair. Think what a thing it will be to be able to boast that you by force of arms compelled the Russians to give you back your son whom the Great White Sultan treasured as if he were his own.' 'It would be even better to get the money too,' replied Shamyl. But Gramov went away with the feeling that he had made some impression.

A day or two later the princesses received a visit from Zeidate's old father the Mulla Djemmal-Eddin, who promised to do his best for them and held out hopes of success. 'But what if the people will not accept a smaller ransom?' asked the princesses. 'There is a way of convincing the people,' said the old Mulla mysteriously and left them trying to think what it could be.

They were to discover the answer a day or two later, when a celebrated local hermit emerged from his cave in the mountains and came down to the Great Aul, where he was received with much ceremony by Shamyl, who, having announced that the fate of the prisoners would be decided by the holy man, put him up to preach from the balcony of his own apartments.

Through the chinks in their door, the princesses could see the hermit on the balcony. '*Astafiour! Alafiour! Allah!*' he sang in a piercing voice, at the same time 'giving his body the grinding, circular movements of a pestle and mortar', while Shamyl and his foremost *naïbs* joined in, until they were all screaming and whirling like dervishes and Madame Drancy's strained nerves could stand it no longer. '*Assez!*' she screamed. '*Assez de ces prières!*' But by now her own little charges had started to mimic the anchorite and the noise both inside and outside the room was tremendous. Finally, when he had finished praying, the hermit started to preach, at enormous length. 'Money is grass,' was his theme. 'Money withers and is gone. We must serve not money, but Allah.'

The holy man's praying and preaching went on day and night. Great crowds flocked in from the mountains to hear him. The emotion he aroused was terrific. Shamyl, too, was at prayer in the mosque. Already it was becoming clear to all that by renouncing the million roubles the Imam would be saving his soul.

By now it was Friday. At their last meeting Prince David had made it clear to Shamyl's messengers that if the princesses were not free by Saturday, the deal would be off. And now, suddenly on Saturday evening, Shamyl's steward Hadjio burst into their room followed by Shouanete. 'You are free! You are free!' they cried. And to Madame Drancy, who had at once started to sob, 'Don't cry, Frenchwoman,' they said. 'You, too, will go home and be happy again.' The Imam, it seemed, had finally settled for 40,000 silver roubles.

It had been agreed between Shamyl and the Russians that the exchange should take place at a ford across the River Michik on Thursday 11 March. Thursday, it appeared was Shamyl's lucky day.

The River Michik lay on the fringes of the Imam's territory, the hills which he controlled sloping down to the water's edge. Beyond it an open plain stretched away for several miles. The night before, the officers at the neighbouring Russian fort gave a farewell dinner in honour of Djemmal-Eddin. Those present noted the sadness of their principal guest's expression.

Next morning at sunrise the princesses set out on the last stage of their journey. By the time they reached the river, they were accompanied by an escort of several thousand Murids, who came pouring down from the hills all round, their *cherkesskas* sewn with silver lace, orders and decorations, their arms shining, their horses magnificent. 'A brilliant *cortège*', wrote Madame Drancy. With them rode Shamyl himself, who now formally took leave of his captives, embracing the children one by one. 'His noble face', we are told, 'was literally shining with joy.'

From where they were, they could see, far away across the valley, a Russian column advancing towards them with men and horses and guns. Shamyl now placed himself on a knoll under a yellow or, according to other accounts, blue umbrella, surrounded by his *naïbs*. Instead of his usual plain black or white *cherkesska*, he was wearing, according to an eye-witness, a green woollen robe, a red silk undergarment, a huge white turban and bright yellow boots. From time to time he surveyed the Russians through a great brass telescope. Behind him were drawn up row upon row of Murid cavalry. Across the river the Russians, too, were taking up their positions with infantry and artillery in the centre and cavalry on the flanks.

The meeting point had been fixed half-way between the two positions. A single horseman now galloped out from the Murid ranks and brandished his lance. At this Djemmal-Eddin, still wearing Russian uniform and accompanied by the Russian Commander, Baron Nikolai, and by Prince David Chavchavadze, started towards the right bank of the river together with a cart containing the ransom in gold and silver coins and an escort of thirty-five soldiers. Meanwhile from the far side Shamyl's younger son, Kazi Mohammed, was approaching with a cart containing the princesses and guarded by an equivalent number of Murids.

'Look Mamma! There's Papa on a white horse!' screamed one of the children. And so Prince David, after eight long months, was reunited with his wife and children. Baron Nikolai and Prince David now crossed to the left bank with Djemmal-Eddin and the cart containing the money. At the same time the cart with the princesses crossed to the right bank, where they alighted and climbed thankfully into the carriage which was to take them to Grozni.

All this time Shamyl was watching the proceedings through his telescope. Having crossed the river, Djemmal-Eddin now took off his Russian uniform and put on a magnificent *cherkesska* which the Murids had brought with them for him. Then silence fell on the assembled multitude and he went forward to where his father was sitting, bowed and knelt before him, at which Shamyl, with tears streaming down his face, embraced his son. The Russian officers who had accompanied Djemmal-Eddin now took their leave of him and of Shamyl and withdrew, while Shamyl, putting his arm round his son's shoulders, led him off towards the assembled *naïbs*. At this a great shout went up from the Murid ranks, while faintly from beyond the river came the sound of a Russian military band playing Russian national airs.

In St Petersburg, meanwhile, Tsar Nicholas had died and on this very same day, Thursday 11 March, 1855, to the beat of muffled drums and the roar of ceremonial cannon, his funeral procession wound slowly through the streets under a wintry sun. Djemmal-Eddin had been told of the Tsar's death some days before. On learning of it, he had withdrawn to his room, there to mourn in solitude the loss of his friend and protector.

9 Prince Alexander Baryatinski

Among a number of other things, the Crimean War had brought home to the Russians the danger of having what amounted to a hostile power within their own frontiers. With the conclusion of the Peace of Paris in 1856, they turned all their energies and resources to the final subjugation of the Caucasus. In July 1856 the new Tsar, Alexander II, appointed his friend, contemporary and cousin, Prince Alexander Baryatinski to be Viceroy and Commander-in-Chief of the Caucasus in succession to Prince Vorontsov, who, now in his seventy-fifth year, had at long last retired.

Alexander Baryatinski was by any standards a remarkable man. He was just forty-one. In its origin and collateral connections his family was second to none in Russia. Tall, rich, good-looking and dissolute, his innumerable love-affairs had for years been the talk of St Petersburg. By 1831, when he was sixteen, he had already achieved an enviable reputation. In 1833, at eighteen, he had been sent in disgrace to the Caucasus to join a regiment of Cossacks. In the Caucasus he had at once distinguished himself in a spectacular engagement against a greatly superior enemy force; had been badly wounded; and had returned to the capital a hero and more irresistible than ever. Thereafter he was to spend most of his military career in the Caucasus, winning wounds and glory and returning periodically to St Petersburg to resume contact and find relaxation. In 1838, at twenty-three, he had gone to Windsor with the Tsar on the occasion of his State Visit to the young Queen Victoria and had been elected a temporary member of several London clubs. Marriage he somehow managed to avoid.

His advancement in his chosen career had been rapid. In 1847 he had, at Prince Vorontsov's instance, been appointed to command a regiment and at the same time direct the operations of the Left Flank.

On his way to take up this appointment he had sailed down the Volga with a flotilla of river-boats flying his family colours, blue and yellow, and carrying his servants, his horses, his silver, his cellar, his pianos, and his library. In 1848, after the capture of Ghergebil, he had been promoted to Major-General.

Though he had now cut his long curls and taken to wearing shaggy side-whiskers and a shabby old uniform plastered with decorations, and though a combination of gout and old wounds had given him a severe limp, he was, at thirty-three, more devastating than ever to the opposite sex. The constant presence at his Headquarters of Princess Marie Vorontsova, the Commander-in-Chief's daughter-in-law, and of Madame Davidova, born Princess Elizabeth Orbeliani, the wife of one of his officers, served further to enhance his reputation. 'The mere thought of Baryatinski', said Prince Gorchakov to his friend Count Leo Tolstoi, 'shatters all my dreams of married happiness. The man is so brilliant in every way, possesses so many outward qualities superior to mine, that I cannot but imagine that my wife might, one day, prefer him to me.'

But, whatever his private life, Alexander Baryatinski was first and foremost a soldier and an extremely formidable one. In 1851 he had taken over command of the vitally important Left Flank and now, five years later, the new Tsar, brushing aside the objections of the scandal-mongers, had advanced him to the supreme command with the rank of Field-Marshal.

To the conduct of the war against Shamyl, he brought a new and infinitely more effective strategy. A guerrilla's most valuable weapons are mobility and surprise and the support, when he can get it, of the local population. He also needs a background, a hinterland, from which to emerge and into which to withdraw. Baryatinski's plan was to deprive Shamyl of these assets by a process of gradual blockade and encirclement, by extending his sources of intelligence and by methodically felling the forests on which he relied for cover, and then to pin him down and exterminate him. As a first step, the new Commander-in-Chief divided the troops in the Caucasus into five different armies, all under his own overall control. Of these, three covered the Eastern Caucasus: the Army of the Left Flank, facing Chechnia; the Pre-Caspian, covering Daghestan; and the Army of the Lesghian Line, based at the south-eastern foot of the main mountain range.

During the year 1857 three columns from these three forces gradually closed in on the Murid heartland in the wild mountain country between Chechnia and Daghestan, building roads and cutting broad rides through the forest as they advanced. By the end of the year the Army of the Left Flank under General Count Yevdokimov, an outstanding commander with prolonged experience of the Caucasus, had occupied all Lower Chechnia and the other two columns had also made good progress. And now, in more and more areas, the population, tired of the incessant fighting, and encouraged by the greater clemency shown them, willingly made their submission to the Russians, now at last in a position to afford them effective protection against the Murids.

Shamyl, meanwhile, though he had suffered heavy losses, was still at the head of a considerable force in country which gave him every advantage. He still enjoyed, moreover, the support of the greater part of the population. Finally, in the wooded mountains enclosing the upper gorges of the Argoun River, he still had at his disposal what seemed a practically impregnable second refuge, barely a dozen miles from Veden, on which to fall back in case of need.

It was now, in mid-winter, that, in accordance with a plan jointly drawn up by Yevdokimov and Baryatinski, three columns under Yevdokimov's command rapidly and secretly converged on the upper valley of the Argoun. Despite deep snow, the operation succeeded and by the end of January 1858, after a single brush with the enemy, who for once were completely taken by surprise, both branches of the Argoun River were in Russian hands and the Russians were busy burning down every *aul* within reach. Shamyl had lost his last refuge. He was also now cut off from all contact with the Western Caucasus. It is said that, when the loss of the Argoun defile was reported to him, he broke down and wept.

And now he was to suffer a heavier and more personal blow. On a wintry day in February 1858 a Tartar messenger galloped into the Russian Headquarters at Hassif Yurt. He came, he declared, from the Imam Shamyl and begged to see the Commandant. He was allowed to deliver his message to Colonel Prince Mitshi: the Imam's son, Djemmal-Eddin, he said, was desperately ill in the mountains. Such medicines as they had were of no use. Shamyl, knowing his son's trust in the Russians and the Russians' love for his son, asked that the medicines he needed should be sent to him.

This strange request was the first news the Russians had had of Djemmal-Eddin since the meeting on the River Michik three years earlier. Having agreed to Shamyl's request, Prince Mitshi sent for his senior medical officer, Dr Petrovski, who, after questioning the Tartar about the young man's symptoms, which seemed to indicate consumption, prepared a package of medicines for the Tartar to take away with him.

Three months later Shamyl's messenger returned. Djemmal-Eddin, he said, was worse. Shamyl begged the Russians to send a doctor. Dr Petrovski volunteered to go himself and Prince Mitshi agreed on condition that three of Shamyl's *naïbs* were handed over as hostages. This condition presented no difficulty. Shamyl had foreseen the Colonel's request and, at an agreed signal from the messenger, five *naïbs* came galloping into the little town. Three stayed behind as hostages, while the other two set out with Dr Petrovski and the messenger.

Dr Petrovski was not told where he was going. It took them almost a week's hard riding through the mountains and then a hair-raising five hours on foot down the sheer mountainside to reach their destination: the towering rock pinnacles of the Audi Gates and, beyond them, the hidden *aul* of Sul-Kadi, where, in one of the houses, Djemmal-Eddin lay dying.

The young man seemed pleased enough to see the doctor and to be able to speak Russian again and talk of that other, remote existence which had meant so much to him. During the three days he spent at Sul-Kadi, Dr Petrovski had no difficulty in discovering what ailed Djemmal-Eddin. He was simply pining away, pining for St Petersburg and Warsaw and for his Russian friends. From the first he had never been able to reconcile himself to life among the Murids. On arriving at the Great Aul he had been given an intensive course of instruction in Muridism and had been sent on a tour of his father's domains. But he found himself repelled by the fanaticism of the Murids and could not feel any sympathy for their resistance to the Russians. On the contrary, he tried to convince his father that the wisest course would be to lay down his arms and come to terms with the Tsar.

Soon it became clear to Shamyl that the high hopes he had had of his son were not to be fulfilled. Djemmal-Eddin was lost to him. The fifteen years he had spent with the Russians had turned him into a Russian. The

Murids, their fierce faith and their even fiercer struggle for freedom meant nothing to him, no more than did the graceful Circassian bride his father had found for him. And so Shamyl saw his son less and less. Finally, as the Russian threat to the Great Aul increased, he had sent him away to the safety and solitude of Sul-Kadi. There, as he grew weaker, Djemmal-Eddin would have himself carried up in the hot summer evenings to the flat roof of the little house in which he lay. And there on the night of 12 July, 1858 he died.

By now the Russians were pressing Shamyl harder than ever. Already they had started to fell the surrounding forest and the carts of the Chechen inhabitants were requisitioned to carry away the timber. Before long the scene had changed completely. 'Shops were opened', writes an eye-witness, 'and booths set up by vendors of food and drink and every sort of petty trader. Soon the wild, gloomy, remote defile was like a busy market, and ladies were even coming out from Grozni to visit the camp.' Everywhere woods were being felled, roads made and bridges built and a fort was strategically sited at the junction of the two branches of the Argoun. Soon a clearing nearly a mile wide reached to the summit of the Dargan Doukh, the high ridge above the right bank of the Sharo Argoun, and from the top of the ridge it was now possible to see quite clearly Shamyl's plateau of Veden barely a dozen miles away to the east.

By the beginning of July everything was ready for the next phase of the campaign and once again the Russians, led by General Yevdokimov, marched in strength up the Argoun valley. Their advance met with very little resistance and in a few weeks the whole of the upper Argoun was in their hands as well as most of the surrounding hills. Not only had they driven the Murids from their innermost refuge; they had also opened up a new line of approach to Daghestan. Meanwhile, everywhere the tribes were coming over to their side. Shamyl had by now lost a guerrilla's greatest asset, the initiative and, apart from a couple of attempted diversions in the summer of 1858, did nothing whatever to check Yevdokimov's advance.

'Yevdokimov', wrote Prince Baryatinski later in a personal report to the Emperor, 'never once gave the enemy a chance of fighting where they meant to fight and where they might have had the advantage. Shamyl's strongest positions fell almost without a fight as a result of superior strategy ... His mountain tribesmen were not afraid of fighting

... fighting implies a kind of equality. So long as they could fight, they never thought of giving in. But when, time after time, they failed to make contact with us, the weapons fell from their hands'.

For some time now, the net had been drawing ever closer round Veden. At the beginning of February 1859 Yevdokimov lay siege to it and on 1 April took it by assault with only slight casualties. Shamyl himself had already withdrawn into the forest. There another blow struck him: the news that in his absence his black and white cat had pined away and died. It had been buried with full military honours and a funeral oration pronounced over its grave. But Shamyl was inconsolable. 'Now', he said sadly, 'things will go badly for me.'

The fall of Veden had an immense psychological effect throughout Chechnia and soon even the most warlike of the Chechen tribes sought to make their peace with Russia. By the middle of July the preparations for the final phase of the campaign had been completed. Prince Baryatinski joined Yevdokimov at his camp near Veden and the general advance began. By the end of July contact had been made with the other two task forces and the combined strength of the Russian force now amounted to some 40,000 men with forty-eight guns.

Seeing that all was indeed lost, Shamyl, accompanied by a small band of loyal followers, now fled south into his native Daghestan. His intention was to make a last stand on the natural stronghold of Gounib, a high mountain plateau surrounded by precipitous escarpments six or seven thousand feet above sea level. On their way there, he and his party were attacked more than once by their own fellow-countrymen and their baggage was looted by the women of the villages they were passing through. But the people of Gounib itself, he found, had remained loyal and were ready to throw in their lot with him. Altogether there were on the plateau just four hundred men.

Prince Baryatinski's march through Daghestan in pursuit of Shamyl quickly turned into a triumphal progress. At dawn on 25 August, the day before the Emperor's birthday, having completed his preparations, he gave the order for the assault on Gounib to begin and from all sides the Russian infantry swarmed up the escarpment.

Soon only a handful of the four hundred defenders were left alive. Had he been alone, Shamyl might have fought on to the end. As it was, fearing for the lives of his wives and children, he sent two emissaries to treat with the Russians. On learning that, if he surrendered, his life and the lives of those with him would be spared, he mounted his horse and rode out to make his submission to Prince Baryatinski. But on his appearance, the Russian soldiers, seeing their old adversary humbled at last, gave a cheer. This was more than Shamyl could bear. He abruptly turned his horse and was about to ride back, when a quick-thinking Armenian colonel ran forward to assure him that the soldiers' cheer was a mark of their respect for a gallant foe. Reassured, he turned and again went forward to where Prince Baryatinski was waiting for him, seated on a stone. Baryatinski now personally repeated to him the assurance he had already been given that his own life and that of those with him would be spared, adding that all else must depend on the wishes of the Emperor. Bowing his head in silence, Shamyl handed his sword to Prince Baryatinski and was led away to captivity. It was just thirty years since Shamyl and Kazi Mulla had proclaimed their holy war against the Russians.

A week after the battle, on 3 September, 1859, Shamyl, 'God's poor pilgrim', as he called himself, left Daghestan for ever, with very little idea of what his fate was likely to be. With him went his son Kazi Mohammed and some of his *naïbs* and servants; his wives and the rest of his family and retinue were to follow later.

Tsar Alexander II, who by nature was generous and humane, had given orders that the Imam was to be treated with every mark of respect. A comfortable travelling carriage was put at his disposal and all along the route arrangements were made for him to stay with the governors of the different provinces through which he passed. At each stop large crowds flocked to see him.

On reaching Kharkov, he was greeted by one of the Tsar's *aides-de-camp* with the news that His Imperial Majesty was reviewing his troops in the neighbourhood and would be glad if the Imam would join him. Their meeting took place during an immense parade, amid marching troops, and to the blare of military bands. Shamyl, wearing his long white *cherkesska* and towering headdress, was a proud figure as he rode out to meet the Tsar. 'I am delighted that you are here in Russia,' said Alexander, embracing him. 'I wish it could have happened sooner. You will not regret it ... We shall be friends.' And he invited Shamyl to ride beside him while he reviewed his cavalry.

From Kharkov, Shamyl was taken to Moscow, where he was shown the Crown Jewels and the other wonders of the Kremlin, including

Peter the Great's gigantic boots, which impressed him most of all. He also called on old General Yermolov and in the evening was taken to see a gala performance of *Les Naïades* at the Bolshoi Theatre. From Moscow he travelled by train to St Petersburg, arriving there just a month after the fall of Gounib. By now his journey had turned into a triumphal progress and an immense crowd had gathered to welcome him at the railway station. From the station he was taken to the Snaminski Hotel, where he was to stay during his visit to the capital, enjoying the rich Russian food, seeing the sights and going to the opera and ballet, which he watched eagerly through a telescope. At the Zoological Gardens he shook hands delightedly with the monkeys, explaining to his companions that they were simply Jews who had been turned into monkeys because they had angered God. Finally, bowing ceremoniously from the window of his private Pullman coach to the immense crowd which followed him wherever he went, he boarded the train for Kaluga, the little provincial town a hundred miles to the south of Moscow, where it had been decided that he should in future reside.

At Kaluga he was given a pretty, old, two-storeyed house surrounded by acacia trees and flowering shrubs, where his family joined him some weeks later. A little mosque was built in the garden and his library, which had followed him from the Caucasus, was accommodated in a pleasant green and white room.

There he remained for the next ten years, occasionally visiting Moscow or St Petersburg for celebrations of one kind or another, dining with the Tsar at the Winter Palace and attending parades and royal weddings. He would also often visit, either in Moscow or on his estates at Ivanovskoye, his former adversary, Prince Baryatinski – 'our Field-Marshal', as he called him.

Alexander Baryatinski's brilliant career had come to a sudden end at the early age of forty-five. For years, he had been living openly with the beautiful Madame Davidova, formerly Princess Orbeliani and known to all as '*La Maréchale*'. Then in 1861, just as he was beginning to lose interest in her, her husband, Colonel Davidov, who up to then had raised no objection to the liaison, had suddenly initiated divorce proceedings, cited the Viceroy as co-respondent and challenged him to a duel. As the Tsar's personal representative, Baryatinski could neither fight a duel nor be involved in divorce proceedings. Even the Emperor himself could not save him. The only course open to him was to resign his great office and leave Tiflis as quietly as he could, taking Madame Davidova with him. They were later married in Brussels, and spent their honeymoon at a watering place in the south of England. To the new Princess Baryatinska this solution was no doubt a satisfactory one; to the Field-Marshal possibly less so. Indeed it was suggested by some that, in acting as he did, Colonel Davidov had only been doing a final kindness to his wife. Shamyl was much concerned on hearing the news. To him it seemed deplorable that so splendid a career could have been brought to an end simply because of a woman.

In March 1870 Shamyl, feeling that he had not much longer to live, asked for and was granted leave to go to Mecca. Taking his wives with him, he travelled by way of the Black Sea to Constantinople, where the Sultan received him with due ceremony and whence he continued his journey eastwards by caravan to Mecca. By now his strength was beginning to fail. From Mecca he went to the holy city of Medina, and in Medina, where Mohammed himself had died twelve centuries earlier, he too died on 4 February, 1871 and was laid to rest near the tomb of the Prophet.

To Shamyl Russia's present rulers have not always shown themselves as generous as their Imperial predecessors. For some years after the Revolution he ranked, it is true, as a leader of resistance to Tsarist imperialism, as something of a hero. Had not Karl Marx himself, after all, declared him, however improbably, a great democrat? But gradually, as the Soviet sense of empire developed and the hunt for bourgeois nationalists became keener, the Great Imam began to appear in an ever less favourable light, being curtly dismissed in the 1953 edition of the *Great Soviet Encyclopedia* as 'an Anglo-Turkish agent'. Of late, however, it is pleasant to record that Shamyl has enjoyed a measure of rehabilitation and that the gates through which you approach Gounib now bear his name.

This summer, after years of waiting, I was granted a visa for Daghestan, the Land of Mountains. In three hours a jet plane took me from Moscow to the little Caspian port of Makhach Kala, once Petrovsk and now capital of the Autonomous Soviet Socialist Republic of Daghestan. Already I was at the centre of things. Just to the north of Petrovsk lay Burnaya, Fort Stormy, securing the Caspian end of the Left Flank, while Russian Headquarters were at Hassif Yurt, forty miles away across the coastal plain.

From Makhach Kala an hour's motoring brought us to Buynaksk and soon we started to climb in earnest, passing through little hill-towns where mosques and turbaned gravestones showed we were in Moslem country. The apple-trees were in flower and the green of the poplars stood out vividly against the rough stone houses and the barren, rocky hills. Crossing a first mountain range, we came steeply down on Shamyl's much fought-over stronghold of Ghergebil, at the junction of the Sulak River and its fast-flowing tributary the Karakoysu. On the hill-sides men carrying long daggers watched herds of sheep, cattle or horses. Avars, in all probability, but there are forty different races in Daghes-tan, including the famous Mountain Jews, who still speak Hebrew. In the villages the girls wore plaids over their heads and shoulders to keep off the rain, like women in Victorian prints of the West Highlands.

As we turned up the valley of the Karakoysu, the great mountains loomed all round us, their peaks wreathed in mist. Ten miles beyond Ghergebil the valley widened and we found ourselves looking across to where the great rock-fortress of Gounib rose massively and abruptly above the river, its almost perpendicular escarpment presenting a seemingly insuperable barrier to any assailant. Climbing steeply from the foot of the escarpment, we left the new village of Gounib behind us and came to the summit, emerging unexpectedly into a shallow green valley five or six miles long and three or four across, watered by natural springs and enclosed by the rocky rim of the escarpment. Here we were to spend the night and here, half a mile from the original *aul* of Gounib, I found, on a grassy bank beneath a birch tree, the stone on which, an inscription told me, Prince Baryatinski sat on that August morning in 1859 to receive the surrender of the Imam Shamyl. In such a place, I thought, with their flocks and herds and crops of oats and barley, more men might have held out indefinitely. But not four hundred against forty thousand.

Next day, swinging further into the mountains, we came to Khoun-zakh, poised dizzily above a precipice from which a mighty waterfall drops into distant depths. Here Hadji Murad was born and here, in the mosque, he murdered Hamzad Bey. The mosque has gone, but the massive fortress built by the Tsar's troops still remains. What I had seen in a few hours helped me, more than a month with manuals and maps, to understand the war waged by Shamyl and grasp the drama of those last desperate days.

10 *The End of Ane Old Sang*

With Shamyl's capitulation resistance quickly came to an end in the Caucasus. For another four or five years, it is true, the Circassians, encouraged by the Sultan of Turkey, kept up their fight in the western Caucasus and on the Black Sea littoral. But by 1864 they, too, had been crushed and their territory occupied by the Russians. In that same year their massive exodus to Turkey took place, where the Sultan granted asylum to some six hundred thousand of them. Following the Russo-Turkish War of 1877–8, the Treaty of Berlin awarded to Russia substantial areas of Turkish territory, which had once formed part of medieval Georgia, notably the port of Batumi and the fortress of Kars and Ardahan.

For another forty years or so, Transcaucasia was governed from Tbilisi as a Russian province by a Russian Viceroy. Tsarist rule did not weigh less heavily on Transcaucasia than on any other of the Tsar's dominions. Various revolutionary and semi-revolutionary movements, some Socialist, some Agrarian and some Nationalist in flavour, were repressed with varying degrees of vigour and in August 1905 something approaching a massacre took place when a regiment of Cossacks, firing through the windows, poured volley after volley into a Socialist meeting in Tbilisi Town Hall. This, needless to say, only served to fan the flames of rebellion. One of the more active members of the Bolshevik faction of the Georgian Social-Democrats at this time was the young Joseb or Soso Vissarionovich Djugashvili, a shoemaker's son from Gori, later to become more widely known as Stalin.

In February 1917 the outbreak of the Russian Revolution threw the whole of Transcaucasia into confusion, further aggravated eight months later by the ensuing Bolshevik Revolution. Since 1915 Transcaucasia had been a theatre of war; but, even before Trotski's conclusion of peace with the Central Powers at Brest-Litovsk early in 1918, Russia's armies on the Caucasus front had begun to disintegrate. The consequent haphazard return from the front of scores of thousands of self-demobilized soldiers and the simultaneous breakdown of communications and acute food-shortage all added to the chaos.

It was against this unpromising background that at the end of November 1917 power in Transcaucasia passed into the hands of an amorphous body of moderate Social-Democratic tendencies, composed in roughly equal proportions of Georgians, Armenians and Azerbaijanis, with a couple of Russians thrown in for luck, and known as the Transcaucasian Commissariat.

Though vaguely Marxist in theory, the new government of Transcaucasia was strongly anti-Bolshevik in sentiment and stoutly refused to recognize the Bolshevik takeover in Petrograd. It also refused to recognize the provisions of the Treaty of Brest-Litovsk and in April 1918, after some thoroughly unpromising independent armistice negotiations, re-declared war on the Turks, who for their part were demanding the surrender of large areas of Armenia and Georgia, including Batumi. At this the Turks immediately occupied the Port of Batumi, easily overcoming such resistance as there was. After which armistice negotiations were once more resumed.

Though refusing to recognize the Bolsheviks (or indeed their White Russian opponents), the Transcaucasian Commissariat, still hoping for the emergence of a more democratic regime in Petrograd, did not at first aspire to independence from Russia. Indeed at the end of March 1918 the newly constituted Transcaucasian Diet voted 'categorically and irrevocably' against it. But events continued to take their somewhat confused course and at the end of April, after further debate, a majority of the Diet rather half-heartedly decided to proclaim Transcaucasia an Independent Democratic Federative Republic.

The new Federative Republic was to have a short and troubled existence. The Turks, having recognized it, at once occupied the great Armenian fortress and town of Kars, from which the Christian population immediately streamed out in panic, rightly expecting the worst. Meanwhile in Azerbaijan an insoluble conflict had arisen in March between the Bolshevik-controlled Baku Soviet and an Azerbaijani nationalist organization known as the Musavat. This was followed by an outbreak of savage street-fighting between the local Tartars and

Garni

Garni

Armenians, at the end of which the Baku Bolsheviks set up their own Council of People's Commissars in open defiance of Tbilisi.

In May 1918, in Turkish-occupied Batumi, fresh peace-talks were opened between the Turks and the new Transcaucasian Government. Though Turkey's territorial demands were manifestly unacceptable, there was equally no apparent means of stopping her from occupying all the territory she wanted. It was at this moment, however, that her German allies, with a clear sense of where their own interests lay, as opposed to Turkey's, decided that the time had come for them to intervene by sending a strong German delegation to the Batumi Peace Conference.

The new Federation's prospects of survival were clearly not good. The Azerbaijanis, as Moslems, had no wish to go on fighting the Turks. The Armenians, after all they had endured, were exhausted and disorganized. There was obviously nothing to prevent the Turks from taking over the whole of Transcaucasia, should they so desire. But this would not have suited the Germans, who, controlling as they did the Ukraine and the Crimea, now saw an opportunity to extend their influence to Transcaucasia and at the same time gain access to the all-important oilfields of Baku. And so, going behind the backs of their Turkish allies, they now encouraged the Georgians to break away from the Federation and proclaim Georgia a sovereign state under German protection. The Transcaucasian Federation was dissolved and at the end of May 1918 an agreement was signed between Germany and Georgia, granting Germany effective control of the ports and railways, the right to station German troops at strategic points in Georgia and various other important advantages. An important member of the German Delegation was Count Friedrich-Werner von der Schulenburg, a German career diplomat of great ability and charm who before the war had been German Consul in Tbilisi and now did much to help establish a harmonious relationship between Germans and Georgians.*

A week after signing their agreement with Germany, the Georgians concluded a treaty of peace with the Turks. This purported to give Turkey Batumi and the other disputed territories. But in fact the treaty

---

*Some twenty years later, just before the outbreak of the Second World War, though certainly no supporter of the Nazi Party, Count von der Schulenburg, by now a courtly old gentleman with pink cheeks and a white moustache, was German Ambassador in Moscow, well liked by everyone in the strange diplomatic ghetto in which we lived. Five years after this, he was to meet a terrible end as one of the participants in Count Stauffenberg's abortive plot against Hitler.

was never ratified, and, when the Turks sought to take possession of their new territories, they were, to their pained surprise, driven back by a combined force of German and Georgian troops.

Meanwhile in neighbouring Azerbaijan and Armenia, where independent republics under moderate Socialist or Nationalist governments had also been formed, events were taking an even stormier course. In July 1918 the Bolsheviks – the famous Baku Soviet – had been driven from Baku by a force of Tartar guerrillas with Turkish support. The town had next been taken over by a coalition of Social Revolutionaries and Armenian Nationalists with the support of a small British expeditionary force under General Dunsterville, the original Stalky of Kipling's *Stalky and Co*. In September Dunsterville had been forced in his turn to evacuate Baku by the combined efforts of the Turks and Moslem guerrillas. It was at this juncture that twenty-six Bolshevik Commissars, who had somehow managed to escape from Baku and had been evacuated across the Caspian to Krasnovodsk, there fell into the hands of a group of vindictive Social Revolutionaries, who at once took them out into the desert and shot them, an act for which Britain has, for no very good reason, ever since been held responsible.

On other fronts, meanwhile, the first World War had been moving slowly and painfully to a close. As early as September 1918 the members of a Georgian delegation in Berlin had gained a fairly clear impression of the way things were going and had reached the conclusion that the moment had arrived for Georgia to move into a position of neutrality with the object of coming to terms with the Western Allies.

In October and November 1918 the defeat first of Turkey and then of Germany by the Allies completely transformed the situation in Transcaucasia. By the end of 1918 all German and Turkish troops had been withdrawn and their place taken by the victorious British. On 17 November, 1918 a British force reoccupied Baku and soon after this arrangements were made for the British occupation of Georgia.

At first the British, who were more concerned with what was happening in European Russia, showed relatively little enthusiasm for the idea of Georgian independence which the Germans had so sedulously fostered, and relations between Great Britain and the new republic were far from happy. But the appointment in 1919 of Mr Oliver Wardrop, a friend of Georgia and an expert on Georgian history and literature, as Chief British Commissioner to the Republic of Georgia, Armenia and

Azerbaijan, led to a gradual modification of this attitude. Further factors in Georgia's favour were the completely free and democratic elections for a Constituent Assembly held in February 1919, in which no less than fifteen parties put up candidates, but which resulted in a substantial majority for the Social-Democrats, the party of Noe Zhordania, who had held the office of Prime Minister since June 1918.

By the end of 1919 the British Foreign Office, under Lord Curzon, finally realizing that in Russia the Whites, on whom they had hitherto pinned their hopes, were now doomed to defeat, had come to regard the three Transcausian Republics as a potential barrier against Bolshevik expansion in the Middle East. The trouble was that the three were for ever at each other's throats.

The hostility between Armenians and Azerbaijanis was of long standing, and during 1918 had flared up in bitter fighting. Serious trouble had followed between Georgia and Armenia. When the time had come for the Turks to evacuate Transcaucasia, they had, in a spirit of mischief, deliberately encouraged both the Georgians and the Armenians to move into certain of the evacuated areas, notably Lori and Borchalo and the town of Akhalkalaki, giving the Georgians a couple of day's start. They then sat back to watch the fun. Finding the Georgians in possession of what they had hoped was going to be part of a greatly enlarged Armenia, the Armenians at once attacked them and, encouraged by their initial success, marched on Tbilisi. The Georgians responded by taking a speedy revenge on the large Armenian population of that city and then, collecting all the troops they could muster, heavily defeated the Armenians at Shulaveri and chased them back into Armenia. In the end the newly-arrived and not very popular British managed to separate the two armies by force, but not unnaturally the ill-feeling between them persisted, making even limited co-operation impossible. To the north, meanwhile, beyond the Caucasus, the Russians, both Red and White, devoted such energy as they could spare from fighting each other to blockading and doing any other damage they could to the independent countries of Transcaucasia, whose mere existence both factions strongly resented.

For the Western Allies, still hoping to use Transcaucasia as a barrier against Bolshevism, the prospects were scarcely encouraging. At the Paris Peace Conference Allied officials were bewildered by the high living, the incessant bickering and the exorbitant demands of these and numerous other emergent nations. Ritzo-Slovaks, one cynic called them. The Armenians, for example, encouraged by the apparent support of President Wilson and Mr Lloyd George, had sent to Versailles not one but two rival delegations who were asking, not only for the seven eastern *vilayets* of Turkey and the four *sanjaks* of Cilicia, but for large parts of Georgia as well, including Batumi and much of the country round Tbilisi. In the end it began to seem doubtful to many impartial observers whether any of the countries of Transcaucasia would ever be able to stand on their own feet. Little wonder that the expressive face of Mr Robert Vansittart, the British Foreign Office official in charge of Caucasian problems, was seen to register 'perplexity, weariness and boredom'. 'In the circles of the Supreme Council', he told a mixed group of delegates from the Caucasus, 'many are of the opinion that the Transcaucasian Republics have no future at all, as they are unable to achieve any sort of solidarity, and are exhausting themselves in conflicts with each other.' 'Is it not clear to you', he asked, 'that the dispatch of arms and ammunition for you has been delayed precisely because of your divergences, because of the fear that these arms would be used in your conflicts with each other?'

The Transcaucasian delegates, for their part, were equally exasperated by the delays and by what no doubt seemed to them the equivocations of the Great Powers, and one eye-witness, Zurab Avalishvili, has left a dramatic account of the principal Georgian delegate 'standing with his head thrown back, his eyes starting from the sockets and his face purple, infuriated by the French texts and formulae, the *nuances* of which he could not quite grasp, all his coolness and self-control gone by the board.' Finally, in January 1920, the Allies decided to grant *de facto* recognition to all three new republics, the assumption being that *de jure* recognition would follow in due course. For the reasons given by Mr Vansittart, however, little or nothing was done about supplying arms to them or otherwise strengthening their defences.

Meanwhile the threat to the newly found independence of the three Republics was becoming daily more real. Nearly three years had now passed since the October Revolution of 1917; almost everywhere in Russia, in the Ukraine and the Crimea, resistance to the new regime had collapsed or been crushed and the Bolsheviks were firmly in power. They were now ready to extend their activities further afield. In February 1920 a Special Committee was set up for the establishment of

Soviet authority in the Caucasus. Its Chairman was a leading Georgian Communist, Sergo Ordzhonikidze and its Deputy Chairman S. M. Kirov, both men of considerable ability and, incidentally, close friends of J. V. Stalin, the shoemaker's son from Gori, who had by now become an extremely important figure in the Bolshevik hierarchy.

During the weeks that followed other bodies were set up with the same objective and with direct links with the Red Army. It was not long before they began to produce results. At the end of April 1920 a boldly executed raid on Baku by a Bolshevik armoured train was followed by the overthrow of the independent Government of Azerbaijan at the hands of the Eleventh Red Army and its replacement by a Bolshevik Government under the control of Moscow. A few days later, at the beginning of May, a Bolshevik *coup* was attempted in Tbilisi when twenty-five local Bolsheviks, mostly Armenians, tried unsuccessfully to seize the Military Academy, while units of the Eleventh Red Army sought simultaneously to cross the Georgian frontier from Azerbaijan but were driven off by Georgian frontier troops.

Having failed in this direct attempt to seize power in Georgia, the Russians at once tried a new approach, offering the Georgians *de jure* recognition and a treaty of friendship. This offer the Georgian Socialist Prime Minister, Noe Zhordania, over-ruling his Foreign Minister, decided to accept and on 7 May, less than a week after the attempted *coup*, a treaty was signed in Moscow. By one of its clauses the Georgian Government agreed to allow full freedom of action to the Georgian Communist Party, while by another they pledged themselves to work for the withdrawal of all foreign troops from Georgian soil.

The British occupation, latterly limited to the Batumi area, had never been particularly popular with the Georgian Government, who, elated by the utterances of President Wilson, firmly believed their independence to be more than adequately safeguarded by the provisions of the Paris Peace Conference and the fine new machinery of the League of Nations, and regarded the presence of foreign troops on their territory as an affront to their new-found sovereignty. The British, for their part, had been under pressure to withdraw ever since their troops had first reached Georgia in 1918 and were by this time certainly not looking for additional military commitments. Moreover, Lord Curzon's policy of propping up the Transcaucasian Republics as a barrier to Bolshevism did not have the support of the Prime Minister, Mr Lloyd George, who for his part was more interested in doing some kind of a deal with Moscow. And so in the end it was agreed that all British troops should be withdrawn from Georgia and the last of these finally sailed from Batumi on 7 July amid the applause of the population.

Their rejoicing was to be short-lived. From now onwards events in Georgia moved swiftly. Under the able direction of S. M. Kirov, who had arrived in Tbilisi in June in the role of first Soviet Ambassador to Georgia, the newly emancipated Georgian Communist Party started an intensive campaign of agitation and subversion, openly aimed at the overthrow of the existing government, and the British High Commissioner was shocked to observe his Soviet colleague violently haranguing the crowds that almost daily assembled outside his Embassy. Meanwhile in South Ossetia trouble stirred up from across the Russian border in North Ossetia led to a large-scale rising against the Georgians. The latter, who had never liked the Ossetians, repressed it ruthlessly. Thousands of Ossetians were killed and many thousands more sought refuge across the Soviet border, with the result that the whole of this already sensitive and strategically important frontier area became a potential powder-keg.

And now pressure was building up from another quarter. Under the Treaty of Sèvres, signed on 10 August, 1920, the Sultan of Turkey had undertaken to recognize Armenia as an independent country. But almost immediately the Turkish Nationalists under Mustafa Kemal seized power in Anatolia, denounced the Treaty of Sèvres, declared themselves once more at war with the Allies and established friendly relations with Soviet Russia. After which, in September, the Turks suddenly invaded Armenia, seizing both Kars and Alexandropol. The Russians, for their part, chose this moment to present to the Armenian Government an ultimatum, demanding free passage through Armenian territory for their troops and those of Turkey, the renunciation of the Treaty of Sèvres and the immediate rupture of relations with the Allies. Then, just as the Armenians were trying to come to terms with the Turks, the Bolsheviks crossed the border in strength from Baku and on 2 December, 1920 declared Armenia a Soviet Republic. Thus by the end of 1920 two of the three independent states of Transcaucasia had disappeared from the map without their Western sponsors doing anything whatever to help them.

During the summer and autumn of 1920 Georgian statesmen spent a good deal of time touring Western Europe, seeking contacts, loans and diplomatic recognition. In this they were not unsuccessful. In due course, various concessions in Georgia were granted to French and Italian industrialists, a loan was floated in London, a French naval flotilla visited Batumi, a delegation of leading Western Socialists toured Georgia, enjoying the lavish Georgian hospitality, and finally on 27 January, 1921, *de jure* recognition was accorded to Georgia by the Western Allies. This happy event was celebrated at a State banquet which was held in Tbilisi on 7 February. It was attended by a representative of the Soviet Embassy who drank, 'with complete sincerity', to the health of Georgia's Socialist Prime Minister. Next day a statement was issued by the Soviet Ambassador to say that Soviet Russia welcomed Georgia's recognition by the Western Powers and only wanted to live in peace and friendship with her.

But by this time Soviet troops were already massing on the Georgian frontier for a full-scale invasion. A detailed plan of attack had been drawn up a couple of months earlier by A. I. Gekker, the Commander of the Eleventh Red Army. It was put into execution during the second week in February 1921. On 11 February disorders broke out simultaneously in the Lori district to the south of Tbilisi and at Shulaveri, near the frontier with Armenia and Azerbaijan, the insurgents being in the main Armenians and Russians. On 14 February fighting started on the Armenian border near Vorontsovka and on 15 February the Soviet Embassy in Tbilisi received a top-secret telegram from Gekker announcing his decision to 'cross the Rubicon'. At first light on 16 February the Eleventh Red Army, to the accompaniment of suitable proclamations, crossed the border between Georgia and Soviet Azerbaijan in strength.

Hopelessly outnumbered, the little Georgian Army retreated westwards, blowing up the roads and bridges as they went, in the hope of delaying the enemy's advance. But already other Red Army units were preparing to enter Georgia by the Georgian Military Highway and along the Black Sea coast by way of Sukhumi, while back in Moscow the Soviet People's Commissar for Foreign Affairs strenuously denied all knowledge of any Soviet military action.

Fighting fiercely against overwhelming odds, the Georgians managed to hold the approaches to Tbilisi for a week. But now from Kazim Karabekir Pasha, the Turkish commander across the border, came, in collusion with the Russians, an ultimatum to the Georgians to evacuate the towns of Ardahan and Artvin. This in the circumstances they could only accept. Tbilisi was by now untenable. During the night of 24 February Zhordania and his government left on the last train for Kutaisi in Western Georgia. On 25 February the Red Army entered the town, led by Sergo Ordzhonikidze, and Tbilisi, not for the first time in its history, was given over to massacre, pillage and rape. A few days later a Revolutionary Committee, or Revcom, which had been waiting in the wings, arrived in Tbilisi and proclaimed the end of Georgian independence and the establishment of a Georgian Soviet Republic.

Zhordania had originally hoped to hold out in Western Georgia, but the rapid advance of further Red Army units across the Mamison Pass and down the Rioni Valley quickly put paid to this and, after some half-hearted attempts at negotiation with the Bolsheviks and an even more half-hearted attempt at intervention by the French Navy, he and his government set sail for Constantinople on 17 March, 1921. The day before, as it happened, a trade agreement had been signed between the British and Soviet Governments, which, amongst other things, effectively precluded any intervention by Great Britain on behalf of any of the countries of Transcaucasia. Lord Curzon had been outmanœuvred; the Welsh Wizard had had his way.

Not long after, a Treaty of Friendship was signed in Moscow between the Soviet Government and the new Government of Turkey under which the Georgian towns of Akhalkalaki, Akhaltsikhe and Batumi were awarded to the Soviet Union, but other large areas of what was historically Georgia were retained by Turkey.

Across the border in Armenia, the Soviet invasion of Georgia had an interesting side-effect. While the invasion was in progress, the supporters of Armenian independence rose in strength, and, marching on Erivan, overthrew the Bolshevik regime there. The insurgents, with no outside help, somehow managed to hold out for two more months, and it was not until April 1921 that the rising was finally crushed, Soviet rule once more established and what remained of Armenia divided between Turkey and Soviet Russia. Such was the fate of President Woodrow Wilson's favourite doctrine of self-determination in what had at one time been going to be one of his favourite small countries.

Thus it was that by the spring of 1921 Azerbaijan, Georgia and Armenia had all been re-absorbed by their mighty northern neighbour.

A leading part in these events had been played by Joseb Vissarionovich Djugashvili or Stalin, who, as Lenin's Commissar for Nationalities, had directed operations from Moscow through his friend Sergo Ordzhonikidze. This had given him a welcome opportunity to work off some personal scores against a number of his former fellow-revolutionaries.

It has been said that the degree of armed force used against the Georgians and the brutal repression which followed came as a surprise to Lenin and made him begin to wonder whether Stalin was entirely suited for leadership. But by then Lenin was partially paralysed and Stalin well launched on what already promised to be a remarkable career. For a time, however, Stalin's popularity suffered considerably in his native Georgia. His friend Sergo Ordzhonikidze continued to serve him loyally for the next fifteen or sixteen years, notably as Commissar for Heavy Industry. In February 1937, however, he suddenly fell out of favour and at Stalin's urgent suggestion committed suicide, being granted in return a State Funeral. At this, as it happened, the present author, having arrived in Moscow for the first time half an hour earlier, was an interested onlooker, without however realizing, any more than anyone else then did, just what had precipitated this splendid ceremony.

The Georgians in general did not take kindly to Soviet rule. In April 1921 a meeting at the Tbilisi Opera House of several thousand workers' representatives, passed resolutions calling for free elections, self-determination and independence and when Stalin came to Tbilisi in July he was given a rough reception by some of his former comrades. Within a year a secret Georgian Independence Committee and Military Centre had been set up by opponents of the regime to prepare for an eventual insurrection and during the next couple of years underground resistance kept breaking out in sporadic guerrilla activities. Finally in the summer of 1924 firm plans were made for a general armed rising at the end of August. These were put into execution and, despite initial confusion, the insurgents achieved a considerable measure of success, various Red Army units being wiped out. But in the long run the odds were too great. The Russian Commander, Mogilevski, hastily reinforced the approaches to Tbilisi and, though he himself was killed by his Georgian pilot who deliberately crashed his own plane with Mogilevski in it, after three weeks' savage fighting the insurrection was crushed.

It was followed, as was to be expected, by severe reprisals, many thousands of Georgian prisoners and hostages being liquidated out of hand and many thousands more being sent to Siberia.

By now Lenin was dead and the Stalin era had begun, not only for Georgia, but for the whole of the Soviet Union. It was to last for almost thirty years and in Transcaucasia, as elsewhere, was marked by massive collectivization and industrialization and by no less massive purges and counter-purges. By the end of the 1930s it had developed into a reign of terror which had few parallels even in Russian history and which Stalin's presence in the Kremlin made no more readily endurable for his fellow Georgians.

For all this, in the second World War, when Hitler's armies reached the foothills of the Caucasus, the peoples of Transcaucasia on the whole fought loyally and bravely for the Soviet Union. German plans to raise a Georgian Legion from *emigrés* and prisoners-of-war to fight for Hitler were frustrated by, amongst other things, Alfred Rosenberg's belated discovery that Georgians were non-Aryans and, instead of being enlisted as allies, should therefore logically be exterminated. Some of the mountain tribes, it is true, are said to have shown less enthusiasm than they might have for the Soviet cause. At any rate after the German retreat in March 1944 the Karachay-Balkar and Chechen-Ingush were deported *en masse* to Siberia and Central Asia and the Kabardan-Balkar and Chechen-Ingush Autonomous Republics abolished and removed from the map.

Since Stalin's death in March 1953 the three Transcaucasian Republics have, like the rest of the Soviet Union, experienced a gradual relaxation of tension, a greater degree of decentralization and a relative improvement in living standards. At the same time, within the strict limits imposed by the system, each of them has developed in its own particular way and according to the national characteristics of its people. Even the Chechen-Ingush and Kabardàn-Balkar Autonomous Republics have been reconstituted and restored to the map, and their peoples, in so far as they had survived deportation, allowed to return home. Indeed, not long ago the former was awarded a high Soviet decoration for the outstanding part its people played in the War.

Of open dissatisfaction with the regime there are today few signs. Indeed, it is both significant and highly ironical that almost the only serious disturbances which are known to have occurred in the Soviet Union in the last thirty years are the riots which broke out in Tbilisi in 1956 as a protest against Khrushchev's savage posthumous attacks on Stalin, whom the Georgians, once he was safely dead, had come to regard as a kind of national hero.

11 *Tbilisi*

What are the Caucasus and Transcaucasia like today, after close on sixty years of Soviet rule? In general, I would choose, I think, to approach Transcaucasia from the north by way of the highly dramatic Georgian Military Highway. But on a recent visit, Veronica and I decided to take the through train from Moscow to Tbilisi and then come home by car.

Soviet trains are to me a source of endless pleasure and amusement. The train we caught on this occasion left, mysteriously, two hours earlier than was expected and arrived, less unexpectedly, several hours late. This necessitated a headlong departure and caused some inconvenience to the friends who were meeting us at the other end. But the journey itself was uniformly enjoyable. We had managed to get a two-berthed compartment to ourselves and for forty-eight hours this became our travelling home.

Russia was having the hottest summer for a century and we were delighted to find that our coach (made in East Germany) was air-conditioned. So was the dining-car, where we had long discursive meals, served to us by a friendly team of waiters, waitresses and cooks, headed by a brisk young man in a blue football-jersey. Afterwards, while the vast Russian plain rolled by outside tightly closed windows, we lay on our berths and read and drank the endless glasses of tea which the conductor brought us from his *samovar*. At the stations we got out and walked up and down and went to see what we could buy at the kiosks in the way of eatables and drinkables. Or else we just stood in the corridor and talked to the other passengers, mostly Georgians on their way home from Moscow and including two or three girls and young women possessing that particular Georgian style of beauty which is one of the things that makes Georgia so attractive to visit. Another equally agreeable national characteristic is that instinctive and often overwhelming Georgian hospitality which caused our neighbours on the train to lavish on us innumerable presents of fruit, cakes, chocolate and wine. It was, as I well knew, only a foretaste of things to come.

124

On the second morning out from Moscow we woke to find ourselves at Sukhumi on the Black Sea coast, with its crowded beaches, palm-trees, blue sea and dazzling white buildings. Then, turning inland, we chugged gently all day along a fertile valley, where the lush green of tea-plantations alternated with golden fields of ripening Indian corn. Beyond lines of Lombardy poplars we caught from time to time a glimpse of distant blue mountains. Then in the late afternoon we began to recognize familiar landmarks; the dining-car staff entertained us to a parting tumbler of Soviet champagne on the house; and, after shaking hands all round, we stepped from our cool sleeping-car into the swelter-ing heat of Tbilisi railway station.

We had decided to make Tbilisi our centre of operations. On earlier visits we had always put up at one or other of the pre-revolutionary hotels, the old *Orient* (now *Intourist*) where my grandfather used to stay in the 1880s, or the splendidly Edwardian *Palace* (now the *Tbilisi*) with its magnificent pillared ballroom. This time we found ourselves in the *Iveria*, a newly completed skyscraper, strong on bathrooms, balconies and other modern conveniences, but definitely lacking in old-world charm. But the *Iveria*, we found, had its compensations. After a brief reconnaissance we discovered in the *bufyet*, or snack-bar, on the fifteenth floor a marvellously cheerful young woman who would pro-vide us at almost any hour with meals of eggs and sausages and tea and jam and sour cream in less than a quarter of the time it would have taken us to feed ourselves amid the turmoil of the grand restaurant down-stairs, and would even cook specially for us the strange foodstuffs we sometimes brought back from the bazaar.

But we had not come to Georgia to sit in a hotel. Tbilisi, capital of Georgia since the sixth century, is one of my favourite towns anywhere. In Georgian *tbili* means hot and Tbilisi owes its name to its hot sulphur springs. These, it is said, were first discovered by King Vakhtang while out hunting over fifteen hundred years ago. A wounded deer fell into the bubbling hot water and re-emerged as vigorous as before it had been hit. This so impressed the monarch that he at once built a town there. It is even said that the water's potency is such that it will restore his lost manhood to a eunuch.

Like Rome, Tbilisi is built on several hills and stands, like Rome, on the banks of a rushing river, the Kura. A long narrow town, with a population of around a million, 80 per cent of whom are Georgian and a high proportion of the remainder Armenian or Tartar, it stretches for several miles along both banks. According to an old Georgian saying, whoever once drinks of the waters of the Kura will drink of them again. This has certainly proved true in my case, for I have returned to Tbilisi a dozen times or more since my first visit there nearly forty years ago.

In the course of its long history, Tbilisi has, as we have seen, been conquered by Mongols, Persians, Greeks and Turks. The oldest part of the town lies to the south-east, where the hills come suddenly together in two rocky promontories. Perched high on the northernmost of these stand the Avlabar, the old Georgian citadel, and the ancient church of the Metekhi Virgin, built originally in the fifth century, sacked by the Mongols and rebuilt in its present form in the thirteenth century. All along the high rocky cliffs which here form the river bank, the houses of the old Georgian quarter, with their deep verandas, overhang the fast swirling waters of the Kura, the original bridge across which is said to have been built by Alexander the Great. Splendidly poised above the river near the Metekhi, a gigantic new equestrian statue of King Vakhtang, the city's founder and builder of the Avlabar, serves to remind the Georgians of their glorious past. Built into the battlements of the Avlabar is an elegant little pavilion which once formed part of the Queen Mother's palace, and here it was, one presumes, that after the death of their respective husbands, Queens Darejan and Mariam conducted the intrigues which were even further to bedevil an already complicated situation.

Facing the Metekhi across the river from the high serrated ridge of the Solokaky stands the old Persian fortress of Narykalà dominating the confused tangle of little streets and terraces and alleyways which once constituted the old Persian, Tartar and Armenian and Jewish quarters, their clustered houses clinging in serried ranks to the steep hillside. Originally built in the fourth century, it was put back into working order by the Turks under Mustafa Pasha in the second half of the sixteenth century. Beneath it, among tumbledown shacks and balconied houses that have seen better days, are a mosque, an Armenian Church, a Synagogue and finally the mosque-like Hammam or Turkish bath, all still in use.

In a street near the mosque, where the Mohammedans live, we were addressed in faultless French by a friendly and also extremely pretty local Azerbaijani girl, home for the holidays from the University of

Baku, who, after taking us back to her parents' house near by and entertaining us to tea and preserved cherries, escorted us, with her little brother, round the admirable Botanical Gardens, founded during his Vice-Royalty by Prince Michael Vorontsov, who also founded the no less splendid gardens at Yalta in the Crimea.

On a subsequent visit, bearing this time a letter of introduction from the Royal Botanical Society in Edinburgh, we called on the Director of the Gardens and were furnished, not only with much valuable information concerning the flora of Georgia, but also with some fascinating botanical specimens, the bulk of which made their way in due course to Edinburgh, though a few, I must admit, eventually ended up in our own garden at Strachur, where at the time of writing they are making good progress. From the planting-out area, which we had been taken to see by a particularly charming plant expert, we gained an admirable view of the massive bulk of Narykalà looming above the neighbouring greenery.

Armenians stick together, and all round their well-attended church the shops and houses we visited were mostly occupied by Armenians, including some Armenian bakers producing their flat, unleavened loaves, and a team of muscular Armenian weightlifters practising their strange sport in the privacy of their own back yard. In the little churchyard are the graves of several Armenian generals who distinguished themselves fighting for the Russians in the early nineteenth century.

Finding ourselves one day in the old quarter around lunch-time and not wanting to go all the way back to the hotel, we thought we would have a quick snack in a rather promising looking *shashlichnaya* – or eating-place specializing in *shashliks* – which we had noticed in a cellar or dive below street-level not far from the back yard of our friends the Armenian weightlifters. The *shashliks* and *lavash*, the Georgian flatbread that usually accompanies them, were excellent and all was going well when Veronica's culinary curiosity was aroused by some kind of savoury stew full of strange herbs that was being eaten with obvious relish by our neighbours at the next table, a knowing-looking group of Georgians or possibly Armenians. She had no sooner got up to look at it, however, than the whole dish of stew, together with two litre-bottles of wine, was immediately sent across to our table with our neighbours' compliments.

Feeling that so generous a gesture called for some return on our part,

Veronica now pulled out her Polaroid camera and took their picture. At once the chef and everyone else in the restaurant, which happened to be full of rather cheerful soldiers, wanted to have their pictures taken too. This was fine so long as Veronica's supply of film held out. But there was one serious drawback. To a Georgian in a restaurant there can only be one possible response to someone who takes his photograph: to send them another bottle or two of wine and some more food. By the time we emerged from that dive it was five in the afternoon and it was all we could do to totter to a bench in a nearby park, where Veronica, worn out by her exertions, went peacefully to sleep with her head on my shoulder.

The Jewish community in Georgia have been established there for more than a thousand years and seem, possibly for this reason, to enjoy a more privileged position than their co-religionaries elsewhere in the Soviet Union. 'There has never been any anti-Semitism *here*,' a Georgian said to me with some emphasis. The Synagogue at any rate is in good condition and, besides being well attended, seems to act as a centre for Jewish social activity.

But of all the institutions, religious or otherwise, that cluster under the shadow of the old fortress, none is busier than the Hammam. From the outside, with its handsome, blue-tiled façade, dating back to the eighteenth century or earlier, it resembles a mosque. Inside, after paying fifty kopeks, and collecting a clean towel, you are conducted to a private suite of bathroom and dressing-room. Both are magnificently tiled with fine old Persian tiles, the former being equipped with a capacious marble bath fed from a natural spring with a constant flow of bubbling hot mineral water of strongly sulphurous flavour and smell, and the latter with a massive marble slab on which for another fifty kopeks you can be vigorously massaged and scrubbed. I cannot vouch for the effect on a eunuch but Veronica and I certainly emerged from the experience feeling much refreshed and invigorated.

But not all its visitors seem to have appreciated the Hammam as much as we did. Dumas Père tells the sad story of an Armenian Archbishop who, owing to his own exaggerated modesty and the clumsiness of his attendant deacons, was allowed to slide by mistake into a bath of scalding-hot water in which he seems to have been boiled alive. '*Il était trop tard*,' the dramatic narrative concludes, '*Monseigneur était cuit*.'

Another account of the Hammam comes from Sir Robert Ker Porter, a Captain of the Westminster Militia who, by a series of strange chances, became Court Painter to Tsar Alexander I and married a Russian princess. Sir Robert arrived in Tbilisi in 1817, well provided with letters of introduction to numerous worthwhile people. After a quick look round the men's baths. which do not seem to have interested him, he and his companion enterprisingly decided 'to try if we could not get a glimpse into the baths dedicated to the fair sex.' This presented no difficulty. 'An old woman was standing at the door, and she, without the least scruple, not only showed us the way, but played our sybil the whole while.' 'We found', he continues, 'a vast cavern-like chamber, gloomily lighted, and smelling most potently of sulphuric evaporations, which ascended from nearly twenty deep excavations. Through these filmy vapours, wreathing like smoke over the surface of a boiling caldron, we could distinguish the figures of women, in every posture, perhaps, which the fancy of man could devise for the sculpture of bathing goddesses.' But even now he was not satisfied. 'We were', he writes, 'as much shocked as surprised, at the unblushing coolness with which the Georgian Venuses continued their ablutions, after they had observed our entrance; they seemed to have as little modest covering on their minds, as on their bodies; and the whole scene became so unpleasant, that, declining our conductress's offer to show us farther, we made good our retreat, fully satisfied with the extent of our gratified curiosity.'

Before leaving this fruitful subject, Sir Robert, interfering to the last, suggests that the baths, with their conveniently secluded cubicles, were clearly much used by the ladies who frequented them for pursuits quite other than bathing. Changing his subject, he goes on, a page or two later, to demolish in all seriousness and great detail the pleasant local tradition that the great cleft at the summit of Mount Elbruz was caused by Noah's Ark running aground there on its way to Mount Ararat. One is left, I am afraid, with the feeling that Sir Robert, though possibly a great traveller and a fine horseman, and no doubt an adequate artist, must by nature have been both sanctimonious and lubricious and, as perhaps befits a court painter, sadly lacking any sense of humour. His original interest in painting dated back, we are told, to an early encounter with the aged Flora Macdonald, who fired his childish imagination by showing him a picture of the Hanoverians massacring the Clans at the Battle of Culloden.

Beneath the Solokaky, too, were once the bazaars, where you could then find in profusion silversmiths and goldsmiths, carpet-sellers, weaponsmiths, makers of daggers, the furriers who made the high, black sheepskin fur hats or *papakhas*, the makers of musical instruments and a dozen other types of craftsmen and merchants. Now only a few poky little booths and shops remain, their place having been taken by the big new department stores and supermarkets of the modern town, which lies to the north of the old town and was built for the most part in the last century when Tbilisi was the capital of the Russian Vice-Royalty of the Caucasus.

On the way from the old town to the new, you pass the Sioni Cathedral, built in the seventh century or even earlier, and, like the town itself, destroyed and rebuilt many times since. It is said that when Jelal-eddin, Sultan of Khorassan, took Tbilisi in 1225 he at once demolished the spire of the Cathedral and then threw a bridge across from his palace to its roof, in order that, whenever he felt so inclined, he could personally trample on a Christian temple. But for all this the Sioni Cathedral still stands and in it you may see, in a splendid silver shrine, the miraculous cross which in the fourth century Saint Nino plaited from vine-stems and bound with her own hair. In front of the Sioni Cathedral stands the handsome classical campanile built by Prince Tsitsianov before he died in 1806 at the hands of the treacherous Khan of Baku, his body being finally brought back and buried in the Cathedral. His head, sent by the Khan to the Shah of Persia as a good-will gift, presumably rests elsewhere.

The singing in the Cathedral is magnificent and after the service a well-dressed congregation gathers in little groups outside the porch to gossip, much as congregations do anywhere on a Sunday morning. Tbilisi is the seat of the Katholikos, the Patriarch of Georgia, a portly figure with a white beard who lives, tended by devoted old ladies, in a comfortable house next to the Cathedral. Unlike the Armenian Church, from which it broke away towards the end of the fifth century, the Church of Georgia, though once again autocephalous, is in communion with the Russian Orthodox Church and services in both languages can be conducted in the same building. Under Stalin, the Georgian Church, it is said, was not as savagely persecuted as the church elsewhere in the Soviet Union, for the reason that the Generalissimo was afraid of his mother, a devout old lady who had

The Georgian National Dancers at rehearsal

The Georgian National Dancers at rehearsal

Old Tbilisi

Lermontov's House, Tbilisi

◀ St David's Monastery, Tbilisi

The Metekhi, Tbilisi

◄ The Old Quarter, Tbilisi

The Nary Kalà, Tbilisi

A Moslem girl, Tbilisi

The Metekhi from the Queen Mother's Palace, Tbilisi

Dominoes

always wanted to make a priest of him and who lived on in Tbilisi until her death just before the war aged nearly a hundred.

A little further on you come to the Picture Gallery, a handsome classical building standing back from the main square of the town. This was once a hotel and, before that, a theological seminary, where Stalin was brought up to be a priest before embarking on his career as a revolutionary. For a time after 1956 the marble plaque informing the public of this interesting fact was taken down, but now it has been proudly restored to its original position.

In Georgia, by a strange quirk of fortune, Stalin is today more popular than he ever was during his lifetime, providing as he does, now that he is safely buried, an outlet for Georgian nationalism – a sentiment of which one very soon becomes aware. ('It's all Georgian this and Georgian that!' said an old Russian I met in the street, and spat vigorously on the pavement.) The Georgians are tremendously unlike the Russians and their language, which they speak at a great rate, is as different from Russian as Chinese is from English. This, and much else besides, the Russians are inclined to find bewildering. One is always being told, in awed tones, terrifying tales of Georgian business acumen. The story, for example, of the operator who, by simply booking all the seats, managed to charter a complete Aeroflot plane to fly masses of mimosa from the Black Sea to Moscow, selling it at an enormous profit to the flower-starved Muscovites and then flying back with a cargo of Dresden china from East Germany for sale at an equally large profit in Tbilisi. And then, of course, endless, rather envious, stories of the success the handsome Georgians have with the opposite sex.

It is also significant that, when in February 1956 Khrushchev made the first speech of his de-Stalinization campaign, rioting should have broken out in the streets of Tbilisi in protest against this insult to the name of a great son of Georgia. It is true that the great statue which today dominates the main square of Tbilisi is of Lenin, not Stalin. But there are fewer reminders of the dead Russian leader in Georgia than in most of the other Republics of the Union and perhaps also fewer exhortations to unity and conformity.

Out of the main square in a northerly direction runs the main street of Tbilisi. This was known in Tsarist days as the Golovinski Prospekt, presumably after the unfortunate General Golovin, but was renamed by the Georgians Prospekt Rustaveli in honour of the medieval Georgian poet, Shota Rustaveli, whose statue adorns the far end of it.

As far as Tbilisi is concerned the Prospekt Rustaveli is the hub of the universe. With its handsome lines of plane-trees, happily-mingled architectural fantasies and cheerful, chattering crowds of pedestrians, this bustling boulevard possesses an unexpectedly Parisian quality to which the Georgians point with pride and which did not escape Alexandre Dumas. This is where you will find the best shops and the best hotels and restaurants and snack-bars and cafés and soda-fountains. Here, opposite the comfortable old-fashioned Hotel Orient is the imposing new building which houses the Government of the Soviet Socialist Republic of Georgia. Here is the former palace of the Tsar's Viceroy, now a children's club. Here, a little further along, is the *Café Metro*, a daringly modern establishment named rather prematurely in anticipation of a projected underground railway which was only to follow several years later. Here are the cinemas and theatres. Here, like their predecessors a century ago, all that is brightest and best in Georgian society gathers each evening towards sunset to walk up and down and take the air and look at each other: boys arm in arm, girls arm in arm, in groups that rarely mingle, at any rate in the street, for this is an eastern country.

In Tbilisi, in the summer, both in the old town and the new, life is very largely lived out of doors, in the street or in the courtyards of the old houses. Wherever you go, something is always happening and there is always a crowd looking on. People are buying and selling things, or playing games, or playing instruments, or looking in the shop windows or looking at each other. There is never a dull moment.

Before the Revolution, it was calculated that one in seven of the male population of Georgia were Princes. Walking up and down the Prospekt Rustaveli of an evening one is tempted to the conclusion that today an even higher proportion must be *stilyagi* – as youthful trend-setters are known in the Soviet Union. Never were there such winkle-pickers, such skin-tight jeans, such sideburns and mustachios and startling shirts, all worn with the same tremendous air with which their grandfathers used to wear the old Georgian national dress. The girls do their best, but their valiant attempts at trouser-suits, mini-skirts, pony-tails and beehive coiffures pale before such masculine glory.

The Georgians are one of the best-looking races in the world. They have a style and an elegance all of their own: the men with their marvellous bearing and fierce, hawk-like good looks; the women darkly beautiful with their flashing eyes, white skins, aquiline features and slender, pliant bodies. They are also a proud race and an excitable and pugnacious one – almost any evening you can see a fight or two in progress up and down the street. And there can be no doubt that in a jolly, southern way they enjoy showing off. But they are not arrogant. They are among the friendliest, gayest, most convivial and most hospitable people I know.

Many of the Georgian national characteristics, dash, elegance, pride, gaiety, even pugnacity, come out in their dancing, which means as much to them as our own Highland dancing – with which it has much in common – means to the Highlander. Quite apart from the consummate mastery of the Georgian National Dance Company, whose fame has now spread all over the world, Georgians old and young will dance at the drop of a hat, wherever they find themselves, in the street, by the roadside, in a restaurant, anywhere where there is room to manoeuvre and where they can find someone to play the drums and accordion.

Not that the Georgians are only interested in their own national dances. Amongst the younger generation there is the same passion for the twist and its various successors that you find everywhere in the Soviet Union. A good American jazz record (like a foreign fashion magazine) was until recently worth its weight in gold, and the sound of jazz coming through an open window would soon collect a crowd of jiving youth.

Now, by one means or another, a domestic source of supply seems to have sprung up to meet the growing demand and, walking along Prospekt Rustaveli, I came upon a street-vendor of home-made records with a transistorized gramophone grinding out tunes which to the untutored ear were indistinguishable from those so continuously played by our own rising generation. This astute operator was also offering for sale what appeared to be privately produced postcards, and in this enclave of private enterprise I was delighted to find a handsome portrait of the late Generalissimo Stalin in full uniform occupying the place of honour between the Beatles on the one hand and the Rolling Stones on the other – a revealing glimpse for the connoisseur of current popularity ratings.

Half way up St David's Mountain, the great hill above the town, stand the ancient church and monastery of St David. Here, in a neat classical sarcophagus, are buried the remains of the writer Alexander Sergeyich Griboyedov, author of the famous satirical play *Woe from Wit or the Misfortunes of being Clever*. Griboyedov was for a time Russian Minister Plenipotentiary in Teheran and there in February 1829 was torn limb from limb by an angry mob of Persians following a dispute over the nationality of two Armenian harem girls and a Court Eunuch. His friend Pushkin tells how one day, when out riding near the fortress of Ghergey, he met some Georgians with a cart drawn by two oxen, which contained something covered by a tarpaulin. 'Where are you from?' he idly asked them. 'Teheran,' they replied. 'What load are you carrying?' 'Griboyedov,' they said. It was thus that he learned of his friend's death. With Griboyedov is buried his young widow, Princess Nina, sister of Prince David Chavchavadze and sister-in-law of the Princess Anna who twenty years later was to become the prisoner of Shamyl.

If you climb right to the top of St David's Mountain and look out over Tbilisi from the vast colonnaded restaurant that has been built there, or when you drive out into the country, you quickly realize the rate at which the city is growing. In a determined effort to solve the housing problem, which here, as almost everywhere in the Soviet Union is acute, enormous new apartment houses are being built everywhere as well as the impressive public buildings from which the still under-housed population presumably derive a vicarious satisfaction. Side by side with the old town, of which the inhabitants are justly proud and which they have had the good taste to cherish and preserve, a new town is springing up and spreading out in every direction – a handsome town, well laid out with avenues and parks in which clever use has been made of the lie of the land and where contemporary Georgian architecture blends the modern with the traditional.

In other fields, too, the Georgians have struck out a line of their own. The films produced by Gruziafilm, the Georgian State Film Enterprise, are technically excellent and have, by Soviet standards, a highly individual flavour. And in the Picture Gallery, in addition to some very oriental-looking Royal family portraits, I found some strange nineteenth-century peasant primitives and some striking examples of an even stranger school of rather decadent painters who flourished in Tbilisi in the 1920s. The leading spirit seems to have been a young man called Djokidze who was clearly quite a considerable painter. His paintings depict a kind of rake's progress with himself in the title role. But all I could find out about him was that he spent some time in Paris and died young. And, looking at his pictures, one is, I must say, hardly surprised.

The Picture Gallery also possesses a collection of magnificent medieval Georgian ikons which anyone interested in Georgian history should on no account miss and which give one a clear idea of the high degree of artistic achievement attained in Georgia in the Middle Ages, during the reign, for example, of David the Builder. Of quite exceptional interest is the magnificent Kakhuli Triptych, a masterpiece of Georgian medieval craftsmanship, some five feet high and six feet broad. The triptych consists of a central panel containing a fine, though unfortunately incomplete, early ikon of the Virgin, with two side panels in the form of doors made to close over the ikon. The central panel is of solid red gold, beautifully tooled and patterned with intricate designs and arabesques, while the two side panels, also patterned in a rather different style, are made from an amalgam of gold and silver. All three panels are thickly studded with precious stones, singly and in groups and patterns, and with exquisite smaller enamel ikons and crosses. Though they form an entirely harmonious whole, the triptych and its ikons are known to be the work of a number of different craftsmen and artists, the earlier portion dating back to the beginning of the tenth century.

To save the triptych from the Seljuks then raiding south-western Georgia, King David the Builder took it to the Monastery of Gelati, in northern Georgia, where it was later further embellished by his successor Dmitri I. Thereafter it remained intact until the year 1859 when it seems to have been plundered and parts of it removed by unscrupulous private collectors. Recovered, re-assembled and returned to Gelati in 1923, it was brought to Tbilisi in 1952.

To those concerned with a still earlier period, the Historical Museum, half way along the Prospekt Rustaveli, offers a collection of early golden torques, crowns, drinking vessels, ornaments and other artefacts, some going back two or three thousand years, which show that already in classical, and even pre-classical times Transcaucasia enjoyed an astonishing high level of civilization.

It is perhaps symbolic of Georgian gaiety and effervescence that one of the more important industrial undertakings in Georgia is the State

Champagne Factory outside Tbilisi, with its output of ten or more million bottles a year – a fact in which all concerned take immense pride. For me Georgian champagne does not have the same appeal as the traditional Georgian wines from Kakhetia and Imeretia, but Georgian vineyards, on the sunny foothills of the Caucasus, produce excellent grapes; the Georgians have studied French methods of champagne production with the greatest care; nothing is put into it that should not be put into it; and the end-product, after two or three glasses well iced, strikes one, especially in hot weather, as a refreshing and stimulating beverage. If you include the production of wine, tea and tobacco, agriculture of one kind or another forms the basis of Georgia's economy.

From a linguistic point of view, it is interesting to find that the Georgian word for wine is *ghvino*. Bearing in mind that the Georgian language is entirely separate from the Turkish, Semitic and Indo-European groups of languages, some experts assume that the word must have been borrowed, probably from the Indo-European. But others, on the contrary, find in this evidence that Georgia is the primordial home of viticulture. Certainly, having sampled the quality of their vintages and observed the astonishing quantities of wine they drink themselves, I incline strongly to the latter theory. 'We may assert', wrote the good Chevalier Chardin (who after all hailed from France) 'that there is no country where they drink more or better wine.' 'In truth,' he continues, 'had I drunk as much as my neighbours, I had dy'd upon the Spot.' And Alexandre Dumas had the same experience a couple of hundred years later. 'In Georgia', he wrote, 'food is a very minor consideration . . . *Quant à la liquide, c'est autre chose.* Even the most moderate drinkers manage five or six bottles of wine and the average is twelve or fifteen.' Certainly our own experience was that things have not changed much over the years – as regards either the quality or the quantity of the wine consumed.

12 *The Land of Georgia*

Kakhetia or Eastern Georgia is a place I had long wanted to visit. Partly because of its excellent wine and the ancient churches for which it is famous. But partly also for its memories of the three beautiful young princesses who in the year 1854 were snatched from Prince David Chavchavadze's house at Tsinandali by the wild Moslem tribesmen of the Imam Shamyl. And so, on a recent trip Veronica and I, having provided ourselves with a hired car and a heavily mustachioed Georgian driver, set out one morning from Tbilisi in an easterly direction.

Soon we had left the wide, dusty valley of the Kura and were crossing a range of thickly wooded hills into the parallel valley of the Alazani. Here, as we entered Kakhetia, the landscape changed; the country became more fertile; and we emerged from the hills to find ourselves looking out through a screen of poplars across vast fields of vines and Indian corn to a line of distant blue mountains, the main range of the Caucasus.

Tsinandali lay at the foot of the hills we had just crossed. The house and estate, approached through a pair of handsome wrought-iron gates, have been preserved just as they were in memory of the early nineteenth-century poet Prince Alexander Chavchavadze. Thanks to his reputedly progressive ideas, Prince Alexander has posthumously won the approval of the Soviet regime; his house has been preserved as a museum; and, allowing for the damage done during the raid itself, the scene today cannot be so very different from what it was in that hot June dawn one hundred and twenty years ago, when Shamyl's Murids swooped down from the hills and carried off their shrieking victims.

The house, built of local pinkish-grey sandstone, is a medium-sized, not very elaborate, two-storeyed country house, with the big windows of the large, airy rooms on the first floor opening on to two sides of a wide veranda, where, in summer, as in most Georgian houses, much of the life of the family was no doubt lived. Across the broad, fertile valley

137

of the Alazani it faces almost due north to where, beyond the green of the vineyards and the spreading fields of ripening corn, stand the distant highlands of Daghestan, a massive mountain wall, which even today retains a hint of the hidden menace it once held for the unsuspecting princesses.

All round the house is a fine park in the English manner, full of splendidly-grown specimens of innumerable different trees, familiar and unfamiliar, domestic and exotic, coniferous and deciduous: great umbrella pines, spreading cedars, giant magnolias with their burnished leaves and heady perfume and perhaps the most beautiful lime tree I have ever seen. At the back of the park are the outbuildings and stables where the Murids began their attack. Today they are used for the production of the delicious white wine to which Tsinandali gives its name, and of which, needless to say, we drank our fill.

From Tsinandali we next made our way to Telavi, the principal town of Kakhetia. Telavi is dominated by the Batonistsikhe, a massive fortified compound containing various churches and palaces, which in the seventeenth and eighteenth centuries served as the residence of the Kakhetian and, later, of the Georgian Kings, notably King Hercules II, who used it as a convenient refuge when Tbilisi, as so often happened, was in the hands of the Persians or Turks. Within easy reach of Telavi are several of the most remarkable churches and monasteries of medieval Georgia. To the north-east, across the Alazani, is Gremi, which in the sixteenth century was capital of Kakhetia. Of the ancient city only a few crumbling ruins remain. But, perched on a fortified hilltop above them, stand two churches of the period which, perhaps thanks to their strategic position and massive walls, survived the ravages of time and the disasters which overtook their neighbours below. There is no town at Gremi today, but at a truck-drivers' rest we lunched off freshly caught fish from the river and a bottle of the local wine.

Not many miles north-west from Telavi are the ancient monastery and academy of Ikalto and the famous cathedral church of Alaverdi, built at the beginning of the eleventh century by King Bagrat III in the shape of a gigantic cross. The sun was setting as we approached Alaverdi. Ringed round with crumbling walls and watchtowers the great cathedral rises white and austere above the green of the surrounding plain, while far away to the north, beyond the cornfields and vineyards, the sunlight still just touched the distant peaks of the Caucasus. Carved in relief on one of the flagstones of the floor, the image of a single human hand recalls the heroic end of a local prince who, captured by the Turks and facing death, cut off his hand and sent it home so that it at least might be buried in holy ground, a typically Georgian gesture. Alaverdi, as it happens, is also regarded as a place of great sanctity by the Moslem tribesmen who live in the surrounding hills and they too, strangely enough, have a Moslem shrine of their own within the precincts of the Christian cathedral.

From Alaverdi it is only a few miles to Ikalto. As far back as the sixth century Ikalto was the seat of a Christian monastery and of an academy famous throughout Georgia. Of the monastery and academy only a few crumbling walls still stand, but the adjoining three churches, of which two date back to the seventh and eighth centuries respectively, have stayed in good repair. A little striped grey kitten, prowling in the long grass, like a tiger at dusk in the jungle, was the only sign of life.

By now it was getting dark and we reluctantly abandoned the idea of going on to see the churches and monasteries at Shuamtha near by. But, just as we were climbing back into our car, we were hailed by a group of village worthies sitting down to dinner under a tree. Georgian hospitality is spontaneous and lavish and five minutes later each of us was facing a flagon of wine, a great slice of watermelon and a gigantic lamb *shashlik*. It was not until a great many healths had been drunk and speeches made and the flagons endlessly filled and refilled that we finally set out in pitch darkness on the long drive back to Tbilisi.

Though among complete strangers, our driver had, without a moment's hesitation, assumed the role of *tamada* or toastmaster, which, as he later rather unnecessarily pointed out, involved drinking even more than he would otherwise have done. Our drive home across the mountains in the darkness to the accompaniment of a blaring radio was an exciting one, our driver waving his arms and kicking the accelerator in time to the music. One of the more spectacular incidents, besides a head-on collision with a gigantic heap of stones, was the sudden appearance in our headlights of a tall, slender Georgian girl with her arms outstretched and her long black hair streaming down her back. She was, she rather breathlessly explained, seeking protection from the unwelcome attentions of a lustful truck-driver, with whom she had hitched a ride. This we duly afforded her. At which the frustrated and infuriated truck-driver immediately tried to ram us. A race through the night ensued and our lives, by my reckoning, were only saved by the timely blue light of a roving police-car, to which I forcibly drew our driver's attention. Our experiences had not quite equalled those of the kidnapped princesses. But we came back from Kakhetia having certainly drunk deeply of the local vintages and with the distinct impression that life there still had its thrills.

After exploring eastern Georgia, our next target was the deep south. Here I particularly wanted to see the famous cave-monastery of Vardzia and the reputably impregnable town of Akhaltsikhe, so successfully stormed by Prince Paskevich in 1828. But to penetrate as far as this into the frontier zone, a special permit was necessary, and this, I was told, was only very rarely granted to foreigners. There followed the usual day or two of uncertainty and suspense, and then, to our great delight, the necessary permit suddenly materialized and on the appointed day we set out again north-westwards from Tbilisi along the wide valley of the Kura in the direction of Gori with a long list of things we wanted to see. The first of these, only a short way from the main road, was the elegantly proportioned, eleventh-century church at Samthavissi with a great cross standing out in sharp relief on its eastern façade. Next, a few miles from Gori, we came to the cave-city of Uplistsikhe, first carved out of the rock in the Bronze Age and finally destroyed by the Mongols in the thirteenth century.

Gori's chief claim to fame is that Stalin was born there in 1879. It was a fine day and we ate our sandwiches on a bench among the flower-beds of the neatly laid-out public park which now surrounds the little flat-roofed house in which the Generalissimo first saw the light of day. This consists of two sparsely furnished white-washed rooms, each about ten feet square, and a veranda. One room, it appears, was occupied by the landlord and the other by Stalin's father and mother. The whole structure is now enclosed within a magnificent, pillared marble pavilion with a glass roof. As we sat and ate our sandwiches, a continuous stream of visitors went in, looked around and came out again.

In the main square of the little town a massive statue of its most famous son stands guard in front of the fine municipal building with which he endowed it, while from a hill on its fringes the battered mass of a ruined fortress, Goristsikhe, broods over everything, as it has done for the past two thousand years and more.

Not many miles south of Gori, standing at the head of a narrow valley, high on a rock above a rushing mountain stream, we found a little church which made as great an impression on me as any in Georgia – Ateni Sion – built in the first part of the seventh century and containing a famous fresco of the eleventh century. Like other churches of this period, the Church of the Cross at Dzhvari in particular, its dome rests on a faceted drum above a cruciform ground plan, the arms of the cross ending in four half-circles. Architecturally, Ateni Sion impresses by its simplicity, but what struck me most of all was its magnificent position and the feeling it gave me of age, serenity and strength.

From Gori we continued westwards along the valley of the Kura to Kashuri. Here the valley turns southwards, climbing steeply between the thickly-wooded hillsides to Borzhomi where we were to spend the night. For the last hundred years and more Borzhomi has been famous as a spa. Various Grand Dukes had their villas there and Chekhov and Tchaikovski and later the giants of the Revolution came to take the waters and enjoy the mountain air. On my last visit it had rained incessantly and I had gone away with an unhappy impression of low cloud and dripping pine trees. This time the weather was perfect; our suite in the hotel, built in Stalin's day on a generous scale, was a comfortable one and the mayor, an eminently cheerful character, was kind enough to ask us to dine with him. After an excellent dinner consisting of *khachapuri*, a delicious kind of toasted cheese, a magnificent *shashlik* and, needless to say, bottle after bottle of local wine, we wandered happily by moonlight along the banks of the Borzhomka, a rushing, poplar-lined tributary of the Kura, flowing between opposite rows of pretty, nineteenth-century stucco villas. One in particular, a fantasy in the Oriental manner, caught the eye by its brilliant patterns of looking-glass spangles sparkling in the light of the moon. This I took to be what Baedeker, writing in the year 1914, describes as 'the Moorish-looking château of the Grand-Duke Mikhail Nikolayevich'. Our stroll took us next to the famous mineral spring in the park, where we all drank as much of the warm, effervescent, sulphurous water as we could get down – a proceeding much to be recommended after such an abundance of rich food and drink.

Next morning, feeling surprisingly well, we set out in a south-westerly direction for Akhaltsikhe and Vardzia. Once again we were following the valley of the Kura. At Atskuri, where, on entering the frontier zone, we showed our special passes to a detachment of smart, green-capped Frontier Troops, an ancient fortress stands high on a rock above the checkpoint, a reminder of the enduring strategic importance of the road along which we were now travelling. For intending invaders, coming from either direction, this has always been a gateway to Georgia or, alternatively an outlet to Turkey, and from now onwards the ruins of some ancient castle or fortification looked down from almost every point of vantage along our route.

Akhaltsikhe, or New Castle, stands at four thousand feet above sea level. Before you reach it the valley opens out and the town itself, with the old citadel rising above it, lies in a bowl ringed round by mountains. It was not at first sight clear to me why it should ever have been regarded as impregnable, but then, once Prince Paskevich Erivanski put his mind to the problem, it turned out not to be after all.

Beyond Akhaltsikhe the valley narrows again, the craggy, rock-strewn hills on either side become higher and more precipitous and the Kura, as you approach its source, more and more of a mountain torrent. Soon we came to the great medieval castle of Khertvissi, standing high above the river on a great rocky cliff, and further on to Tmogvi or Tamara's Gates, where, towering above the valley, the mighty ruins of an ancient fortress, destroyed by Persian invaders in the sixteenth century and also, it is said, by a subsequent earthquake, are now almost indistinguishable from the rocks on which they stand.

As you approach Vardzia, the mighty volcanic cliffs on either side of the valley are honeycombed with what were once cave-dwellings and everywhere you can see traces of early terraced cultivation. But Vardzia itself is on an altogether different scale from these early burrowings. Here, half-way up the cliff, a whole city has been hollowed and tun-nelled out of the rock with room for several thousand inhabitants as well as for churches, palaces, forts, monasteries, banqueting-halls, barracks, stables and wine-cellars, all interconnected by an endless labyrinth of caves and tunnels and passages and stairways, the pattern of which has been even more clearly revealed by an earthquake which at some period sliced away a part of the rockface. Here, having first climbed up a steep winding path from the valley below, you may see, when your eyes become accustomed to the darkness, the stalls in which the King's horses were stabled, the frescoed chapel in which he worshipped, the wine presses from which his wine gushed forth, the great jars in which it

Tsinandali, looking out on the mountains

Tsinandali, Prince David Chavchavadze's house

Tsinandali, the gateway to the estate   Telavi, the Citadel

Gremi

Ikalto, the Academy

◀ Alaverdi, the Cathedral

Ikalto: Georgian hospitality is spontaneous and lavish

The approach to Gounib

A man of Daghestan

Gounib from below

The road to Khounzakh

Stalin's Birthplace, Gori

Gori, Town Hall ▶

Towards Ateni Sion

Ateni Sion ▶

Borzhomi, 'the Moorish-looking chateau of
the Grand Duke Mikhail Nikolayevich'

Khertvissi

◄ The road to Vardzia

Kutaisi, the Cathedral of King Bagrat III

◀ Vardzia

Kutaisi, the receptionist

Kutaisi

Gelati, Belfry

◀ Kutaisi, the
Cathedral of King Bagrat III

Nikortsminda, Belfry

Nikortsminda, the Ascension (11th century)

was stored, and the dining-room in which he and his friends drank it. And, if you know where to look, you may also see, as you enter the royal dining-room, the slit in the rock above, just wide enough for a lance to be driven down through it into the neck of an unwelcome guest. Across the river, at a discreet distance from the monastery, was, we were told, a convent for nuns.

Vardzia was completed in the twelfth century and devastated by the Persians in 1552. A contemporary Moslem historian has left a vivid, if somewhat bigoted, account of Vardzia and of its sacking. 'In strength', he writes, 'it was like the wall of Alexander and the castle of Khaybar. In the middle of the fort they had hollowed out a place ten cubits high, and made a church of four rooms and a long bench, and had painted its walls without and within with gold and lapis lazuli and pictures of idols and arranged a throne in the second room, and an idol gilt and covered with precious stones, with two rubies for the eyes of that lifeless form; within the church was a narrow way one hundred and fifty cubits long to go up, cut in the solid rock. They had two hidden kiosks for use in times of trouble, and there were doors of iron and steel in the outer rooms, and a golden door in the inner ones. Then the Ghazis fell upon that place and climbed above that fort, and slew the men and took captive their wives and children. The Shah and his nobles went to see the church, and they slew twenty evil priests and broke the bell of seventeen maunds weight seven times cast, and destroyed the doors of iron and gold, and sent them to the Treasury . . . Thus the Shah got great booty; and in it were two rubies being the eyes of the idol, each worth fifty tumans. And they levelled the fort to the ground.'

Having scrambled back down the rocky track under the glare of the August sun, we were more than ready for a swim in the fast-flowing stream of the Kura. A toe, gingerly inserted from the brink, registered that it was breathtakingly cold. But gushing from the ground near by we found a hot sulphur spring in which we soaked ourselves before plunging into its rushing, icy waters. After which, before setting out on the long journey back, we threw ourselves with considerable appetite on the bottle of wine, Georgian unleavened bread and cold Soviet sausage we had brought with us.

We had deliberately kept western Georgia until the end of our stay. Imeretia and its capital, Kutaisi, were places I had always wanted to see. This, after all, is Colchis, the Kingdom of Medea's father. This is where Jason and his Argonauts sought their fortunes and to this day the town of Kutaisi bears as its municipal crest the Golden Fleece they went in search of. In the museum I was delighted to find a handsome moustachioed portrait of the famous Emperor Solomon II of Imeretia who put up such a sturdy resistance to the various invaders of his country, before appealing in vain to his fellow-emperor Napoleon.

We had travelled by train from Tbilisi through the night to Kutaisi, arriving early the next morning. The local hotel, again in the Stalinist style of the 1930s, was chiefly remarkable for the excellent service in the restaurant, clearly a centre of life in Kutaisi, and for the good looks of the receptionist, who, with her ivory skin and elaborate coils of jet black hair, might have served as a model for Medea herself. Our room looked out on to an agreeably laid-out park and, after a copious breakfast of fried eggs, sour cream, bread and jam and tea, we set out to explore the town.

Not far from the hotel is the Green Market, where the peasants bring their own produce to sell. At this time of year, almost everything was in season and there was an abundance of fruit and vegetables, as well as more exotic products such as spices and home-grown tea. Clearly the process of buying and selling serves to bring out various deep-seated human instincts which are not supposed to exist under Communism, and some pretty vigorous bargaining was in progress. But as soon as it became known that we were foreigners, this at once gave way to the spontaneous generosity which is such a characteristic of the Georgians and we found ourselves literally overwhelmed with presents of peaches, apples, grapes and water-melons as well as some mysterious packets of spices which have since lent an entirely new dimension to Veronica's cooking.

Kutaisi is pleasantly situated on the Rioni River, the Phasis of the ancients. This rises further north in the main range of the Caucasus, its fertile valley, rich with vineyards and tea plantations, being reputedly the ancestral home of the pheasant or *phasianus colchicus*. High on a rock above the river stand the splendid ruins of the great cathedral church of King Bagrat III of Georgia, built around the year 1000 when Tbilisi was still in the hands of the Arabs and Kutaisi had for the time being become the capital of the Georgian kings. It was blown up by the Turks almost exactly seven centuries later. Behind the church are the remains of a massive fortress tower from which on a clear day you get a fine view of the great mountains away to the north.

A few miles to the north-west of Kutaisi, beautifully situated on a hillside above a river in full view of the main chain of the Caucasus, is the monastery of Gelati, endowed at the beginning of the twelfth century by King David the Builder, who, it is said, fell from the scaffolding and injured himself while supervising the workmen. In King David's day Gelati became one of the most important religious and also cultural centres in medieval Georgia. Within its precincts stand three churches, a bell-tower and the ruins of an academy which quickly became famous as a centre of learning and in particular as the seat of a school of metaphysical philosophy founded with King David's support by the great Georgian neo-Platonist, Petritsi.

Of the three churches, the largest is the great sandstone Cathedral of the Virgin Mary, beautifully proportioned and containing some remarkable twelfth-century mosaics and frescoes. These include a magnificent mosaic of the Virgin and Child with the Archangels Michael and Gabriel, dating from the twelfth century and presented to the monastery, it is said, by the Emperor of Byzantium, and a full-length imaginary portrait of King David done in the sixteenth century, showing him as a tall, bearded figure with a halo, proudly carrying a small model church. The two lesser churches are dedicated to St George and St Nicholas respectively, the latter being built on two storeys. From under the little free-standing belfry rises a spring of clear fresh water at which, after our long, hot drive we gratefully quenched our thirst.

King David the Builder lies buried under the archway of one of the gates of the monastery. It is said that, as a token of humility, he wished his grave to be walked on by as many people as possible. 'This', runs the inscription on his gravestone, 'is my home for all eternity. Here shall I dwell, for I have willed it.' A rather battered iron gate which hangs, swinging back and forth above the grave, is said to have been brought back by David's son Dimitri from one of his campaigns against the Persians. Of Petritsi's Academy, with its great windows looking across the valley to the mountains beyond, enough remains to convey a feeling of scholastic serenity and calm.

In the district of Racha, forty or fifty miles beyond Gelati, high up in the foothills of the Caucasus, stands another masterpiece of Georgian medieval architecture: the church of Nikortsminda. We approached it through a green fertile valley, the lower slopes of the hills on either side of the road being taken up with vines and tea-plantations, where women wearing brightly coloured head-shawls were busy gathering the young shoots. The little church stands on a low green mound on the outskirts of a village. Over the wall, the children from the village school were scampering merrily about enjoying their midday break. On another side green orchards and vineyards sloped steeply down to a mountain stream. The church is built of mellow, golden-coloured stone. Its ground-plan is hexagonal, the conical cupola or spire being carried by a splendid drum, the twelve facets of which are pierced by tall narrow windows – scarcely more than loopholes – with beautifully carved architraves. The carving, characteristic of the Imeretian stonework of the period, is superb. High on the north wall above three perfectly proportioned blind arches is a splendid figure of Christ. The frescoes inside the church are five or six hundred years later in period and include portraits of various local notabilities of the day.

Beyond Nikortsminda the valley of the Rioni narrows and the road – the Ossetian Military Highway – climbs up to the town of Oni and beyond it to over 9,000 feet at the Mamison Pass, whence it descends to Alagir on the other side of the Caucasus, and thence, like the Georgian Military Highway, with which it runs parallel, to Ordzhonikidze.

While Georgia abounds in magnificent examples of church architecture of all periods, old secular buildings, other than fortresses, are much rarer. One of the relatively few surviving Georgian non-ecclesiastical buildings of feudal times is the great ruined palace of the Georgian Kings at Geguti, four or five miles to the south of Kutaisi, where the Rioni Valley opens out into a wide plain, and water buffaloes wallow happily in muddy rivulets. 'In the autumn of 1123', we are told, 'King David the Builder arrived at Geguti, where he hunted and rested, and, having settled all local affairs, departed for Karthli in March.' Here in 1179, King George III proclaimed his daughter Tamara his co-ruler and here in 1207 the same Queen Tamara resided with her ministers. Here, too, a century and a half later, in 1360, King David VII, son of King George the Magnificent, met his end.

For anyone who is not a connoisseur of ruins it requires a fairly vivid imagination to gain from this tumbled mass of bricks and masonry a very definite impression of anything much except size. Clearly, the palace or castle, the ruins of which are said to extend over two thousand square metres, was on a grandiose scale and the monarchs who resided there must have been able to hold court without fear of feeling cramped in the Great Hall with its fifty foot dome, one shattered arch of which is still standing.

Imeretia, like Kakhetia, is wine-growing country and, to my taste, the light, rather flowery white wines produced there can more than hold their own with the heavier vintages of Tsinandali and Gurjani. It goes without saying that in Western, as in Eastern Georgia, we were given every opportunity of tasting them as well as the local cuisine, with its wide range of highly spiced and highly flavoured dishes. The surprise farewell luncheon party given in our honour before we left, by a local prince of our acquaintance (also a leading Party member), began without warning at eleven in the morning and lasted till five in the afternoon. It took place in the spacious, massively furnished, town house of one of our host's cousins and was attended by at least three generations of his family and a further number of friends and connexions, who dropped in for an hour or two as and when their various occupations permitted. It was, as usual, punctuated by toasts in honour of everybody and everything.

We had intended to fly back to Tbilisi that morning, but this improbable idea soon faded into unreality and in the end we caught a plane at eight in the evening and that only by the skin of our teeth. At the last moment an immense demijohn of Imeretian wine was thrust on board with us as a parting gift. On reaching Tbilisi we were wondering what to do with this bulky addition to our luggage, when our pretty and enterprising air-hostess promptly commandeered the airport's electrically propelled steps on which we then careered merrily across the tarmac, air-hostess, demijohn and all.

13 *Across the Caucasus*

After a couple of weeks in the sultry heat of Georgia we were ready for the cooler air of the Northern Caucasus. Bright and early on the morning after our return to Tbilisi we set out in a sky-blue self-drive *Moskvich* rent-a-car, with the firm intention of crossing the main range of the Caucasus by way of the Georgian Military Highway. We had asked for a *Volga*, heavier built and more powerful, but when it came to the point, no *Volga* was available and so we had to make do with the *Moskvich*. This we were to regret the first time we switched the engine off, only to find that it would not start again except on a steep incline – a performance repeated with sickening regularity throughout our journey. Fortunately, however, there are plenty of steep inclines in the Caucasus and, by making intelligent use of them, we managed better than might have been expected. (It is only fair to say, however, that on our next trip we were provided with a sprightly little car called a *Zhiguli*, which carried us over the highest passes and along the stoniest and roughest mountain roads without a murmur.)

Our first stopping place was Mtzkhet, the ancient capital of Georgia and one of the oldest inhabited towns in the world. On a hill near by stand the crumbling ruins of Harmotsikhe, in pre-Christian days the fortress of the ancient Georgian kings, while not far away lies a vast burial ground dating back to the Iron Age. Now little more than a village ('a wretched village', says Baedeker disparagingly and unjustly), Mtzkhet stands at the confluence of the Aragva and Kura rivers a dozen miles to the north of Tbilisi. It clusters round the great cathedral church of *Sveti Tzkhoveli*, the Life-Giving Pillar, built on the site of King Mirian's miraculously constructed wooden church. In one of the aisles of the cathedral, rebuilt in the fifteenth century after the earlier building had been destroyed by Tamerlane's invading hordes, stands a tiny stone chapel ten or twelve feet high, which, it is said, faithfully reproduces the original building.

Here in Sveti Tzkhoveli, the kings of Georgia were crowned, and here they were buried, right down to George XII and last who, after making over his country to the Russians, died in Tbilisi in the year 1800. Like many churches in Georgia, Sveti Tzkhoveli is strongly fortified, being ringed around by a high, battlemented wall with towers and look-out points at intervals. Within the precincts they were getting in the hay and the pointed haystacks in the field below matched the cathedral's soaring central spire.

High up on the north wall of the cathedral is the carving of a single human hand holding a set-square. This commemorates the fate of Arsukidze, the Master Builder of the cathedral, who, despite his lowly birth, dared to vie, all too successfully, with his sovereign King George I, for the love of Shorena, the daughter of a neighbouring duke. Their love was discovered and the romance ended badly for both of them, Arsukidze's right hand being at once cut off and the fair Shorena immured in a convent.

To the Georgians Mtzkhet is a place of great sanctity and the services in the cathedral are well attended. Often, after the service, you will see members of the congregation going round the outside of the church, touching its walls as they go, as though to absorb some of its holiness through their fingertips, and often you will see beggars, who have nothing else to give, bringing bunches of wild flowers to lay on its floor-stones. Near by are the Church and Convent of Samtavro, in which is buried Mirian, the first Christian King of Georgia. Outside it on a bench sat the Mother Superior, a lady of immense dignity, taking the air in company with a majestically bearded, black-robed, high-hatted priest and a great, white, shaggy sheep-dog.

On a steep hill, high above Mtzkhet and offering, as it were an aerial view of it, is Dzhvari, the Church of the Cross, built fourteen centuries ago on the spot where, another two centuries before that, Nino or Nouni, the holy slave-woman from Cappadocia who converted the Georgians to Christianity, first set up the Cross and whence she is said to have looked down in sorrow and anger on the people of Mtzkhet, as they obstinately continued to worship at the shrines of the old pagan gods and goddesses. Above the south door is an exceptionally fine bas-relief of a pair of winged angels bearing the cross. The dome, like that of the seventh century church at Ateni Sion, rests on an octagonal faceted drum based in turn on a cruciform ground plan. Dzhvari was to be a prototype of church architecture in Transcaucasia.

Anyone who arrives at Mtzkhet in a robust frame of mind and with plenty of time to spare should look in at the local restaurant. This is massively built in the ancient Georgian style, and consists of a low stone dome, under which, in a cavernous room with a dark, smoky and highly convivial atmosphere, you will, with luck, drink the best wine and eat the finest *shashlik* in Georgia. In my own experience, all one needs to do is put one's nose round the corner of the door to be immediately greeted with welcoming yells and find oneself involved in a christening, a wedding or a wake and guest at a feast which may last for any number of hours.

This time, however, we had, or thought we had, a programme to keep to and so, leaving Mtzkhet behind us, we pressed on in the direction of Ananuri. We did, however, allow ourselves one detour. Branching off the high road at Zhingali, we turned up the valley of the Pshavskaya Aragvi into Khevsuretia, the land of the Khevsurs, who, claiming descent from the Crusaders, though nominally Christians, until recently worshipped St George as the God of War. The scenery was magnificent and the road, while it lasted, left nothing to be desired. But in the end we came to a sizeable unbridged river and when even Veronica, having bravely waded across it, declared it impassable for an ordinary light car, I decided that we had better turn back and continue our journey to Ananuri.

At Ananuri the true mountains begin, and at the junction of two valleys stands a magnificent fortress, looking out across the foothills to the plain beyond. From within its battlements rise a massive square watchtower and two ancient churches, their golden-yellow walls elaborately adorned with figures of lions and other creatures carved in relief and surrounded with arabesques. On the wall of the larger church is a striking relief of St Nino's cross of intertwined vine-stems, supported by two chained lions, while demons devour the grapes. Beneath the ramparts lies a secret hiding-place, whence reserve bodies of men-at-arms once sprang out to surprise the enemy. And in the church wall just behind the altar you can still see the spy-hole from which during a service the lookout man kept watch for the approach of a foe. In the Caucasus reminders of a heroic and blood-stained past are never far to seek.

It was at Ananuri that in the year 1727 Prince Bardsig, the Eristav of the Aragvi, while feasting with his kinsmen and friends, happened to glance out of the window and catch sight of what was clearly some great lady, riding along the valley in the direction of his castle, accompanied by her chaplain, her two falconers and a number of retainers. At this the Eristav called his guests to the window and one of them, with sharper eyes than the rest, at once recognized the traveller as the wife of Prince Chanche, the Eristav of Ksani, a neighbouring nobleman with whom Aragvi's relations were far from friendly. As she approached, they saw that the object of their curiosity was young and beautiful. They had dined well and it was all they needed to know. Mounting their horses and calling out their men-at-arms, they swooped down on the little party, chased away the chaplain, the falconers and the serving-men, and carried off the princess. An hour later her pink pantaloons were hoisted like a standard above the castle keep.

The princess did not return home immediately. When she did, without her pantaloons, her husband, the Eristav of Ksani, was not unnaturally incensed and swore a great oath to eradicate and exterminate the whole accursed brood of the Eristav of the Aragvi right down to the last man jack of them.

This was easier said than done. The Eristav of the Aragvi was no weakling. And so Prince Chanche sought allies. Though a Christian, he allied himself with the Mohammedan Lesghians and with their help seized the nearby fort of Khamchistsikhe. Thence he marched on Ananuri. When he came within view of the castle, the sight of his wife's pink pantaloons floating above the keep infuriated him still further. To his first oath he added another: to replace this symbol of shame with the head of the Eristav of Aragvi.

The siege was a long one, but with the help of the Lesghians the fortress was finally stormed, the garrison massacred to the last man, and the pink pantaloons taken down and replaced by the severed head of Prince Bardsig. For the Lesghians, too, as good Mohammedans, the occasion was a particularly happy one. Bursting into the two churches that stood within the fortifications, they completely sacked them both, taking the greatest pleasure in poking out with their daggers the eyes of the Christian saints and apostles depicted on the walls. As for the pink pantaloons, they have, it is said, been preserved through the generations in the family of the Eristav of Ksani, in much the same way as the MacLeods religiously preserve their Fairy Flag at Dunvegan.

After Ananuri the Military Highway, leaving behind the mellow

Georgian countryside, enters the mountains and really starts to climb. Having eaten our sandwiches and set the engine going with a sharp push backwards, we drove on up the valley of the Aragvi, between the green, thickly wooded hillsides, rather reminiscent of Perthshire, to Pasanauri, where we planned to stay the night. News of our arrival had not reached the little rest-house that has now been built there. (The self-driven foreigner is still a novelty.) But in the end a room was found for us.

Pasanauri is a pleasant enough village with the great hills rising steeply all around. It stands at the confluence of two rivers, the Black Aragvi and the White, and from it you can see how, where they meet, the two different-coloured streams remain distinct. Having two or three hours to spare before dark, we decided to spend them exploring the valley of the Black Aragvi by a track which, according to one of our maps would, with luck, have eventually brought us back to the Georgian Military Highway somewhere between Kobi and Kazbek. On reaching a point, however, from which we had a marvellous view of the big mountains and having no other immediate objective except dinner, we decided, with night coming on, to turn back to Pasanauri and its excellent outdoor restaurant, where we dined off highly spiced meatballs in a green arbour. The wooded hills above the road are full of bears and on previous visits there had always been a tame one in residence, for the customers to feed with sugar-lumps, but this time there was none.

Next day was market day and early that morning we walked down to where the peasants from the neighbouring valleys were beginning to assemble, bringing with them their beasts and farm produce. Then, having packed our bags, paid the bill and prodded the car into motion, we started on the long pull up towards the Krestovi Pass or Pass of the Cross.

As far as Mleti, we followed the valley of the White Aragvi. Here the road crosses the river and then begins to climb in a series of eighteen startling bends up the almost perpendicular rock walls of the valley to Gudauri. First the Red Mountains come into sight and next the Seven Brothers, both massive ranges of red volcanic rock; then all at once at Gudauri a magnificent mountain panorama opens out before you with Mount Gud on one side and Mount Krestovaya, the Mountain of the Cross on the other. From Gudauri the road winds its way along the edge

Sveti Tskhoveli, Mtzkhet

Dzhvari

Holy Beggar, Mtzkhet ▶

Samtavro, the Mother Superior and companion

Lute player

Sveti Tzkhoveli

Sveti Tzkhoveli, a church within a church

Dzhvari

Ananuri

◄ Khevsuretia, a sizeable unbridged river

Ananuri

◀ Ananuri, St Nino's Cross

Ananuri, the Castle Keep

The Georgian Military Highway ▶

Wayside shrine, Georgian Military Highway

The Valley of the Black Aragvi ▶

Across the Caucasus, hill sheep

The Georgian Military Highway, the top of the pass

Mount Gud ▶

The Georgian Military Highway

The Georgian Military Highway, a side valley

◄ The Mountain of the Cross

At the bottom of a valley, the Georgian Military Highway

Kazbek

The Georgian Military Highway ▶

The Georgian Military Highway

The Georgian Military Highway, across the watershed

of thousand-foot precipices to reach the summit of the Krestovi Pass, where Queen Tamara, it is said, first erected a gigantic cross.

Here the road flattened out and we were amongst pleasant Alpine meadows, where, at almost eight thousand feet, peasants with gigantic scythes and rakes were harvesting the hay, while far beneath us we could see the little villages nestling at the bottom of the valleys or clinging like swallows' nests to their sides. It was now that the sky-blue *Moskvich*, having reached the only flat stretch of road for miles, stalled irretrievably, resisting all attempts to push or pull it into action. My own temper was not at its best and Veronica, her patience tried beyond endurance both by me and the car, which she had bravely driven most of the way while I stopped endlessly to photograph, finally stamped off into the middle distance, announcing angrily that she was leaving us both for ever – only to come scampering hurriedly back two minutes later when the self-starter, responding, with a thoroughly unfair sense of timing, to a masculine hand, suddenly did what it was supposed to do and set the engine in motion, as if nothing had ever been the matter with it. After this it was downhill all the way.

Once across the watershed, the mountains become wilder and even more precipitous. High above us, hovering and swooping among the pinnacles of rock were a pair of splendid white-tailed eagles which with their enormous wing-span and brilliant golden-white plumage struck me as the most spectacular birds I had ever seen. From now onwards the road follows the valley of the Terek, which has its source near by. At Kobi, if you are lucky with the weather, you get your first sight of the snowy dome and black precipitous flanks of Mount Kazbek. An extinct volcano, first climbed by an Englishman a hundred years or so ago, it stands over 16,500 feet above sea-level and 11,000 feet above the valley at its foot in which is situated the little village of the same name. At the summit, they say, up in the eternal snows, is pitched the tent of Abraham and inside it, strangely enough, the Holy Manger from Bethlehem. But the only climber who ever went to look for it is reputed to have come down stark, staring mad.

In the middle of Kazbek village stands a handsome statue to the Prince of Kazbek, a noble native poet who lived here in the second half of the last century and ruled benevolently over the surrounding country. Across the valley, a green plain with patches of oats and rye and groups of little flat-roofed houses stretches away to the foot of more mountains which rise precipitously from it to a height of ten or twelve thousand feet.

Not far beyond Kazbek village we crossed the Terek and were soon following a narrow shelf cut out of the face of the rock above the rushing torrent. On both sides vertical precipices of granite five or six thousand feet high towered directly above us. This was the celebrated Darial Gorge – Dar-i-Alan – the Gate of the Alans, as the forefathers of the Ossetians, Persian in origin, were formerly called. High on a precipice above the river stand the ruins of an ancient fortress. Here, according to a legend made famous by Lermontov's poem *The Demon*, dwelt a queen called Tamara, or, some say, Daria, who caused her dis- carded lovers to be thrown headlong from it into the torrent below. Here, too, it is believed, were the famous Iberian gates which marked the furthest point of the Roman advance under Pompey, while a little further on are the ruins of an eighteenth- or early nineteenth-century Russian fortress and a great ninety-foot boulder weighing 1,500 tons and called appropriately enough after General Yermolov, who in his way was also something of a blockbuster. It was, it appears, deposited here in 1832 by an avalanche that blocked the road for two years.

On either side of the valley wooded limestone foothills rise sharply to a height of five or six thousand feet. Behind them, above the tree-line, bare rocky peaks stand out and in the side valleys you catch glimpses of villages, with their watchtowers and clusters of huts perched on the high ground against sudden attack. The population of the valley are by now mostly Ossetians of whom it is said that, before the advent of the Russians, it was their picturesque custom, when a man died, to cut off his widow's right ear and throw it into his grave, so that he might be better able to claim her in the next world. To the east, beyond the mountains, lies the territory of the Ingushes, who less than a century ago were still pagans, and beyond them dwell Shamyl's loyal supporters, the Mohammedan Chechens, a group of tribes quite dis- tinct from their neighbours in speech and racial origin.

14 *The Northern Caucasus*

Not far from Kazbek village we crossed the border between Southern and Northern Ossetia and at the same time the frontier between Georgia and Russia. As it issues from the gorge, the valley of the Terek widens out and for some miles its bed is strewn with enormous boulders. A few miles further on, the road finally emerges from the mountains into the open plain and soon we were in sight of the celebrated town of Vladikavkaz, the Ruler of the Caucasus, now endowed with the name of Ordzhonikidze, in honour of the former People's Commissar of that name, and for the past fifty years or so the capital of the North Ossetian Autonomous Republic.

I had not been to Ordzhonikidze for thirty-five years, and then only briefly and had forgotten, or never realized, what an attractive town it was. Since my last visit its name had again twice been changed: once (after Sergo Ordzhonikidze's disgrace and involuntary suicide) to Dzauikau and then (after his posthumous rehabilitation) back to Ordzhonikidze. Founded by Count Paul Potyomkin in 1783 as a jumping-off place for the conquest of the Caucasus, it retained its strategic significance during the years that followed right down to 1942, when the German thrust towards Transcaucasia was turned back only four miles from its outskirts.

Since my first visit Ordzhonikidze had increased enormously in size, but to this day the older part of the town has kept its air of a nineteenth-century garrison town cum fashionable resort. One of the smarter restaurants still bore, I noticed, the name of Garrison Diner. Down the middle of the main street, once the Alexandrovskaya, with its brightly painted stucco houses, runs a much-frequented promenade between a double avenue of lime trees. Near by are the Public Gardens with their ornamental boating lake and white stucco statues of nubile sports-girls, and beyond them the broad, fast-flowing stream of the River Terek, on the far bank of which stands a single, brightly tiled mosque, a late-nineteenth-century concession to the local Mohammedan population. From our 1914 Baedeker we knew that the hotel we were aiming for was in this immediate vicinity and we were able without too much difficulty to find it, and better still, get a room there, resisting all attempts to shunt us off to an unattractive-sounding new motel ten miles outside the town. Here, for once, our *Moskvich* did us a good turn by obligingly breaking down right in front of the hotel entrance and utterly refusing to move.

The charming, balconied hotel, a hundred years old or more, fully justified our expectations. Behind it was a pleasant garden restaurant where throughout our stay a private vine arbour was specially reserved for us. But we were not in search of privacy. On our very first night we quickly became aware that one of the party in the next arbour was playing an immense Ossetian bagpipe. This was a link between nations that could not possibly be overlooked and soon we were in the neighbouring arbour with the piper and his friends, all drinking endless toasts to friendship between Ossetia and Scotland. Later another party of Ossetians took over the dance-floor, where they insisted on dancing their own wild Ossetian reels until the management, amid loud protests, sternly and finally removed the band.

Our chief purpose in stopping off at Ordzhonikidze was to explore this part of Ossetia and, if possible, some of the neighbouring mountain valleys. Having had the *Moskvich* looked at by a knowledgeable garage-hand who diagnosed it without difficulty as 'capricious', we set off in a westerly direction along the road to Alagir until we reached the valley of the Fiagdon or Crazy River, where, pushing our way through the flocks and herds that thronged the road, we boldly turned south along the river valley in the general direction of Mount Kazbek.

We could not, as it turned out, have made a happier choice. Narrowing, the valley first led us through the Kurtatinski or Kurdish Gorge, a narrow gap in the mountains named, we were told, after some medieval Kurdish warrior in the service of the Mongols who was so impressed by the heroism of his Ossetian adversaries that, being unable to beat them, he decided to join them and, taking an Ossetian wife, settled in this very valley, where, or so it is said, a strong Kurdish strain still persists.

A little further on, not far from the mouth of the Gorge, on the bank of the Fiagdon River, we found a group of five carved and painted standing stones with another, single stone two or three yards away. These commemorate the sad fate, a century or more ago, of five brothers and their only sister. The brothers, it seems, had been hunting in the hills near by and had left their dinner cooking by the river in a pot. But, while they were away, a snake was careless enough to fall into the pot and was cooked with the dinner, so that, when they returned and ate it, they were poisoned. When they failed to come home that evening, their sister went out to search for them and in the end found them on the river bank, sprawled around the fire, stone-dead. At this she was so stricken with grief that, seizing the *kinjal* or dagger, which, like all good Ossetian girls, she always carried, she plunged it into her heart. The five brothers were buried together where they died, by the river. Two of them were twins and their stones are of the same size and stand side by side. As a woman, their sister was buried a few feet away and so her stone stands on its own.

Following the course of the river, we next came to a succession of ancient fortified Ossetian villages dating back to the days of the Mongol invasions. The first of these was Dzivgis. Our only warning of it was a lonely watchtower silhouetted against the sky six hundred feet above us. Then, rounding a bend in the road, we suddenly came on the village itself, clinging to the foot of the rocky hillside immediately above the rushing stream of the Fiagdon. From it the Ossetian inhabitants, every bit as wild and wiry-looking as in Shamyl's day, came flocking out to greet us, feed us with magnificent apples and show us round. In return we distributed to the children of these hardy highlanders boiled sweets and brightly coloured balloons, which greatly enhanced our popularity.

At first sight there had been no great change in the life of the Fiagdon Valley since the days of the Mongol invaders. The houses were built in the shape of towers: high watchtowers, from which to watch for the approach of an enemy; fighting-towers for warriors, with arrow-slits and loopholes from which to meet an attack; dwelling-towers into which animals, women and children and old people could be herded in case of danger; and towers for the dead, each with a narrow hole through which the family's corpses could be pushed until there was room for no more. Only the very poorest families, we were told, did not possess a tower for their own dead. In the last six or seven hundred years some of the towers have fallen down and been rebuilt and some have been extended and adapted. But the people who live here still lead a simple, pastoral existence with which they seem well content, and which, they proudly tell you, produces a phenomenal number of centenarians. Not far beyond Dzivgis we came to several more villages. In one, which lay among some orchards and green meadows by the banks of the Fiagdon and had a more peaceable look, many of the towers had been turned into ordinary farmhouses.

A little further on by the roadside, with the mountains all around, stands a memorial to those killed in the last war, which I found most moving: a statue of a horse, with empty saddle, its head down and the reins on its neck, for most of the dead were cavalrymen. On a bronze tablet were their names, perhaps two hundred individual names, but, as you will find on such memorials in any tribal society, whether it be in the Highlands of Scotland or in Montenegro, with only five or six different surnames between them.

High above us on the skyline we could now see our next objective, a village called Tsimitar. This stands splendidly perched on a kind of rocky promontory four or five hundred feet above the river, commanding the valley in both directions. Perhaps because of its relative remoteness and stronger strategic position, it is in a far better state of preservation than the other villages. Here watchtowers, fighting-towers and dwelling-towers are all clearly identifiable, standing out proudly against the skyline, while a group of half a dozen death-towers stand apart, a little further up the hill.

According to the local experts, the Alans, who held sway in these parts from the fifth to the ninth centuries of our era, buried their dead in underground vaults. From the ninth to the twelfth century the dead were buried in tombs which were half above ground and half below. And from the twelfth to the eighteenth century entirely above ground in death-towers like those at which we were looking.

But then, wandering over the hillside, we happened to look into a hole in the ground, which, on closer inspection, we found to contain two or three complete skeletons, some with scraps of skin and shreds of clothing or shrouds still on them. These left us wondering whether such remarkably new-looking remains could really date back to the ninth century A.D., as in theory they should have done, or whether they belonged to some more recent, but equally troubled period.

Tsimitar can no longer boast a great many contemporary inhabitants, but, firmly established in one of the dwelling-towers, we found two neat little girls and their father. Their mother, or possibly aunt, a cheerful character much given to shouting, came in later, with a merry yell, from picking mushrooms on the hillside. These, she planned to cook with sour cream and grated cheese, a piece of information which particularly incensed Veronica, all of whose carefully gathered mushrooms had been thrown away that morning by the hotel cook on the grounds that they were bound to be poisonous.

Looking out across the valley to the great hills on the other side, our new-found friends had contrived a wide veranda. Here they were entertaining various relations and passers-by from all around, including one sturdy, good-looking old lady in her seventies, who seemed to me to say that she was on her way to take some food and a bottle of wine to her sick grandmother, who lived in the next valley. There were also, for contrast, some teenagers, one of whom, pert and rather pretty, was being closely questioned by all present about her sex-life and marital prospects and clearly enjoying every moment of it.

Carrying on up the valley, now veiled in mist, we came, four or five miles further on, upon a single stone, erected to the memory of one of the local inhabitants. These, owing to the good air, the healthy life they lead and their large intake of yoghourt, are said to live to a very great age. 'To Giso Gigoevich Marzaganov', said this particular inscription, '1745–1913' – an old man by any standards, linking, as he did, my own life-span with that of my ancestor who fought at Culloden. Perhaps, we reflected, we had after all been right in understanding the old lady at Tsimitar to say that she was on her way to see her grandmother. Or could it have been her great-grandmother?

Next day, continuing our exploration of the North Ossetian foot-hills, we followed the course of another mountain stream, the Gizeldon or Red River, which, it appears, earned this name after a particularly hard-fought battle with the Mongols in which its stream ran red with the blood of all concerned. Not far away stands a monument put up at the point where, in 1942, some seven centuries later, the Germans were in their turn thrown back, once again with great slaughter on both sides.

Continuing up the valley of the Gizeldon, we now drove on up through a breathtaking beautiful gorge to which the snowy peaks of the Caucasus provide a highly dramatic backdrop, and then over a grassy shoulder into another valley, that of the Karmadon, where, on a hill-side, we came on a complete city of the dead, a settlement, if that is the word, of three or four dozen death-towers. Here there were no watchtowers, dwelling-towers or fighting-towers. For what need, we reflected, as we ate our cold Soviet sausage under a steady drizzle, could there be for any of these in a city of the dead?

The valley of the Gizeldon lies five or ten miles east of the Fiagdon. The map showed us that, running roughly parallel to the Fiagdon, a score of miles further west was the valley of another tributary of the Terek, the Ardon. This to me was of particular interest as being the starting point for the second of the two main routes across the Caucasus: the Ossetian Military Highway, of which we had already explored the southern half when we drove up the Rioni valley from Kutaisi. Refusing to be deterred by stories of landslides, crumbling verges and falling boulders, we accordingly now set out westwards, at first keeping the main range of the Caucasus on our left and then turning southwards off the main road at Alagir, a rather nondescript modern town with a large nineteenth-century Orthodox church in the middle of it.

Here a gap in the hills marked the mouth of the Ardon valley. At first the road followed the left bank of the Ardon, climbing slowly through a wide green valley full of orchards and villages with rocky hills on either side and the sunny, snow-covered peaks of the main range in the distance. From time to time side valleys brought in tributary streams. Above the road, opposite the entrance to one of these, a single carved memorial stone depicts, standing stiffly to attention, some long-forgotten local *dzhigit* or warrior who had presumably met his end near by.

Twenty miles or so from Alagir, near the little copper-mining village of Mizur, the Ardon, now a rushing mountain stream, is joined by the Sadon, another wild torrent rising among the high snow-capped peaks visible to the west of the road, which at this point crosses the river by an iron bridge. Here the Ardon valley narrows abruptly and from this point the river flows between steep hillsides covered with an agreeably mixed forest of pines and hardwoods.

Soon after crossing the bridge, we reached the ancient hamlet of Nuzal, reputed, rightly or wrongly, to be the cradle of the Ossetian race, and where, carved out of the sheer rock face above the river you can still see traces of medieval fortifications commanding the approaches to the village. In the village itself, after some inquiry, we found what we were looking for: a tiny Christian chapel, ten or twelve feet square, built of great, unhewn blocks of stone. Following a heated debate among the village elders, most of whom were strongly on our side, we eventually prevailed upon them to open it for us. It contained, we found on inspection, some really remarkable early medieval frescoes depicting the Virgin, St George mounted on a spirited horse and a figure believed to be David Soslan, the second (and better) husband of Queen Tamara of Georgia, himself an Ossetian prince, whose bones, or so the excavator believed, were found buried under the floor when it was opened up some thirty years ago. This chapel, with its frescoes and bones, is accepted by historians as evidence of the spread of Georgian (and Christian) influence in Ossetia in the eleventh and twelfth centuries.

From Nuzal the road starts to climb much more steeply in a series of alarming zigzags towards the Mamison Pass, and plentiful signs of landslides, crumbling verges and newly fallen boulders now began to justify the warnings lavished on us before our departure. Above us, as we approached the treeline, pines began to predominate on the thickly wooded slopes above us and above them we could now see in all their glory the snowy peaks beyond, while the glaciers appearing level with us in the neighbouring valleys showed us how high we had already climbed.

Near the village of Tsei, where we made our next stop, are the remains of some kind of shrine or place of sanctuary, said to date back to early Christian or pre-Christian times and still decorated with the horns of the innumerable beasts sacrificed there at one time or another and in one cause or another. According to legend, a castle which once stood here was built under the personal supervision of St George, from stones carried miraculously up the mountain by teams of oxen in waggons without human drivers.

A little way below the village we came to another shrine, dedicated this time to the late Generalissimo Stalin, whose portrait, in full dress with decorations has been painted in vivid hues on an enormous rock by the roadside. From the two young Ossetians to whom we had given a lift we at once received an earnest request to let them get down and be photographed in front of the great man's likeness. With this perfectly reasonable plea we readily complied and, peeling the finished product from Veronica's invaluable Polaroid camera, sent them on their way delighted.

By the time we reached Tsei, night was beginning to fall and, abandoning the idea of pressing on by a reputedly impassable road to the Mamison pass still two or three thousand feet above us, we reluctantly turned back to Ordzhonikidze.

Before returning to Moscow, we had one more assignment to fulfil. We wanted to visit the town of Pyatigorsk, partly because of its associations with the poet Lermontov, that strange, romantic figure, the lineal descendant, through the Learmonths of Ercildoune, of our own Thomas the Rhymer, and partly as a possible starting-point for further expeditions into the mountains.

Much to our surprise, the *Moskvich* started this time without a murmur and so, packing ourselves back into it, we set off westwards and northwards, skirting, as we went, along the northern foothills of the Caucasus. Some forty miles west of Ordzhonikidze we came to the River Terek, encountering it this time at the point where, finally emerging from the foothills, it starts on the last stage of its long journey to the Caspian Sea. Here, not far from the road and looking rather like a factory-chimney, stands the lonely Minaret of Tartartub, which for centuries has marked the famous ford across the Terek, (now replaced by a solid iron bridge), where in 1395 Tamerlane defeated Toktamish; where in 1785 Sheikh Mansur was beaten by Count Potyomkin; and where in 1846 Shamyl for once allowed himself to be outmanœuvred by General Freitag.

Passing through a village a little further on and hearing the insistent note of a horn, I saw, looking in the driving mirror, that we were being pursued by a police-car. This was it. We had been too lucky for too long. Now we were in trouble, though why, I could not imagine. With sinking heart, I pulled obediently into the side of the road, only to be briskly saluted by an incredibly smart local village policeman and handed a message to say (surprise, surprise) that Veronica had left her new mackintosh behind at Ordzhonikidze and that it was being sent after her by train.

We reached Pyatigorsk in darkness and in a downpour of rain. The journey, like all journeys, had taken longer than we expected, we were lost, and Veronica in a moment of impetuosity had managed to get the *Moskvich* inextricably jammed athwart some tramlines, set on a collision course with an oncoming tram, a situation from which it was only rescued by the combined exertions of the entire local police force. All this was rather hard on the nervous system and we were accordingly delighted, on finally making our way to the Hotel Mashuk, to find that we were expected and, further, that it was undoubtedly one of the best hotels in the Soviet Union, the management being friendly and co-operative and our room with its spacious balcony and shining bathroom leaving, by any standards, nothing to be desired. A perusal of our 1914 Baedeker seemed to show that this was the old Bristol, while a plaque on the wall indicated that some discerning Bolshevik leaders had very sensibly made it their headquarters during the Civil War. The news that a new Intourist skyscraper, with so many hundreds, if not thousands, of beds, was under construction did not in any way alter our resolution to return to the Mashuk on our next visit and if possible to Room 208.

When we woke up, the sun was shining and we set out to explore the town. In Russian Pyatigorsk means Five Hills, and the hills in question, volcanic in origin and known as *Beshtau*, spring abruptly from the plain, a sixth, Mount Mashuk, rising immediately behind the town to the north-east. Far away to the south above the mists, the main range of the Caucasus was now visible with the great snow-capped peak of Elbruz towering above all the rest and, unless I am much mistaken, above every other mountain in Europe, always assuming, that is, that, geographically, Elbruz is in Europe.

Pyatigorsk is first and foremost a watering-place and the first thing we did was to take the waters. These are of varying strengths and consistencies and flow freely from a series of different hot springs in a number of different buildings. Our hotel looked out directly on the pleasant public gardens in which many of them were situated and, strolling through these before breakfast, we found a number of other seekers after health doing the same, all with their own little drinking cups. Most, I noticed, drank only from one of the springs, but I drank from them all one after the other, with the happiest possible results. I also took, closely supervised at every stage of the proceedings by a motherly figure in a white apron, a most enjoyable hot mineral bath in the old bath-house, a fine, early nineteenth-century building in the classical style; 'Keep your chest *out of* the water, Comrade,' she kept saying, on finding that I had once again slid luxuriously beneath the surface.

From the public gardens a steep, tree-lined path leads up to the Elizabeth Gallery, the colonnade containing the Elizabeth Spring. On a rock seven or eight hundred feet higher stands a kind of belvedere, in which, as in Lermontov's day, there is an Aeolian Harp. This was presumably once played in a haphazard fashion by the wind blowing as it listed, but now, thanks to various built-in electrical and mechanical aids, it emits a continuous, not unmusical, humming sound. One is also shown various grottos and caves, some containing more hot mineral springs and others associated in one way or another with Lermontov, who, it appears, enjoyed giving champagne parties in them.

Lermontov, you very soon find, is the presiding genius of Pyatigorsk under this regime as he was under the last. There is a Lermontov Statue, a Lermontov Street and Square, Lermontov Baths, a Lermontov Gallery and Museum and finally a Lermontov Monument at the spot where the poet met his altogether unnecessary end in a duel on the lower slopes of Mount Mashuk. Indeed one is tempted to wonder what Lermontov himself, an off-beat character if ever there was one and never a very whole-hearted supporter of any government or regime, would make of it all, were he to come back today.

Strongly evocative of Lermontov and his times are the former Assembly and Dining Rooms in the middle of the town with their fine classical portico. This was where he spent much of his time when he was in Pyatigorsk and was the scene of the famous ball described in *A Hero of Our Time*. Indeed the whole of the older part of the town, and particularly the public gardens with their tree-lined promenades and grottos and pump-rooms and even the little Belvedere with its Aeolian Harp, all recall Lermontov both as a man and as a writer, as, for that matter, do the jagged mountains on the skyline, amongst which he fought and of which he wrote.

But most evocative of all is a little thatched, white-washed cottage where the poet once lived and which has remained unchanged to this day. 'Yesterday', he wrote in *Princess Mary*, 'I arrived in Pyatigorsk and rented quarters in the outskirts at the foot of Mashuk; this is the highest part of the town, so high that the clouds will reach down to my roof during thunderstorms. When I opened the window at five o'clock this morning the fragrance of the flowers growing in the modest little front garden flooded my room. The flower-laden branches of the cherry trees peep into my windows, and now and then the wind strews my writing desk with the white petals. I have a marvellous view on three sides. Five-peaked Beshtau looms blue in the west like "the last cloud of a dispersed storm"; in the north rises Mashuk like a shaggy Persian cap concealing this part of the horizon. To the east the view is gayer: down below the clean new town spreads colourfully before me, the medicinal fountains babble and so do the multilingual crowds, farther in the distance the massive amphitheatre of mountains grows ever bluer and mistier, while on the fringe of the horizon stretches the silvery chain of snow-capped peaks beginning with Kazbek and ending with twin-peaked Elbruz ... It is a joy to live in a country like this! A feeling of elation flows in all my veins. The air is pure and fresh like the kiss of a child, the sun is bright and the sky blue – what more could one desire? What place is there left for passions, yearnings and regrets? But it's time to go. I shall walk down to Elizabeth Spring where they say the spa society congregates in the mornings.'

One of the things we had hoped to do while we were in Imeretia was to take a light aircraft from Kutaisi to Mestia, the principal town of Svanetia, high up on the southern slopes of the Caucasus beneath Mount Elbruz. But day after day low cloud on the mountains kept the little plane grounded and in the end we had to abandon the idea. What I now had in mind was to approach Mount Elbruz from the other side. Our sky-blue *Moskvich* had finally packed it in and this time we were lucky enough to secure the use of a powerful, plum-coloured *Volga*. Setting out from Pyatigorsk in this magnificent machine, we first retraced our steps in the direction of Ordzhonikidze as far as the village of Baksan, where the main road crosses the Baksan River, a tributary of the Terek, and then turned off south-westwards along the Baksan Valley in the direction of Elbruz.

We were now in Kabarda, the country of those wild Kabardan tribesmen whose help Shamyl sought so hard to enlist against the Russians in 1846. But the people we encountered along the way looked very much like any other Soviet citizens and the villages, to look at, were very much like Russian villages. The mountains, on the other hand, became higher and wilder at every turn of the road, until, passing through the little township of Elbruz, we found ourselves at the very foot of the Elbruz itself. With the help of a chairlift, we were now hoisted up to one of the starting-points for the ascent of Elbruz, whose snowy bulk loomed immediately above us. But what interested me was not so much Elbruz as a little mountain trail which I discovered leading off in the opposite direction. This, they said, led to Svanetia, only a long day's walk away through the mountains – something, I thought, to look forward to another time.

Returning to Pyatigorsk a year or two later, we were to witness another – to us entirely new – aspect of local life. On once more installing ourselves in Room 208 which had most thoughtfully been reserved for us, we found the Hotel Mashuk filled this time to bursting point with horsy-looking foreigners, male and female: French, Dutch, Italians, West Germans and so on, all ordering large quantities of champagne and generally making their presence felt. They provided, it seemed to me, an interesting change from the delegations of earnest seekers after Socialist truth who are usually to be found in the dining-rooms of Soviet provincial hotels, sucking down sour milk and canned fruit and drinking fizzy lemonade on their way to see State crêches and ball-bearing factories.

What, we wondered, could all these obvious horse-copers have come for? It was then that I remembered *Konni Zavod 2*, in other words Horse Factory Number Two, the second of the great State-owned stud farms, the first of which I had once visited outside Moscow and of which I had always known another to exist somewhere near Pyatigorsk. And, sure enough, on further inquiry, I was told that next morning was the opening day of the big annual sale of two- and three-year-olds from the famous stud.

Next morning at nine we were there, bright and early, by the ringside, eagerly scanning the handsome glossy catalogue we had been given but without, we regretfully noticed, the free champagne and sturgeon sandwiches which were lavished on likely buyers. From the conditions set out in the catalogue, we concluded that these must have brought with them, in ready cash, immense sums of U.S. dollars to be paid down as a deposit immediately on purchase of anything they bought. Little wonder, then, that they were so popular.

The sale lasted most of the day. It was a fine sunny morning and the scene by the ringside was worthy of Newmarket, the colts and fillies, mostly of high quality, being trotted round the ring in style by manifestly dedicated stud-grooms, sweating profusely under the hot sun as they tried to control their sometimes unruly charges. In the intervals we had a look round the stables, which were beautifully kept, and talked to the grooms who obviously knew their job thoroughly and showed tremendous pride in the horses that were being put up for sale. First came the pure-bred Arab colts and fillies. Then Akhal-Tekke Turkoman horses from across the Caspian in Central Asia – the breed that

Tsimitar

Tsimitar

The Fiagdon Valley

Tsimitar, a cheerful character

Tsimitar, the two neat little girls

The Crazy River

... a bottle of wine for her sick grandmother

The Fiagdon Valley, the War Memorial

Karmadon Valley, father

Tsimitar, the pert and rather pretty teenager

. . . and son

Gizeldon, herdsman

The foothills of the Caucasus

Five brothers and their only sister

The Karmadon Valley, the City of the Dead

◄ The Karmadon Valley, the City of the Dead

The Ardon Valley

The Ardon Valley,
a single memorial stone

The Ardon Valley

Generalissimo Stalin ▶

On the Ossetian Military Highway

Сталин для нас был величайшим
авторитетом
Г. Жуков

Худ. Дзабисов

Beshtau

◀ The Ardon Valley

The Minaret of Tatartub

Veronica

A Kuban Cossack

Approaching Mount Elbruz

A Highlander

A latter-day Circassian

Pyatigorsk, Horse factory Number Two. Trotting round the ring

Pyatigorsk, the bidding became brisker

Pyatigorsk, the Assembly Rooms

made the Turkomans such formidable desert-raiders right up to the end of the nineteenth century and were descended, or so we were told, from the horses of Jenghiz Khan and even from Bucephalus, the horse of Alexander the Great. Then Terek horses, for so long the mounts of the Terek Cossacks. And, finally, horses of the famous Kabardan breed (some cross-bred with English thoroughbreds) which had carried the fierce Kabardans into battle in the days of Shamyl.

After a relatively slow start, the bidding, to the patter and banter of a clearly most experienced auctioneer, became much brisker. Two or three West Germans made most of the running, one of them, after a number of other successes, paying the top price of around $8,500. All in all, at the end of the day, with over two hundred horses sold at an average price of $4–5,000 each, Horse Factory Number Two must have netted the best part of a million dollars, a useful contribution, one felt, to the Soviet economy and earned, when you come to think of it, by impeccably Marxist methods.

During this, our second visit to Pyatigorsk, though we did not, as I had hoped, reach Svanetia, we did something else I had always wanted to do, namely, explore the valley of the Teberda. This lies in the Karachayevo–Cherkesskaya Autonomous Region, in other words, Circassia, the territory of those famous Circassians whose warriors gave the Russians so much trouble in the nineteenth century and whose fair maidens were so sought after by successive Sultans to be the stars of their Seraglio.

Setting out from Pyatigorsk, we first drove fifty miles or so due west to Cherkessk and then thirty miles due south to Karachayevsk, thus visiting in rapid succession the two rather uninteresting towns after which the region is called. From Cherkessk to Karachayevsk, we had been following the course of the Kuban, the river which gives its name (or possibly vice-versa) to the Kuban Steppe, the vast rolling plain made famous by the Kuban Cossacks who have roamed over it for the past five centuries or more and which we had now been crossing for the best part of a hundred miles. By the time we reached Karachayevsk (which we did, awash to the axles, in a cataclysmic cloudburst), we were back once more in the foothills of the Caucasus. Following a southwesterly course, we now drove on up the valley of the Teberda River which joins the Kuban at Karachayevsk. By this time the rain had stopped, the clouds were lifting and, as we travelled further up the valley, we began to catch glimpses of wooded hills on either side of us, at first some way back from the road and then, as we went further, closing in steeply on either side. On our way we passed through four straggling villages named, a trifle unimaginatively, New Teberda, Lower Teberda, Upper Teberda and Teberda Proper. Of greater interest were two little ruined Christian churches perched high on the hills above the road and dating back, or so we were told, to the ninth and tenth centuries respectively. These, it seems, were founded by missionaries who reached Circassia, not from Georgia, but from Byzantium, presumably by way of the Black Sea, now not very distant.

At Teberda Proper, we found clearer skies and the first signs of sun. Here the road starts to climb in earnest and the valley narrows abruptly. The river now flowed through a deep canyon several hundred feet below us. To right and left, the steep sides of the valley were covered with a great variety of trees, both hardwoods and softwoods: oak, hazel, poplar, Caucasian elm and a (to me unknown) conifer seventy or eighty feet high and reminiscent of the giant red-woods I had recently seen in California. By the side of the road (when there was a side to the road and not just a precipice) grew shrubs and flowers familiar to us from gardens at home: deutzia, viburnum, cotoneaster, mock orange, azalea, salvia and iris, as well as a profusion of exotic wild flowers.

We were just wondering what there was to stop us from motoring merrily on into the Abkhazian Autonomous Republic, according to the map no more than twenty miles or so further on across the border in Georgia, when, rounding a sudden corner, we got our answer. Towering above us and above the surrounding circle of wooded hills, a tremendous mountain barrier, its snowy peaks glittering in the distant sunlight, rose majestically from the mists and vapours of the valley, conjuring up visions of crampons and ice-axes and climbers dangling precariously over crevasses. Another five or six miles brought us to the Dombai Clearing, where the valley opened right out, offering us on every side a vast panorama of impressive peaks. As we unpacked our picnic of cheese, cold sausage and hard-boiled eggs and put a bottle of beer to cool in the icy torrent of the Teberda, we decided that the rest of the journey was something that might be undertaken on our next visit to the Caucasus, but then only after plenty of preparation.

15 *Armenia*

From Tbilisi, if that is the way you choose to go, the train takes you through the mountains in the night to Erivan, now capital of the Soviet Socialist Republic of Armenia. Though near neighbours and connected by a history and culture which have overlapped and intermingled through the centuries, the Georgians and Armenians possess very different national characters. The Georgians are gay, romantic, heroic extroverts, who like fighting and drinking and dancing and making love and dressing up and showing off and who are swayed by sudden violent emotions, sharing with the Celts what W. E. D. Allen (who knew us both) has called an 'aesthetic irresponsibility' which is one of the secrets of their charm. The Armenians, on the other hand, are dour and dogged, clear thinkers, hard workers, hard fighters and hard bargainers, whose proud boast it is that, while it takes three Greeks to get the better of a Jew, it takes three Jews to get the better of an Armenian. As some Frenchman once said, they have, through the centuries, had *'juste le temps de s'enrichir entre deux massacres'*. Or, as another shrewd observer put it, 'their martyrs are as characteristic as their merchants'.

Anyone who spends any length of time in Armenia cannot fail to be struck by the strength and depth of feeling of the Armenians, especially where their own country and nation are concerned. It is this intensity of feeling, one soon realizes, that has enabled them, like the Jews, whom in some respects they resemble, to survive their diaspora and to retain their national identity, not only, despite successive foreign invasions, in Armenia itself, but in any other country in the world where a larger or smaller number of Armenians are gathered together.

There are, I was told, over three million Armenians in the Soviet Union (of whom a couple of million live in Soviet Armenia) and a million and a half in the rest of the world. To the Armenians in Armenia, their fellow Armenians throughout the world are deeply important, just as these, for their part, are deeply concerned to maintain their ancient, hereditary links with their fatherland. In Erivan every hotel seems full of Armenians from overseas, from America, from Syria and the Lebanon, from India and France and Manchester and Iran, come back to the home of their fathers to see it for themselves and soak themselves in its strongly Armenian atmosphere. Of this togetherness I could have had no better illustration than sitting in Erivan at a display of Armenian national dances next to an elegant, blue-rinsed, Armenian matron from New York City and observing her complete surrender to the music and rhythms of a country she had never before visited but which she felt at once was hers. Or meeting the other day in a Hertfordshire lane an olive-skinned young farm labourer, British-born of Armenian parents, whose eyes suddenly lit up when he heard that I had just come back from an Armenia which neither he nor his parents had ever seen.

These links with the outside world distinguish Soviet Armenia from the other republics of the Union and give it a character all of its own. Just how close and continuous they are became clear in the course of half an hour spent at Holy Etchmiadzin in the company of the Katholikos, Vasgen I, the Head of the Armenian Church throughout the world, a most impressive man of God, who had come to the Soviet Union from his native Romania and whose American-Armenian chaplain repeatedly interrupted our audience to put through long-distance calls from Armenians all over the world.

One is immediately struck, too, by the manifest intelligence and quick-wittedness of the Armenians. Nothing escapes them. They have read one's thoughts almost before they have had time to take shape. Not inappropriately it is to a mythical 'Radio Armenia' that other Soviet citizens invariably attribute any really witty and with-it *bons mots* or poor-taste jokes about the regime that happen to be going the rounds at any given time. I know how dangerously unfashionable it is nowadays to suggest that any given race or nation possesses qualities or characteristics which others do not. But I just cannot help feeling whenever I am in Armenia that the Armenians (as they themselves keep telling you) are much, much cleverer and quicker than most other people.

Whether you are talking to the aged Marshal Bagramian, to a parish priest, to the extremely alert young First Secretary of the Armenian Communist Party, to the head-waiter or to the clerk behind the reception desk in your hotel, you are struck again and again by that same penetrating, concentrated intelligence, gleaming in their dark eyes and reflected in the speed of their reactions.

As for their business sense, this has for several thousand years been famous throughout the world. Under Communism the available opportunities are necessarily limited, but even so, the fact is that every business transaction is conducted with the innate keenness of a Gulbenkian and that overt signs of business acumen and efficiency are everywhere. How revealing, for example, that in Armenia there are more private cars per head of the population than in any other Soviet republic.

Stone, perhaps naturally, plays and has always played a big part in the life of the Armenian people. Though the valleys are exuberantly fertile, much of their country is barren, rocky and boulder-strewn. Indeed they tell the same story of Armenia that the Dalmatians tell of Dalmatia: that when God had finished making the world, he dumped the surplus stones in Armenia. Stone, too, for the most part reddish volcanic tufa, has always been their favourite medium, their chosen means of expression. Not only the innumerable splendid ancient stone churches which are the pride of Armenia bear witness to this, but the secular and domestic buildings of today: theatres, houses, schools, factories, libraries, government buildings and hotels are all built of stone and decorated with the same beautiful designs which distinguished the buildings of an earlier age. And this was equally true when I first visited Erivan almost forty years ago. Many of its citizens were then still living in hovels, but hovels built of stone. Even the statues of Armenian national heroes which adorn the parks and public squares have a lapidary vigour which such monuments normally lack. Hewing stone, carving stone, building in stone, these are all Armenian trades, trades that well befit a people so tough, craggy and enduring, who possess, like the glittering black obsidian chips we found by the roadside on our way to Lake Sevan, an edge and a brilliance all of their own.

Earlier Armenian monuments and buildings bear witness to a considerable degree of sophistication. But without doubt the architectural talents of the Armenians found their highest form of expression in the magnificent monasteries and churches of the early Christian era. From the pagan classical temples of the Hellenistic period was developed the plain, barn-like, domeless vaulted basilica, similar to those found in Georgia, throughout Asia Minor and elsewhere in the Near East. The basilica was not, however, a specifically Armenian or Georgian form of architecture, and by the sixth and seventh centuries the Armenians, like the Georgians, had turned their attention to the problem of setting a central dome on a vaulted roof. This they did at first by building an 'apse-buttressed' or 'niche-buttressed' square, cruciform within and resting on four axial buttresses, on which the dome, supported by corner squinches and covering the entire central space, was then superimposed. All this, it may be observed, being carefully constructed by skilled Armenian master-masons in good Armenian stone and not, as elsewhere in the Middle East, from crumbling mud-bricks. The cruciform church with a centrally placed dome thus became, as it were, the archetypal form of both Armenian and Georgian church architecture, the two most celebrated examples being Dzhvari, the Church of the Cross outside Mtzkhet in Georgia, and the Church of St Hripsime at Etchmiadzin in Armenia.

Needing more space, the Armenians next introduced four free-standing piers to support the central dome, thus making it possible to increase the size of the body of the Church, while, later still, to give more height, barrel vaults were inserted between the base of the dome and the supporting buttresses. Later, having mastered the basic problem of the central dome, the Armenians tried numerous variations on their original theme, building, for example, hexagonal and octagonal in place of cruciform churches or, alternatively, extending the four ends of the cross, so as to produce the effect of two intersecting basilicas with the central dome placed at the intersection. Among the best examples of the latter style of architecture are the principal monastery churches at Sanahin and Akhpat in the mountains of Northern Armenia.

Mainly for strategic reasons the churches and monasteries of Armenia were for the most part sited high up in the mountains or at the head of valleys in readily defensible positions safely out of the way of the main invasion routes. This and the solidity of their construction has meant that large numbers of them are to this day in an admirable state of preservation and also that usually they are splendidly situated against magnificent natural surroundings. To reach them, however, involves in the first place much careful research into their exact locations and then, once permission has been obtained, a voyage of exploration into the unknown, usually offering, it must be said, a lavish return for the effort expended.

For most travellers to Armenia their starting point will of necessity be the capital, Erivan. This is situated at some three or four thousand feet above sea-level in the valley of the Araxes at what historically was once the centre of an Armenia now divided in half by the Soviet border with Turkey. Erivan, they say, was founded by Noah. From it you look across the Turkish frontier to the vast mass of Mount Ararat, where the Ark came to rest after the flood. *'Erivan!'* cried the Patriarch, looking out of the porthole, 'It has shown itself!' and so gave the city its name. Noah's next move, as we know from Genesis IX, was to plant some vines and make (and drink) some wine, thereby starting a tradition which has continued in Armenia to the present day, the wine produced there now being excellent and the brandy even more famous. A hundred miles or so from Erivan, on the Persian frontier, beside the railway line, is the dusty little town of Nakhichevan, or Noahville, where Noah himself, it is said, lies buried in a disused churchyard.

Twenty years had passed between my first and second visits to Erivan, but even so I was not prepared for the remarkable transformation that had taken place there. Hardly anything was left of the old town of roughly built, flat-roofed eastern houses that I remembered. Their place has been taken by an entirely new city of avenues and piazzas laid out in the grandest possible manner and now spreadeagling far beyond the former city limits in vast new suburbs and boulevards, to house a population of more than half a million people, nearly a third of the whole population of Soviet Armenia. Over it all hangs the massive bulk of Ararat, twenty miles or so away to the south, in Turkey.

Like the Georgians, and no less successfully, the Armenians have adapted their country's traditional style of architecture to modern uses, and you can recognize in the Government buildings of present-day Erivan the same designs and motifs, executed in the same reddish-yellow tufa, that you find in Armenian churches and monasteries of the early Middle Ages. One particularly striking new building, the work of a young architect of twenty-four, is the great market which has been built near the site of the former bazaar. Here, but on a larger scale and marked, if anything, by a greater intensity of feeling, one witnesses the same transactions between producer and consumer as in the peasant markets of Tbilisi. The Armenian is nothing if not businesslike.

But, equally, no one is more conscious than the Armenians of their tremendous past. 'The crest of the old Kings of Armenia,' said an

Armenian acquaintance proudly, as we passed an immense heraldic eagle adorning some recently erected monument or other. 'David of Sassoon,' he added a few minutes later, explaining a muscular giant manfully wrestling with a monster outside a fine new block of flats, while round the corner we found an equestrian statue of the same mythical hero prancing no less energetically in front of the railway station. In the National Library, the Matenadaran, you will be shown an unrivalled collection of ancient Armenian books and manuscripts and illuminations stretching back through the centuries. Not far away, the Kok Jami, a handsome, blue-and-yellow tiled mosque and religious college built in the eighteenth century by Nadir Shah, recalls that barely 150 years ago Erivan was still a Persian city. But by now it is almost the only trace that remains of the Persian occupation.

Without wishing to be unduly pedantic, it seems probable that what Noah really said on emerging from the Ark was not 'Erivan!' but 'Erebuni!' This, at any rate, is the name of the ancient walled stronghold perched on a hill in the northern suburbs of Erivan, which is all that is left of the original capital of Urartu and is believed to have given the present city its name. On the other hand, according to a contemporary cuneiform inscription on a solid-looking block of stone near the entrance, Erebuni, or at any rate its citadel, was founded in the year 782 B.C., during the reign of King Argistis, son of Memnon, quite a long time, presumably, after the Flood. (In 1968, incidentally, the people of Erivan proudly celebrated the 2,750th anniversary of the foundation of their city.)

Urartu, the Kingdom over which Argistis reigned, centred, as Armenia did later, round Ararat, from which it derived its name of Urararatu, shortened to Urartu. Mention of Urartu, which, like its rival Assyria, was one of the most powerful states in the Middle East, first occurs in an Assyrian inscription of the thirteenth century B.C. Like Assyria, it seems to have survived until the sixth century B.C. when both countries lost out to a powerful coalition of the Medes and Chaldaeans. It is thus that, with the eclipse of Urartu, its successor-state, Armenia, appears on the scene, as a satrapy, in the first place, of Achaemenidian Persia.

Erebuni, quite clearly, occupied a position of considerable strategic importance and almost certainly continued in use as a fortress long after the eclipse of Urartu. Excavations began there twenty-five years ago.

To the practised eye of the archaeologist (though not to mine) its crumbling ruins clearly reveal a variety of temples, barracks, palaces, colonnades, courtyards, storage-chambers and assembly rooms, which the uninitiated must take on trust, while from a few fragments of wall-paintings whole frescoes have been pieced together. A number of fine ornamental shields, helmets, drinking-cups and other artefacts found in the ruins bear, to the unpractised eye, a certain resemblance to the Persian or Assyrian art of the period. But, for the casual dilettante this is clearly dangerous ground on which to venture. I am not in general a great amateur of such ancient remains, but I enjoyed my visit to the fortress-city of Erebuni and the prospect which on clear days it offers across the plain to the greater and lesser peaks of Ararat.

Something else which helps one to understand the Armenian point of view and frame of mind is the monument which has been erected outside Erivan to the hundreds of thousands of Armenian men, women and children who were massacred by the Turks in 1895 and 1915. Here, on a hill overlooking the city, a flame, sheltered and surrounded by protecting walls, burns perpetually to their memory, while beside it a soaring obelisk points upwards to the sky. The Armenians have long memories and this, one feels, is a memory which it will take centuries to obliterate.

I have always been interested in monuments and, revisiting Erivan, three or four years after Khrushchev's famous de-Stalinization speech of February 1956, I was intrigued to find that, while everywhere else the effigies of the great man had vanished, the colossal bronze statue of Stalin, perhaps a hundred feet high, which dominated the whole city from a strategically-placed piazza looking across to Mount Ararat, was still *in situ*. Clearly it would not be as easy to get rid of as the ordinary run of statues and busts. Nor, once disposed of, would it be particularly easy to replace. How, I wondered, would the problem be solved?

On my next visit to Erivan I got the answer. Of the late, great Dictator, there was no longer a trace. Dynamite, clearly, and the melting pot had done their work. And now, in his place there stood a fresh bronze colossus representing, this time, Mother Armenia, an allegorical concept likely to survive any foreseeable political or ideological change of emphasis or line and made, one presumed, from the metal so conveniently provided by its predecessor. Once again

I was left full of admiration for the flexibility and down-to-earth common sense of the Armenians.

But I had not come to Armenia solely to follow the vagaries of Soviet monumental statuary. A dozen miles outside Erivan, enclosed within a massive wall is the monastery of Etchmiadzin, or Holy Etchmiadzin, as it is usually known, where the Katholikos of Armenia has his See in a Cathedral originally built in 309 by St Gregory The Illuminator, at a time when, as you are constantly reminded, Rome was still a pagan city, but which has since been heavily restored and rebuilt.

In a crypt underneath the Cathedral we were shown the remains of the Temple of Venus, on top of which the original Christian church was built. Also the well into which in the year 303, when Rome was still a pagan city, the good St Gregory pushed the local pagan gods and sealed them off with a marble slab. The priest who showed it to us spoke, we were glad to find, with almost equal affection of the late Mr Nubar Gulbenkian who had presented his church with a fine new Hammond organ.

Near by are the Churches of St Hripsime and St Gayane, both still in use. The former was built in the seventh century to commemorate the martyrdom of Hripsime, a beautiful Christian maiden, who with her nurse Gayane had fled from Rome to escape persecution at the hands of the Emperor Diocletian, only to run into worse trouble in Armenia. Struck at first sight by her quite exceptional beauty, King Trdat III decided to make her his and sent his palace guard to seize her and bring her in. Having more or less successfully repelled the royal advances, Hripsime managed to escape, but was brought back to the palace and tortured to death together with Gayane (in whose honour another church was built nearby).

For this and other misdemeanours Trdat and his entourage were very properly turned by the Almighty into a herd of swine and not allowed to resume human shape until Trdat, as recounted above, had released his cousin Gregory from the snake-pit and agreed, presumably by a series of meaningful grunts, to be, with his court, converted to Christianity. The tale of Trdat's conversion, with numerous variations, is to this day greatly cherished by the Armenians and, as Professor Marshall Lang so rightly observes, 'its fabulous details are not lightly to be called in question, even by historians of a sceptical turn of mind.'

The church of St Hripsime, built in 618 on the site of an earlier *martyrion* or martyr's shrine and never since rebuilt or restored, is one of the most perfect examples of early Armenian Christian architecture. Cruciform, with its lofty central dome resting solidly on four apses and four supporting corner niches, its appearance from the outside is solid and simple to the point of austerity, while within it is surprisingly light and harmonious. It served, one is told, as a prototype for a number of churches of this period. Struck by its resemblance to the monastery of Dzhvari in Georgia, I remarked on this to an Armenian friend, only to be told that Dzhvari had almost certainly been built by the same Armenian architect who built St Hripsime. An interesting and possibly valid theory, but one which I should hesitate to try out in Georgia.

A few hundred yards from St Hripsime and similar to it in style is the church of St Gayane, built some ten or twelve years later, also on the site of an early *martyrion*. Though considerably rebuilt, it is full of interest. An arched portico, added to the front of the church in the seventeenth century and containing the tombs of some high Armenian ecclesiastics, though perhaps detracting from its pristine purity of style, gives it a charm all of its own.

Immediately in front of this was a rough-hewn oblong stone, two or three feet square and perhaps four feet long, with a handful of salt lying on top of it. When I asked the priest what this was for, he replied that on feast-days during the service a lamb was led seven times round the stone. After which its throat was cut, a fire lit and its roasted flesh distributed to the congregation. This, the priest said, was in accordance with ancient tradition. But whether an ancient Christian tradition, or some yet more ancient pagan tradition, or both, one was left wondering.

At the far end of the little graveyard belonging to the church we found the tombstone of Sir John Macdonald, British Envoy to the Court of Fath Ali Shah, who died in Persia in 1830 and was brought thence to Etchmiadzin to receive a Christian burial. Originally buried within the Cathedral precincts, he, or at any rate his tombstone, was moved to its present location some thirty or forty years ago. It was Sir John, it will be recalled, who acted as go-between in the Russian–Persian peace negotiations in 1828 and helped to bring about the peace of Turkmenchai. For this he was decorated, it appears, by both the Russians and the Persians, but lived only two more years to enjoy the fame and general goodwill his peacemaking had brought him.

A mile or two outside Etchmiadzin, looking across a vista of green vineyards to the snow-capped peaks of Ararat are the ruins of Svartnots. These are all that is left of a gigantic, three-storeyed, Christian cathedral, a hundred and fifty feet high, built (as one learns from a contemporary Greek inscription on one of the stones) by the Katholikos Narses in about 643, at the time of the first Arab raids, and destroyed some three hundred years later by an earthquake or, according to other accounts, a Saracen raid. They show it to have been circular in form, rising in three stages to a single central dome. Broken columns, shattered walls, piers and buttresses, the remains of the high altar and crypt are all contained within a great circular rim of faced stone which must once have formed the perimeter of the cathedral and at the same time the three steps you climbed to enter it. Standing proudly out amongst the debris, carved on the capital of broken columns, is the great Spread Eagle of the old Armenian Kings.

Svartnots must, quite clearly, have been different from anything else, representing possibly the peak of Armenian architectural achievement. Though myself no great lover of ruins, I went away delighted to have seen it, only regretting its destruction by that raid or earthquake a thousand years ago.

It is said that, when it was completed, the Byzantine Emperor Constantine III personally attended the consecration of the new building and was so impressed by it that, when he went, he carried its architect off with him so that he might build him another cathedral like it in Constantinople. But on the journey the architect had the misfortune to die and so the Byzantines were left to make do with St Sophia and a number of other, not inadequate places of worship.

On our way back from Etchmiadzin we stopped to pass the time of day with a large and cheerful-looking party who were picnicking in a kind of summerhouse by the roadside. 'Come and join us,' they said at once and, before we knew what was happening, we each had a mug of Armenian wine in one hand and a heavily-laden skewerful of *shashlik* in the other. We were, our hostess told us, commemorating the anniversary of her husband's death, which had occurred some years previously on this very spot following a truck crash. His many friends, she said, had built the summerhouse as a memorial to him from materials unwittingly provided by the factory in which he worked. And now every year on the anniversary of his death they all drove out there to eat and drink to his memory.

The country around Erivan is, not unnaturally, full of places of interest, most of them quite easily accessible, provided you know where to look. Twenty miles or so due east of Erivan, dramatically sited on a triangular promontory high above a valley, with walls of sheer rock falling abruptly away on every side in a splendidly impregnable position, we found the massive ruins of the ancient Urartian fortress of Garni. Built on the site of an even older neolithic stronghold, the ruins of this great fort date back to the eighth century B.C., while stones inscribed in Greek, Aramaic and Armenian bear witness to the continued occupation of the site by a succession of conquerors through the centuries. 'I', reads one cuneiform inscription in the name of an Urartian King, 'came to this place and conquered it.' And an inscription in Greek on a vast block of basalt records that the fortress was rebuilt in A.D. 77 by the Armenian King Trdat or Tiridates I who also built a palace there for his consort. In Hellenistic times, Garni, which stands more than five thousand feet above sea-level, was the summer residence of the Armenian Kings. It also produces, and no doubt produced then, an excellent *vin rosé*. Passing through the crumbling gates of the fortress, you come at once upon a fine classical temple, built in the first century of our era, partly destroyed by an earthquake in 1679 and now carefully restored and rebuilt by a distinguished Armenian archaeologist. During its reconstruction evidence has been found of the existence of no less than three earlier temples on the same site. Other things being equal, it seems possible that, even before the earthquake demolished it, the Graeco-Roman temple now happily restored fell victim a couple of centuries after its construction to the iconoclastic zeal of King Trdat III, who, after his own spectacular conversion, took to persecuting the pagans with as much enthusiasm as he had formerly persecuted the Christians. Near the temple are the remains of a fine Roman bath built in the third century A.D. on regular Roman lines with hot, cold and tepid rooms and a handsome mosaic pavement depicting the sea with a selection of nereids and marine monsters. Outside the walls of the fortress are the ruins of two Christian churches of the fifth and seventh centuries respectively, as well as various buildings of the later Middle Ages.

Not far from Garni, on our way back to Erivan, we turned off the high road and up a secluded side valley which led us to the no less dramatically sited Monastery of the Holy Lance at Geghard. This stands in a commanding position near the head of the valley with precipitous cliffs of rock rising on all sides and a rushing mountain torrent sweeping past it. According to ancient tradition, this has been a place of Christian worship since the fourth century and above the monastery itself are several little cells for hermits cut in the face of the rock and dedicated to St Gregory the Illuminator. Beside them are some fine early stone crosses or *khatchkars*. For Armenians, this is a place of great holiness and all around the rockface is blackened by the smoke of innumerable candles, lit to the greater glory of St Gregory.

Like St Gregory's shrine, the main church of the monastery, the much larger thirteenth-century Church of the Virgin, with its cruciform dome and connecting chapels, is also largely cut out of the living rock. In it are the tombs of some local medieval princes, the Proshyans, whose beautifully carved emblem, two chained lions and an eagle bearing a calf in its claws, still proclaims their glory. This church, too, is still in use and we were proudly shown round by a priest in long black robes with a fine black beard. In spite of having been built at a number of different periods, the monastery, like so many medieval monasteries, retains a remarkable unity of style. As we started back for Erivan, the sun was setting and, rounding a shoulder of rock a mile or two down the valley from Geghard, we suddenly found ourselves looking at the Greater and Lesser peaks of Ararat, which that morning had been completely hidden from sight, but which now stood out in all their magnificence against the evening sky.

Back in Erivan, we decided this time not to take the plane or train, but to go northwards by car to Tbilisi, taking the road across the mountains of the Anti-Caucasus and stopping off on the way to look at some of the fine examples of local medieval architecture which are to be found in Northern Armenia.

The first of these, some twenty miles from Erivan, is the monastery of Kecharis, dating from the eleventh century and standing rather forlornly amid wooded hills on the outskirts of the comparatively uninteresting modern village of the same name. The oldest and most important of the buildings which go to make it up is a large church with its dome now partly open to the sky, built in the year 1003 and dedicated to St Gregory the Illuminator. A fine *khatchkar* or stone cross

Khatchkar (Sevan)

Erivan, the Market. Full measure

Etchmiadzin, the Cathedral ▶

Erivan, the Market

Erivan, the Market

Etchmiadzin, St Hripsime

St Gayane, the Sacrificial Block

Etchmiadzin, St Gayane

St Gayane

An Armenian Reel

An Armenian

Svartnots

Geghard

Mount Ararat

Garni

Geghard, rock shrine

Geghard

Kecharis, St Gregory

Sevan

Haghartsin, St Gregory Altarpiece

Haghartsin, St Gregory Altarpiece

Haghartsin, St Gregory

Haghartsin, the woodcutter

Haghartsin ▶

Lake near Dilijan

Goshavank

◄ Haghartsin, ruined shrine

Sanahin, the caretaker

Sanahin, Akop

Sanahin, the Cathedral of St Saviour

Sanahin

The road to Akhpat

Akhpat

Akhpat, St Cross

Akhpat, fountain

◄ Akhpat, the Cathedral of St Cross

Akhpat, kid and lamb

Akhpat, King Smbat and King Gurgen

standing near by pays a well deserved tribute to its architect, Vetzik. A *gavit* or porch, resting on four columns and used, it appears, for secular as well as ecclesiastical purposes, was added to the original church in the twelfth century. Next to the church of St Gregory stands the smaller chapel of St Cross, also dating back to the eleventh century. Beyond this is the thirteenth-century church of Karoghike, while a hundred yards away is the smaller and slightly older church of Arutyun, with yet another type of *gavit*. Today St Gregory's crumbling dome gives shelter to a flock of pigeons which fly noisily out at your approach, the only other inmate being a bent old man endlessly and despairingly employed in sweeping up their copious droppings.

From Kecharis we drove on to Lake Sevan, some forty miles or so northwestwards from Erivan and lying, like so much of Armenia, at more than six thousand feet above sea-level. It is, one is told (and I had no difficulty in believing this), larger than all the lakes in Switzerland put together. Of it Marco Polo writes: 'There is a great lake at the foot of a mountain. And in this lake are found no fish either great or small through the year until Lent comes. But on the first day of Lent they find in it the finest fish in the world, and great store thereof; and these continue to be found until Easter-Eve. And after that they are found no more till Lent comes round again. And so it is every year.' Today, under a Soviet Government, the fish bite indiscriminately, without reference to the feasts of the Church and at Whitsuntide I have eaten more than one fine salmon trout at a little wooden shack which used to stand by the lakeside. These particular fish are known as *Ishkhan* or Kingfish, in much the same way that in Scotland the salmon has a royal connotation.

On a promontory reaching out into the waters of the lake, which was until quite recently an island, stand two ancient churches dedicated respectively to St Karapet and the Holy Apostles and both dating back to the ninth century. They were founded, it is said, by a princess named Mariam who fell in love with a fisherman. When her father forbade her to see her lover and banished her to a nunnery, she solved her problem by building one for herself by the lakeside, where he could and did visit her nightly. It is, or rather was, a beautiful and romantic place. On my last visit, however, I found to my dismay that a large, aggressively modern, concrete Rest Home for Writers with a luxury restaurant attached had been built a couple of hundred yards away from the churches, thus abruptly transforming the whole site into a lakeside resort for the intelligentsia of Erivan.

From Sevan the road, leaving the great lake behind, carries you through a series of splendidly wooded gorges and over a seven or eight thousand foot pass to Dilijan, a beautifully situated health resort, of which the principal feature, apart from its mineral springs, is a holiday camp of luxury stone cottages belonging, in this case, to the Composers' Union and each, I was pleased to find, when I stayed there, provided with a grand piano. My own chalet, I was told, was usually occupied by the great Khatchaturian himself.

On our way to Dilijan we passed through a completely Russian village, bearing the name of Semyonovka and inhabited by descendants of the Molokans, a sect of eighteenth- or early nineteenth-century dissidents from the Russian Orthodox Church, whose heresy, we were told, consisted in drinking milk (*moloko*) on fast days. That great Victorian pundit, Sir Donald Mackenzie Wallace, comes up, on the other hand, with the interesting discovery that the Molokans were in fact presbyterians, doctrinally allied to the Church of Scotland. However this may be, they soon fell from favour and were consequently sent by some Tsar or other to carry on their unorthodox practices in deepest Armenia at a safe distance from any large centre of population. After so many olive-skinned, aquiline Armenians, there could have been no greater contrast than the pink cheeks, snub noses and flaxen pigtails of the little Russian children and the majestically spreading beards of the village elders. (The beard has always played an important part in Orthodox theology.) The brightly painted houses, too, are essentially Russian in character, as are the farming methods. In fact there is nothing to distinguish Semyonovka from thousands of villages like it in European Russia, except perhaps that, with the years, remoteness and isolation have still further accentuated its essentially Russian characteristics.

Up a secluded valley, a dozen miles from Dilijan, the monastery of Haghartsin stands among splendidly wooded hills. Looking out over the valley to a prospect of distant blue mountains, its three churches, refectory and outbuildings are harmoniously grouped at the head of a green glen above a rushing mountain stream, while all round the wind stirs the leaves of a mixed forest of beech, oak, elm, hornbeam and lime. Near by, on green banks and under the trees, half hidden in the grass, are a number of ancient shrines and finely carved crosses, all testifying to the essential sanctity of the place. Short of actual invasion, the monks who lived there must, I reflected, have led a relatively happy, contented life, sheltered as far as anyone could be from the stresses and strains of the outside world.

Of the three churches the largest is that of St Gregory, built in the tenth century of rough white limestone. Near it is the handsome, larger, thirteenth-century Church of the Virgin as well as another, smaller, thirteenth-century church dedicated to St Stephen. Of considerable architectural interest, too, is the refectory, composed of two connecting halls with a ceiling resting on cross-arches. There was no priest in sight when I went there and no sign of any congregation, only an old man with an axe, chopping wood. But on the high altar of the largest church a sand-tray full of lighted candles stood in front of two strangely archaic pieces of carving – proof that somewhere not far away there were still people who worshipped here.

Up yet another valley, not ten miles from Haghartsin, is Goshavank, or the Monastery of Gosh, Gosh having been apparently a medieval scholar or holy man or both, who also gave his name to the rather untidy village of which the monastery is part. Next to the main church of the monastery, which dates back to the twelfth or thirteenth century, was a library with blackened walls, due, we were told, to the books it contained being burned in it by some invader, either Turk or Mongol. The monastery also possesses some fine carved crosses, but its most interesting feature is what appears to have been a prehistoric fortress, its walls built from gigantic, roughly-hewn stones and incorporated here and there in the other buildings. Certainly these gave the impression of having been there very much longer than anything else, indeed of having been left over from some earlier civilization, presumably that of Urartu. On another hilltop near by was perched another, smaller church. Calves, pigs and hens made their way up and down the village street, while from the open windows of the village school came the clear, shrill sound of children's voices repeating their lessons.

After lunching rather well off *shashlik*, yoghurt and Armenian flat unleavened bread at a truck-drivers' rest by the roadside, we drove on from Dilijan through disheartening rain in search of the famous monastery of Sanahin. This we knew to be somewhere near a village called, like its namesake in Georgia, Alaverdi, a presumably Turkish or

Persian place-name meaning, apparently, something like Godspeed, or God Help Us and also used, I discovered, in drinking toasts. But, on reaching Alaverdi, lying in a narrow gorge at the foot of towering cliffs, we found that, although vaguely aware of the existence of a monastery somewhere in the vicinity, the first six inhabitants we met had no clear idea of its whereabouts. Finally, however, we found someone with much more definite opinions on the subject who in answer to our inquiry pointed firmly skywards. In accordance with his instructions, improbable as they might seem, we now drove up a rocky and more or less vertical track apparently leading straight to the top of the nearest mountain. This emerged eventually on to a high plateau and here, after a certain amount of casting about, we eventually located the monastery, magnificently sited some three thousand feet above sea-level in a position commanding a panoramic view of the surrounding country and looking directly across a precipitous gorge to the dark copper-bearing rock walls on the far side of the valley.

After some delay and a good deal of argument, a courteous, good-looking old man was found who had the key to the monastery buildings and we were able to enter the precincts and inspect them. The oldest is an early tenth-century cruciform Church of the Virgin. Near by stands the much larger Cathedral of St Saviour, built in the second half of the tenth century. St Saviour's is also cruciform, two ends of the cross being extended to give the effect of a basilica. Both churches possess handsome *gavits* of a rather later period. Near the Church of the Virgin is a tiny chapel dedicated to St Gregory the Illuminator, built at the end of the tenth century and later rebuilt. Adjoining this is a most interesting eleventh century library, surmounted by a flattened, tent-shaped, octagonal cupola and possessing a fine, pillared gallery. Its stone shelves and niches are now empty of books, their contents having presumably been pillaged by the Mongols who passed this way in the thirteenth century, or by some subsequent invader. Wedged between the Church of St Saviour and that of the Virgin and thus protecting both from snowdrifts is the long, vaulted and pillared Academy of Gregory the Magister, a leading local medieval scholar and divine who made Sanahin a famous centre of learning and culture. Like the Library, the Academy is of particular interest as a fine example of Armenian secular architecture of the Middle Ages. The monastery also contains the mausoleum of some nearby princes, built in the twelfth and thirteenth centuries, and a fine thirteenth-century belfry. On the splendidly sculptured eastern wall of the Church of the Virgin, high up under the gable, a charmingly executed contemporary carving depicts its founders, King Smbat and King Gurgen Bagratuni. At one time the monastery is said to have housed several hundred people. At some distance from the other buildings stand the ruins of the tenth-century church of Akop, demolished in the eighteenth century, as well as various other chapels and shrines. After we had laboriously investigated all this for an hour or two under a steady downpour, the weather suddenly cleared and we at last got a proper sight of the monastery in all its splendour.

Having first climbed the hill behind the monastery to look at the remarkable view, hitherto shrouded in mist and now beginning to open up before our astonished eyes, we made our way back down into the valley by the same precipitous track we had taken on the way up. After which we set out in an easterly direction and considerably better spirits in search of our next objective, the neighbouring Monastery of Akhpat, which we eventually found some five or ten miles away on another high plateau, looking out across the intervening gorge to Sanahin. On our way there we caught sight of a great ruined keep poised high on a crag above the road and, in its turn, tacitly underlining the importance in medieval Armenia of a strong strategic position for laymen and clerics alike.

Of the six monasteries we saw on our way north, Akhpat in some ways made the greatest impression on me. By the time we reached it, it was bathed in the light of the setting sun and the three churches, belfry and refectory that stand within its outer wall seemed an integral part of the village which clustered round it on the steep hillside. Under a fine thirteenth-century portico a little way up the village street, young girls were drawing water at a fountain as their predecessors had done for the past seven hundred years or more, while white lambs and brown kids scuffled and skipped in the dust outside.

Leaning over the monastery wall, taking the air and watching the sun go down, we found two old men who at once engaged us in friendly conversation, asking, as Armenians so often do, for news of their compatriots abroad. 'I bet they're doing well,' said one of them, discussing the fortunes of the Armenian colony in Great Britain and clearly confident of the ability of his race to make their way anywhere. 'I bet by now they are all lords.'

By this time another friendly villager had found the keys of the monastery for us and, having first taken us to the top of a remarkable, three-storeyed, thirteenth-century belfry to admire the view, opened up the three churches of the monastery for us to see. The oldest and finest of these is the Cathedral of St Cross, built between 977 and 991. On its eastern wall under the gable is carved an even more delightful representation of King Smbat and King Gurgen, the founders it shares with Sanahin across the valley, heavily bearded and turbaned and holding between them a model of the Cathedral itself. On the west side of the Cathedral is a fine *gavit* added two centuries later, with an exceptionally handsome entrance arch. Adjacent to St Cross are two smaller domed churches, that of St Gregory, built in 1005, and that of the Virgin, built some two hundred years later. Also within the precincts of the monastery are a thirteenth-century refectory and a number of *khatchkars* and tombs, notably those of the Ukanants princes who seem to have held sway here at some time in the Middle Ages.

In the Cathedral of St Cross the caretaker had rigged up a makeshift but highly effective lighting system which he now proudly switched on for our benefit and then, momentarily disappearing behind a column, turned another switch which suddenly flooded the whole ancient building with the singing of a great choir. All of which so startled the hundreds of birds roosting in the high stone roof that they flew out in flocks, adding their excited twittering to the splendid *te deum* of the tape recorder. It was, oddly enough, a strangely moving moment. Whether the church was officially in use or not was, like many other things in these parts, not clear. Meanwhile, the dribbles of congealed wax on the altars seemed to suggest that it did not entirely lack a congregation.

By the time we left Akhpat it was dark and the rain had started again. In order to comply with some characteristically incomprehensible local regulation, we were prevented, as foreigners, from taking the direct route through the mountains from Akhpat to Tbilisi and obliged to drive back the whole way to Dilijan and start out again from there, with the result that we finally reached Tbilisi in a rage at one in the morning, still debating whether the direct road clearly marked on the map did not really exist; whether, if it did exist, it would have led us past some vitally important (and in this way clearly pinpointed) secret military installation which we could not be allowed to see, even in the dark; or whether, as also seemed quite probable, it was simply another case of rules for the sake of rules. Such are the occasional minor penalties paid by those who choose to travel off the beaten track in the Soviet Union. But against this, we had on this trip seen everything we had set out to see and thoroughly enjoyed it.

On my next visit to Armenia I broke what was for me new ground by taking a bus ride to Leninakan, the ancient city of Kumairi or Gumrion, as Xenophon calls it in his *Anabasis*, seventy or eighty miles north-west of Erivan and only three or four miles from the frontier with Turkey. Known in Tsarist days as Alexandropol, Leninakan, now Armenia's second city, is famous, in a country of quick-thinking people, for the wit of its inhabitants and innumerable tales are told of their gift for repartee. On this occasion it was to be the scene of the centenary celebrations of the famous local Armenian poet Isaakian.

Setting out on a fine October morning from Erivan, we had soon left the urban sprawl of the capital behind us and were bowling briskly along across the tawny stone-strewn uplands of Western Armenia five or six thousand feet above sea-level. To look at, the landscape bore, not surprisingly, a strong resemblance to that of Eastern Anatolia, a few miles away across the Turkish border. Here and there outcrops of rock, brown, white or pink, varied the barren surface of the plain. More rarely, where a stream or river watered the parched soil, its dusty monotony was broken by patches of vegetation: vines, lines of poplars and sudden rows of neatly planted fruit-trees. Three or four times we passed a flock of dark brown sheep or a herd of dun-coloured cows grazing disconsolately among the stones, watched over by a single lonely herdsman standing motionless on some vantage point above them. Far away on the horizon, to the left and right of the road a line of distant snow-capped peaks emerged from the morning mists.

Twenty or thirty miles out of Erivan we rushed at high speed through the ancient town of Ashtarak, perched above the rocky ravine of the river Kasakh, and for a moment caught a glimpse of an old Christian church with a conical dome. It was tantalizing not to be able to stop and explore further but the bus-driver had a real or imaginary schedule to keep to. Soon we were climbing as we started to skirt the southern flanks of Mount Aragats, Armenia's second highest mountain, the twin peaks of which stayed with us for the rest of the journey, white against the blue of the sky.

Ten miles or so short of Leninakan we stopped in the little village of

Maralik. Here they were already busy celebrating the Isaakian centenary. In the village square long tables had been laid out, loaded with piles of fruit, Armenian unleavened bread, white cheese, smoked and spiced ham, jugs of new wine and great bowls of *matsoni*, the sour milk on which, under one name or another, the peoples of the Caucasus seem to thrive. At one end of the square they were dancing vigorous Armenian reels to the music of a three man band, wind, string and drum. At the other a piper had been found and, after a good many refreshing mugs of new wine, was blowing away manfully, at a rather primitive but gigantic bagpipe, while sixteen or more dancers circled tirelessly around him, first this way and then that. The new wine was heady and I could happily have stayed there all day, but the bus-driver was relentless and after half an hour of unadulterated enjoyment we were once more on our way. In the next village, however, he halted again and this time I was fortunate enough to find an alternative means of transport. By now we were not more than a couple of miles from Leninakan and, transferring myself and my luggage to an open two-horse shay which happened to come up, I made my entry into that city in some style at a brisk canter, loudly cheered along the route by crowds of excited schoolchildren.

Leninakan, like the villages along the way, was in festive mood. Few traces remain of its great antiquity. Several miles of high-rise concrete suburbs converge on a central square, containing a seventeenth-century cathedral, a theatre and a rather handsome hotel in the grand manner of the Stalin era. An entirely new and functional hotel or 'tourist base' some twenty storeys high has recently been erected in a commanding position on the outskirts.

A walk round the older part of the town revealed two or three more churches and some pretty old stone houses, dating from the days of the Turkish occupation. The vaulted cellar of one of these had been turned into a restaurant and there at eight o'clock next morning, after a heavy night spent celebrating the poet's centenary, I went with some friends to have breakfast. This consisted of *Khash*, a kind of stew made from pig's trotters and garlic, followed, quite simply, by sheep's heads, three or four to a dish, hollow eyed and reproachful-looking, the whole washed down by copious libations of wine, vodka and sour milk. I would sooner, quite frankly, have had some dry bread and a cup of tea, but persevered notwithstanding, put to shame yet again by the unfailing resilience and powers of recovery of the Armenian people. Being unable to speak Armenian, I had no real opportunity of forming a valid opinion of the wit or conversational prowess of the inhabitants of Leninakan. Russian, quite clearly, did not offer the same scope. I have, however, rarely come across a more hospitable or friendly lot of people, to every one of whom my comfort and well-being seemed to be a matter of personal concern.

But already the driver of the Erivan bus was sounding his horn and it was time to start on the return journey. A road is in any case apt to look different coming back from going out. This time I woke from an uneasy sleep to find myself looking at something that had simply not been there the day before, the enormous bulk of Ararat, forty miles or so away across the border in Turkey, towering above the vapours of the plain as though suspended between earth and sky. It was a truly magnificent sight. For twenty years or more I have been trying, with remarkable lack of success, to photograph Ararat, both from the Soviet, and from the Turkish sides of the frontier. Invariably, as I get out my camera, it vanishes behind layers of mist and cloud. Now at long last it stood out clearly against the pure blue of the sky in easy reach of a long focus lens. But, the driver had time to make up: nothing would induce him to stop. Photographing a distant mountain through the half open window of a recklessly driven bus as it negotiates a series of hairpin bends at seventy miles an hour is not an entirely simple matter. However, I did my best; my fellow-passengers could not have been more co-operative, making way for me as I lurched from side to side of the gangway, and, though by the time we reached our destination the great mountain was once again veiled in mist, I hoped that this time I should have something to show for my efforts – a hope which, as the illustrations section shows, was not entirely unjustified.

16 Azerbaijan

Azerbaijan, the third of the Transcaucasian republics, has a rather different history and background from the other two. Consisting originally of Baku and several other Tartar Khanates, linked historically with what is now Persian Azerbaijan and overrun through the ages by repeated invasions and migrations, though Tartar by population it was for centuries a more or less integral part of Persia, only annexed by Russia, as we have seen, at the beginning of the nineteenth century.

My own first visit to Azerbaijan, which I have described in greater detail elsewhere, was in 1937. I had arrived in the Soviet Union for the first time a few weeks earlier and was possessed by an overpowering desire to travel. In those days the railway linking Tbilisi with Moscow by way of the Black Sea had not yet been built and the train, skirting round the northern Caucasus to the Caspian and then meandering along the coast of Daghestan by way of Derbend and Makhach Kalà eventually deposited me at Baku, the capital of the republic, with its busy harbour and immensely long seafront and promenade. Since then I have been back there a number of times, though mostly on my way to or from somewhere else. To work up any real enthusiasm for Baku, you need, I think, to be an oil-man.

Today the fifth city of the Soviet Union, Baku was, it will be recalled, finally taken by the Russians in 1806, but not until Prince Tsitsianov had met his death before its gates. Very little is now left to recall its Tartar and Persian past, when it was variously a Khanate on its own or the principal port of the Persian province or later Khanate of Shirvan. It is now an almost entirely western city in which the fancifully ornate buildings of the nineteenth century vie as best they can with the varied products of modern Soviet architecture. Only the ruins of the Khan's Palace and a few fine old fourteenth- and fifteenth-century mosques and caravanserais recall its former rulers, both Tartar and Persian, while on the sea-front the massive masonry of the Maiden's Tower bears witness to a still earlier civilization.

A sad little tale attaches to the Maiden's Tower. One of the early Khans of Baku had an unusually beautiful daughter, so beautiful that he fell in love with her himself. Embarrassed by her parent's incestuous advances, the Princess finally told him that she would only give him what he wanted if he proved his love for her by building her a tower to live in taller than any in the whole town. Work on the tower was started at once and, with the lustful Khan personally urging on the builders, went ahead fast, layer of masonry rising rapidly above layer of masonry. But the Princess was still not satisfied. She wanted it taller still. 'Just one more storey ...' she would tell her father coaxingly.

Soon the tower was far taller than any of the neighbouring buildings, taller even than the minarets in the upper part of the town, and the Khan became more insistent than ever. But now the Princess made it a condition that, before she yielded to his advances, the tower must be becomingly furnished and buyers were accordingly sent out into the bazaars to find the finest carpets and brocades for the Princess's tower. This took a long time; she was a born interior decorator. But eventually the day came when the last carpet had been laid and the final touches put to the furnishings. It was now that, with her father impatiently waiting for her to fulfil her part of the bargain, the Princess announced that she wanted to look at the view. Followed by her ladies-in-waiting, she climbed right to the top of the tower, and thence, leaping lightly over the battlements, cast herself down into the sea below, a maiden to the last, leaving her father a sadder but, we must hope, a wiser man, to console himself as best he could with the ladies of his well-stocked *harem*.

Sited at the junction of innumerable sea and caravan routes, Baku was once a mart and exchange for carpets from all over the Near East and in the museum you may see, if you make friends with the curator, one of the most fascinating collections in the world of carpets from the Caucasus, from Persia, Turkey and Central Asia, while scarcely less splendid carpets are spread out on the floor of the great mosque which overlooks the town.

But for more than a hundred years now Baku, once the haunt of Persian fire-worshippers who adored the sacred flames that sprang mysteriously from the soil and even from the sea, has been above all an oil-town. The smell of oil hangs heavily in the air and the gaunt derricks which mark the oil-wells reach far out into the Caspian and stalk in

serried ranks across the barren hinterland. Its population is a jumble of
Azerbaijanis, Russians, Armenians and other nationalities. By now, as
in so many Soviet cities, European Russians are probably the most
numerous, though in the rest of Azerbaijan the native Turko-Tartars
still predominate.

Having spent a couple of days in Baku and feeling adventurous, I
decided, on my first visit back in 1937, to try a trip to southern Azerbaijan. The news that this was impossible did not deter me. Making
my way down to the harbour I hopefully boarded an ancient paddle-
steamer, which had presumably once belonged to the old Caucasus
and Mercury Steamship Company, and, after a night spent on deck
among a crowd of densely packed Tartars, found myself next morning
coming in to land at the little port of Lenkoran, only a few miles
from the Soviet–Persian frontier and the scene of the famous siege
of 1812, which the Russians rounded off by bayoneting four thousand
Persians.

The climate of the southern Caspian littoral is classed as sub-tropical
and the scene, as a number of high-prowed native boats took us off the
steamer and carried us ashore, was in the sharpest possible contrast with
the barren red hills outside Baku and the even more barren Mugan
steppe which lies to the south of it. Luxuriant green orchards and
steaming tea-plantations grew almost down to the water's edge, while
behind these, in the distance, rose a line of blue mountains. A few red
roofs and whitewashed walls stood out here and there from the vivid
green of the trees, for in those days Lenkoran, taken from the Persians a
century or so before, was still little more than a village. Of the fortress,
rebuilt for the Shah by British engineer officers in 1812, there was no
sign.

In Baku there had been talk of tigers and other exotic fauna and flora
in the hinterland of Lenkoran, not to mention strange Moslem villages.
Was it not here or hereabouts, after all, in the Karabagh, that Tamerlane
himself had hunted the tiger? And so, hiring a horse from an amiable
Tartar blacksmith in the bazaar and taking a friend of his with me for
company, I set out hopefully for that distant range of blue hills. Before
long we had left the orchards and the tea-plantations behind us and
were riding along a dry river bed with, on either side, a tangled mass of
semi-tropical vegetation. A snake slipped from the bushes and slid
across our path; a brightly coloured bird flew out of a tree, its wings

flashing in the sunlight. For the first time in my adult life, I had the agreeable and exciting feeling that I had left Europe far behind.

I was, as it happened, absolutely right. Without realizing it, I was heading straight for the Soviet–Persian frontier, at that time a particularly sensitive area. We had not gone far when I noticed a troop of cavalry riding across country at full gallop. They were well mounted and wore the uniform of the Special Troops of the Commissariat for Internal Affairs. They seemed to be heading in our direction. Suddenly, a broad circling movement brought them face to face with us, and, before I had taken in exactly what was happening, I was staring down the barrels of a pistol and half a dozen carbines. 'Hands up!' said an officer, and up went my hands.

A few moments later I was being led away to what my captors, a grubby-looking band of Tartars, assured me was immediate execution.

After riding for two or three miles with my hands still above my head, I decided it was time to produce the diplomatic pass I was carrying. But this was no easy matter. When I tried to get at my pocket, I was at once rewarded by a sharp dig in the ribs from my neighbour's pistol. In the end he grudgingly consented to take it out for me himself, and having taken it out to look at it.

But it did not produce the effect I had hoped for. Indeed, it produced no effect at all. Then, to my dismay, I noticed that he was holding it upside-down and after a little hedging, he finally admitted that he could read no Russian. 'But wait and see,' he said, 'at headquarters there are many people who can read Russian.'

At N.K.V.D. headquarters the entire force was paraded and each man inspected my card in turn. But without success. Taking advantage of their obvious embarrassment, I said that, as I seemed to be the only person present who could read Russian, perhaps I'd better read it for them. A little guilelessly they agreed and I proceeded to read out, with considerable expression and such improvements as occurred to me, what my pass said about the representatives of friendly Powers. 'Signed,' I concluded, 'Maxim Litvinov, People's Commissar for Foreign Affairs of the Union of Soviet Socialist Republics.' Then I looked up to see what effect this had had on my captors.

It had made a considerable impression. As if by magic, they became amiable and apologetic. I was at once released and after shaking hands with a roomful of Tartar militiamen, I took my leave. A day or two later I caught an even older paddle-steamer back to Baku, taking with me, despite this slight *contretemps*, a pleasant enough impression of southern Azerbaijan, though I cannot say that it is a place I would go out of my way to visit again.

While I was in Lenkoran, I had another not uninteresting experience, which, as I later came to realize, was typical of the Soviet Union in Stalin's day. Hearing a noise one morning and looking out of the window, I saw a succession of lorries being driven down to the shore, filled with gloomy-looking Turko-Tartar peasants under a guard of security troops with fixed bayonet.

As lorry followed lorry, the local population began to take notice; little knots of chattering people gathered at the street corners and some of the bolder spirits even showed mild disapproval of what was happening. But the lorries rolled on down to the harbour whence the deportees were ferried out to several ships waiting to take them across the Caspian to Central Asia. This sort of thing apparently happened quite often. No one seemed to know the reason, but the general view was that it was done as 'a measure of precaution'. While two or three of us were discussing the question, a nondescript man came up to me and pointed to a cartoon in a Soviet comic magazine he was carrying. It depicted, for these were the days of the British Raj, a brutal British officer with a whip herding some sad-looking Indians into a concentration camp. 'Not so different here,' he whispered, and was gone, giving me a momentary glimpse of that in those days largely unknown quantity: Soviet public opinion.

Epilogue

A century and a quarter ago the Russian poet Lermontov, who himself fought in the Caucasus, predicted that the conquered Caucasians would come to say with pride: 'We may truly be slaves, but enslaved by Russia, the Ruler of the Universe.' How does this supremely arrogant remark look today? For how much longer are the various non-Russian races that go to make up the Soviet Union likely to retain their national identity? Or, conversely, what prospect have they of achieving a greater measure of independence?

At the present time, if you include Russia itself, there are altogether fifteen Soviet Socialist Republics, each of which has, in theory, the right of secession from the Union. Each of these Republics has its own President and Government, mainly recruited from its own nationals. Some even have their own Ministers for Foreign Affairs. They also have their own national Communist parties and their own national flags. Moreover, of late there has been a measure of genuine decentralization and it is now possible for local authorities to take quite important decisions on their own initiative, without always referring back to Moscow.

What is the outlook for the future? During a period when everywhere else in the world the colonies of the so-called Imperialist Powers (egged on by the Soviet Union) have been given or have taken their independence, and even some of the Soviet satellites have shown occasional signs of stirring, is Moscow tightening or relaxing her grip on her own non-Russian possessions?

One thing is certain, the rulers of the Soviet Union have no intention of practising what they so readily preach to others. If a Georgian or an Armenian or an Uzbek or a Tajik were to be so simple as to suggest that his country should make use of its constitutional right to secede from the Soviet Union, he would at once be in the worst kind of trouble as a 'bourgeois nationalist'.

This does not mean that a reign of terror still persists in the provinces. Life in Tbilisi or Tashkent, like life in Moscow, is on the whole much freer and more agreeable than it was thirty or forty years ago. The standard of living has improved, and there is no longer the same fear of the secret police. People are free to speak their own language and, up to a point, to practise their own religion. If they want to (and they do), they can talk to foreign tourists and listen to foreign broadcasts.

One of the reasons for this is that their rulers in Moscow feel far more secure in their control over them than they did thirty or forty years ago and far readier to face competition with the outside world. As each fresh generation grows up, the process, not so much of Russification, for that would not be quite the right word for it, but of ideological assimilation, of Sovietization, is carried a stage further. What matters is not that a few old people attend church or go to the mosque, or that on the stage this or that team of dancers or singers wears national costume and dances national dances or sings national songs. Or even that this or that Government is composed of the nationals of one country rather than another. What matters is that Moscow has supreme and absolute control over foreign affairs and defence, over financial and economic policy and, through the Communist Party, over the whole legislative, administrative and executive machine. What matters, finally, is that everywhere in the Union millions and millions of young Soviet citizens, whatever their nationality, are being taught in identical schools, are reading identical books and newspapers, are listening to identical broadcasts and speeches and sucking in identical propaganda.

That, no doubt, is what the Soviet Communist Party Programme meant when it declared some years ago that the boundaries of the constituent republics were 'increasingly losing their former significance' and that, under Communism, 'the spiritual features' would be the same for 'Soviet men and women of all nationalities'. The merger, it added, would take time. 'The effacement of national distinctions and especially of language distinctions is a considerably longer process than the effacement of class distinction.' But the ultimate aim of the programme was not in doubt.

Such is the official theory. How will it work out in practice? It is true that the mills of Communism grind exceedingly small. It is true that everywhere distinctive national usages are dying out and national differences becoming less marked than they were. It is true that everywhere the standard of living is steadily improving and thus removing a potential cause of discontent. It is true, finally, that, as Lermontov predicted a century and a half ago, Russians and non-Russians alike take a very genuine pride in the great empire to which they belong.

But even its originators admit that their new programme will take time and, given time, all kinds of things can happen. Human nature, which Communist planners are rather inclined to leave out of account, can often make hay of the best-laid systems and plans. Increased freedom can be put to many uses. In some of the Republics, notably in Georgia and Armenia, new, elegant, sophisticated trends are beginning to manifest themselves, which are already in advance of anything in Moscow or Leningrad, a difference of standards and of taste, which combined with a genuine local patriotism, could make ultimate absorption far from easy.

Might the flames of nationalism, which the Russians are so busy fanning elsewhere, some day blow back on to their own dominions? It is at any rate conceivable. Meanwhile, it is amusing to hear the Georgians, when they take the aeroplane to Moscow, teasing their Russian friends by announcing that they are 'going to the Soviet Union'.

Strachur, Argyll   F. M.

Index